LAROUSSE
Dictionary of the
FRESHWATER
AQUARIUM

LAROUSSE
Dictionary of the
FRESHWATER
AQUARIUM

Henri Favré

**Translated and adapted by
Gwynne Vevers**

BARRON'S/Woodbury New York

Acknowledgements
The photographs were provided by the following:
J.-F. Boudinot–10, 26 (centre and below), 75 (above),
81, 93, 100, 146, 147 (below), 154. M. Bellieud-
Pitch–99 (below). J.-P. Ferrero–64 (below). Jessueld-
Arepi–131. Leclerc–9, 18, 26 (above), 45, 77, 136.
Lubrano–32 (below), 74, 82 (above), 144, 149
(above). G. Mazza–6, 11, 12, 13, 14, 15, 16, 19, 20,
22, 23, 25, 27 (above), 31, 33 (below), 35, 40, 41, 42,
43, 47, 48, 49, 50, 52 (below), 55, 56, 57, 58, 59, 60,
61, 66 (above), 67, 68, 70, 72 (below), 73, 76, 79, 82
(below), 86, 88, 89, 92, 95, 97, 98, 104, 107, 108, 109,
110 (above), 112, 114, 116, 117, 118, 119, 120, 122,
123, 124, 125, 126, 127, 128, 129, 130, 133, 135, 150,
151 (above), 152 (above), 153, 155, 156, 159, 160. S.
Pecolatto–21, 24, 32 (above), 34, 36, 37, 38, 52
(above), 53, 64 (above), 65, 66 (below), 72 (above), 75
(below), 78, 83 (left), 84, 87, 90, 91, 94, 96, 99
(above), 101, 103, 105, 106, 110 (below), 111, 113,
132, 134, 137, 140, 141, 148, 151 (below), 152 (below).
K. Ross-Jacana–99 (centre), 147 (above), H. Schultz-
Atlas-Photo–17, 33 (above), 62. J. Six–27 (below), 28,
30, 46, 51, 83 (right), 85, 102, 138, 139, 143, 149
(below). P. Summ-Jacana–115.

First U.S. Edition 1977
Barron's Educational Series, Inc.
113 Crossways Park Drive
Woodbury, New York 11797

International Standard Book Number 0-8120-5192-0
Library of Congress No. 77-11664

Library of Congress Cataloging in Publication Data
Main entry under title:

Larousse Dictionary of the freshwater aquarium.

   Translation of Larousse des poissons d'aquarium.
I. Aquarium fishes–Dictionaries. I. Favre, Henri.
II. Title: Dictionary of the freshwater aquarium.
III. Title: Freshwater aquarium.
SF457.L2613   639'.34   77-11664

© Librairie Larousse, France 1975

English translation © Ward Lock Limited 1977

First published in Great Britain in 1977
by Ward Lock Limited, London, a member of the
Pentos Group.

Printed and bound by Lee Fung Asco Printers, Hong Kong.

Preface

The art of keeping fishes is not new. The Chinese were domesticating and breeding goldfish at least 2,000 years ago and their skill and patience in selecting and perpetuating a vast range of different colours and shapes is well known.

In the West, on the other hand, fish were certainly kept for the table by monks during the Middle Ages, but the idea of keeping ornamental fishes is relatively new. In his diary entry for 28th May 1665 Samuel Pepys wrote: 'Thence home and to see my Lady Pen, where my wife and I were shown a fine rarity: of fishes kept in a glass of water, that will live so for ever; and finely marked they are, being foreign'. It must have taken several weeks for the fishes to reach London, whereas their relatives now travel by air and arrive in about 36 hours.

Today the cult of fish-keeping is worldwide, and the number of species imported and bred must certainly run into several hundred. This is a cult which appeals to modern man for it requires techniques which are fascinating in themselves and relatively inexpensive to operate. An aquarium tank can be set up in the smallest urban flat still, I believe, without a frown from the town-hall bureaucrats, and its occupants do not need to be taken for a walk in the park.

This dictionary is designed for those who wish to know not only about those fishes that are suitable for an aquarium, but also about their basic requirements and the principles of aquarium management. These are not difficult to master, and the results of their application will provide much enjoyment and stimulation.

I doubt whether Samuel Pepys was aware that some fishes can breathe air and can even drown if they are denied access to it. There is, however, no doubt at all that he knew nothing of fish mothers that incubate the eggs in their mouth, of fish fathers that build a nest of air bubbles as a shelter for the eggs, or of fish parents of both sexes which feed their brood on a mucus secreted from their own flanks. These are just a few of the interesting habits and adaptations of tropical freshwater fishes that are described in this dictionary.

Gwynne Vevers
January, 1977

The asterisks and the references at the end of the articles will lead the reader to other articles on related subjects.

A

Acanthophthalmus kuhlii

Several related species of loach are marketed under the popular name of kuhli or coolie. These are *A. myersi*, *A. semicinctus*, *A. shelfordi*, *A. cuneovirgatus* and *A. rubiginosus*. The pattern of the markings varies according to the species, but they are always blackish-brown on an orange-yellow background. These are hardy fish in all types of water. They avoid the light, and tend to hide away among rocks and vegetation.

Family: Cobitidae.*

Diet: omnivorous, taking scraps of food and small dead animals.

Sex differences: none apparent.

Length: up to 8 cm (3 in).

Distribution: Malaysia and Indonesia.

Compatibility: excellent.

Temperature range: 18–30°C (64–86°F).

Breeding: details not observed, although they have bred a few times in captivity.

ACARA, see *Aequidens*.

ACCESSORIES, see Maintenance.

Accidents

Although living in a protected environment aquarium fishes do sometimes become the victims of accidents. They may dash themselves against the glass if there is a sudden panic, as when the lights are switched on too abruptly. Fighting can also cause injuries, as can sharp-edged accessories and rockwork*.

Acanthophthalmus kuhlii, the coolie loach (up to 8 cm or 3 in)

Aequidens pulcher, the blue acara (15 cm or 6 in)

Such injuries usually heal. They can be treated in a bath of methylene blue but this involves handling the fish, which should be avoided if possible. It is better to transfer the wounded fish for 2–3 days to a tank of salt water (7 g per litre for 36 hours, increasing gradually to 11 g per litre), (or ½ oz per 3 pints for 36 hours, increasing to ¾ oz per 3 pints). see Setting up the tank.

ACCLIMATIZATION, see Heating.

Aequidens

A genus of American Cichlidae*, formerly known as *Acara,* which reproduce well in captivity. There are several species on the market.

Aequidens pulcher

Also known as *Aequidens latifrons,* this is a typical robust cichlid with an elongated elliptical body. The general coloration is greyish-green with turquoise-blue iridescence and brown markings which may form 5–8 vertical bands. The fins are also beautifully coloured.

This species, known popularly as the blue acara, does not attack the plants or tank decoration.

Family: Cichlidae*.
Diet: omnivorous with a preference for live prey.
Sex difference: dorsal and anal fin pointed in the male, rounded in the female.
Length: up to 15 cm (6 in).
Distribution: Colombia, Panama, Venezuela.
Compatibility: satisfactory with all fishes measuring at least half its own length.
Temperature range: 20–30°C (68–86°F).
Breeding: easy. Spawning at c. 26°C (79°F), under a leaf or on a previously cleaned stone, in almost any kind of water. The parents do not attack the young, which hatch in about three days, and protect them by hiding them in furrows in the sand. When swimming freely, after the yolk sac has been resorbed, the young should be given a plentiful supply of infusorians* and *Artemia*.

Aequidens maronii

A relatively short, brownish cichlid with a dark vertical bar running through the eye. At certain periods two brown markings also appear on the body. The pointed dorsal and anal fins have a blue border.

This is a peaceful, sometimes rather timid fish, known popularly as the keyhole cichlid, which accepts the presence of other small species. It also respects the plants and tank decoration and is recommended for the beginner.

Diet: omnivorous, taking dried food and small live food.
Sex differences: the dorsal and anal fins are rather more elongated in the male, and the abdomen less convex.
Length: c. 12 cm (4¾ in).
Distribution: Guyana.
Compatibility: excellent.
Temperature range: 23–28°C (73–82°F).
Breeding: relatively easy. The breeding pair should be placed in a tank with c. 50 litres (11 gallons) of water, at 26°C (79°F), with filtration and sufficient vegetation for shelter. The water should be slightly acid. The eggs are laid on a flat stone and guarded by the parents who fan them with their pectoral fins, and remove by mouth any unfertilized eggs, which would otherwise rot and contaminate the viable spawn. The eggs hatch in three days, and as soon as they are free-swimming the young should be fed first on infusorians, later on *Artemia*.

Aeration

In most cases it is essential for an aquarium*to have some form of artificial aeration, even if it is not overpopulated. By this means some of the oxygen required for respiration becomes dissolved in the water* and it also provides water movements which help to expel the carbon dioxide produced by the fishes.

Aequidens maronii, the keyhole cichlid (10 cm or 3¾ in)

Aeration is effected by an air pump, which is usually of the vibrator type. It is powered by electricity but it uses very little current. Such pumps can be regulated and they require little or no maintenance or oiling.

The compressed air produced by the pump is led into the aquarium tank by fine flexible plastic tubes which end in diffusers (airstones) or filters.

The purpose of a diffuser or airstone is to break up the incoming air into very fine bubbles. The diffuser normally used looks rather like a lump of sugar and is made of hard, porous material. The air supply to a tank can be divided into two by a T-piece, usually of plastic which is preferable to metal.

The pressure of the air delivered can be regulated by small plastic taps.

An efficient system of aeration has two main functions. First, the diffusers lying on the bottom of the tank cause the water to circulate so that all of it is exposed to the surface for it is there that oxygen is absorbed and carbon dioxide removed. Secondly, the mixing of water resulting from aeration helps to equalize the temperature throughout the tank. see Filtration.

Age

The age of a fish freshly caught from its native waters can in many cases be determined by examination of the scales under a microscope. Scales grow by the concentric deposition of calcareous material, normally in the form of two annual rings, the one deposited in summer being wider than that laid down in winter. This is less pronounced in tropical fish than in those from temperate areas, where the seasonal temperature range is greater.

In most cases the life of aquarium fishes is quite short, on average three years, but it is often somewhat longer than in the wild. Goldfish *(Carassius auratus)* are an exception, for they may live for 15 years or more. When a fish is found dead in a tank where the others appear to be perfectly healthy there is a good chance that it may have died of old age, rather than from any disease.

Algae

Algae are one of the plagues of aquariology★, but they also provide valuable information on certain conditions in the tank. It is therefore advisable to know how to interpret their presence or absence in a tank that has been established for a period of at least several weeks.

The absence of algae suggests that the water tends towards acidity.

The presence of a few patches of green algae on the glass or on the rockwork★ close to the light source indicates that the quantity and quality of the illumination is correct.

If the same green algae grow rapidly there is likely to be too much light.

Algae which have the appearance of a downy coating, whether dark green, deep blue or brownish-black, belong to the Cyanophyceae or blue-green algae. Their presence

Diffuser stone, or airstone

Air pump with tubing and taps

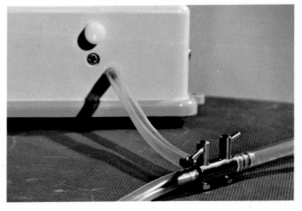

is generally due to excess light and food, the latter derived from fine powdered food left unconsumed by the fish, which quickly breaks down to provide nutrients for the algae.

In contrast to these, the presence of brownish algae in most cases indicates insufficient light.

Finally, there are the filamentous or hairlike algae, usually introduced into the tank with rockwork or decorative plants and these are very difficult to control. They must be removed as soon as they are detected, either by cutting off any leaves on which they have settled or by removing contaminated stones, brushing them with a bleaching liquid, and rinsing them thoroughly in running water.
see Water, Maintenance, Biological equilibrium.

AMBASSIDAE, see Centropomidae.
AMBASSIS, see *Chanda*.

Anabantidae

The labyrinth fishes of the family Anabantidae, which come from tropical Africa and Asia, possess an accessory respiratory organ known as the labyrinth. This is a structure situated in the branchial (gill) cavity on each side of the head and is made up of folded tissue richly supplied with small blood vessels. The fish rises to the surface and takes in fresh air which passes to the labyrinth organ where its oxygen is absorbed by the vascular tissue.

The labyrinth organ is absent in the fry* and starts to develop a few weeks after hatching. It is indispensable to the adults

Green algae first appear on the rocks receiving most light

which could not survive using gill respiration alone. Labyrinth organs enable anabantids to live in waters that are very deficient in oxygen, as so often happens in the tropics.

Most of the genera in the family have another unusual characteristic: their pelvic fins are reduced to two long filaments.

Some of the anabantids can be bred by the amateur aquarist and the process is extremely interesting to watch. In most species the male constructs a nest of air bubbles coated with salivary mucus, which floats at the surface like a raft. When the female is full of ripe eggs she rejoins the male who turns her on her back and encircles her with his body. This stimulates both sexes to spawn and the eggs are fertilized by the sperm in the water. After each mating the couple fall towards the floor of the tank. The male then collects the eggs in his mouth, swims up and spits them out into the nest where they remain among the sticky air bubbles. The process is repeated until the female has laid all her mature eggs. After this she is chased away by the male, sometimes rather brutally. He then works ceaselessly at replacing any eggs which fall out of the nest and after they have hatched in about 36 hours he continues to tend the young fry★. At the end of 2–3 days when they have used up their yolk sac and are free-swimming, it is preferable to remove the male to prevent him from eating his offspring.

An air-bubble nest of an Anabantid (much enlarged)

The tank must then be well covered so that the air above the water surface becomes warm and humid in preparation for the formation of the labyrinth; this is a particularly sensitive period. When small, the fry are fed at first on infusorians★, later on *Artemia*★.

The family includes the well-known fighting fish *(Betta*★*)*, and various species of *Colisa*★, of *Macropodus*★ and of *Trichogaster*★. Other anabantids often kept in the aquarium are the kissing gourami *(Helostoma temmincki)* which becomes rather large for the amateur's tanks, the small *Trichopsis* from southern Vietnam and Thailand, the peaceful but delicate chocolate gourami, *Sphaerichthys*, from Sumatra, and the very aggressive species of *Ctenopoma* which are therefore not much kept in captivity.

Anatomy

Fishes are aquatic vertebrate animals breathing by means of gills and swimming by means of fins. In general, the body is spindle-shaped and well suited for rapid swimming, although there are many other shapes such as the disc-shaped *Symphysodon*, the snake-like eels and the almost spherical pufferfishes.

The fins take on the role played by the limbs of mammals. Some of them serve as organs of propulsion, others are used for maintaining equilibrium and for changing direction.

In most fish families there is a gas-filled swimbladder which serves to keep the fish from sinking or floating.

Respiration is normally with gills which enable the fish to absorb the oxygen dissolved in the water. The gills are leaf-like structures enclosed in a thin membrane and they have an abundant supply of blood vessels. The gills are covered externally by the operculum, or gill cover.

Vibrations in the water are perceived by the lateral line, which extends in a branching system throughout the outer skull bones and usually has a branch extending along the middle of each flank. It consists of a series of narrow canals containing sensory cells.

The exterior of the body is protected by a

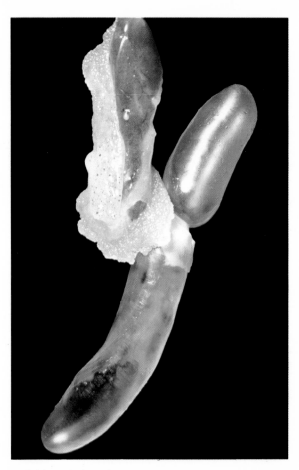

A fish's swimbladder

flexible 'armour', consisting sometimes of fairly large articulated, bony plates, but more often of small, bony scales of various kinds. The scales overlap like the tiles on a roof and are covered by an outer skin layer and by protective mucus.

The digestive tract, running from mouth to anus, is comparable with that of mammals.

The sex organs vary according to the method of reproduction. In livebearing fishes, the eggs are fertilized within the body of the female, and in males the anal fin is modified to form a copulatory organ, such as the gonopodium of the Poecilidae★. However, the males of species that lay eggs do not have this organ.

Visual acuity, whether by day or night, varies considerably according to the species. A few fishes, such as the subterranean form of *Astyanax*★ *mexicanus*, are blind.

Anatomy of the fish (*opposite*)

1 Operculum

2 Ventral fin

3 Pectoral fin

4 Lateral line

5 Anal fin

6 Dorsal fin

7 Caudal fin

Coloration is sometimes stable, sometimes capable of change. Thus the colours may intensify with anger or sexual activity, but tend to fade when the fish is frightened or in poor health.

ANOPTICHTHYS JORDANI, see *Astyanax mexicanus*

Anostomidae
A family of South American fishes related to the Characidae★. They are not widely kept in

A scale seen in polarized light

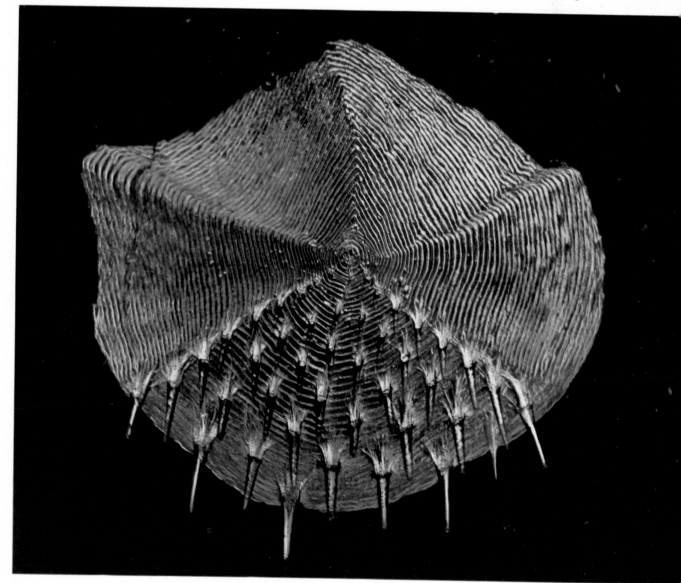

Anostomus anostomus (15–18 cm or 6–7 in)

aquaria, as they are only imported from time to time.

see *Anostomus anostomus, Chilodus punctatus, Leporinus fasciatus.*

Anostomus anostomus

An elegant, spindle-shaped fish with brown and gold markings and reddish fins. It often assumes a vertical position in the water, with the head either up or down. The tank should be large.

Family: Anostomidae.

Diet: omnivorous.

Sex differences: none reliable, but the female is generally described as being slightly stouter.

Length: 15–18 cm (6–7 in).

Distribution: Amazon region and Guyana.

Compatibility: satisfactory with those of its own size, doubtful with smaller fishes.

Temperature range: 23–30°C (73–86°F).

Breeding: not yet reported in captivity.

Aphyocharax rubripinnis

A small, slender, active and hardy fish which prefers to live with others of its own kind. The back is green, the belly white and the fins blood-red, hence the popular name of bloodfin.

Family: Characidae*.

Diet: omnivorous.

Sex differences: female somewhat stouter than the male.

Length: c. 5 cm (2 in).

Distribution: Argentina.

Compatibility: very satisfactory.

Temperature range: 17–26°C (66–79°F).

Breeding: possible in a medium-sized tank with almost any kind of water at 26°C (79°F). The eggs, laid while swimming, drop to the bottom and are liable to be eaten by the parents. They hatch in about 30 hours. The tiny fry will start to eat infusorians* when free-swimming, and will soon accept finely powdered dried food.

Aphyosemion

An African genus of the family Cyprinodontidae. The systematics of the group is somewhat confused. At the present time it is usual to distinguish between the genus *Aphyosemion* with species living to the east of Dahomey and *Roloffia*, a newly created genus for species to the west of this country, but the two genera are so close together that only specialists can distinguish them. All these fishes have the same ecology: they live in

Aphyocharax difficilis, the bloodfin, a species from southern Brazil rarely seen in the aquarium (5 cm or 2 in)

water-holes that may often be only a few centimetres deep and that may disappear completely in the dry season.

Aphyosemion australe

Known popularly as the Cape Lopez this species has an almost cylindrical body with a lyre-shaped tail which gives it a particularly elegant appearance. The male has particularly bright colours, with green iridescence overlying a ground coloration of brownish-red.

This species, the most compatible of the group, was, in fact, the first to be imported and it is still the most popular. There is a selected yellow variety, *A. a. 'hjerreseni'*.

Diet: almost exclusively small live food.
Sex differences: female smaller, duller than male, and with a rounded caudal fin.
Length: male 5 cm (2 in), female less.

Distribution: Africa (Gabon, Cameroon).
Compatibility: satisfactory.
Temperature range: 18–25°C (64–77°F).
Breeding: fairly easy if the following points are strictly adhered to: the tank should be small, with a good cover as these fish are remarkable jumpers, and filled with water at 26°C (79°F), pH about 6.8, hardness up to 10°DH. The substrate should consist of a layer of sand covered by a thin layer of boiled peat. The tank can also have a rock and one or two plants. A filter is not necessary, but diffuse lighting is advisable. Spawning takes place over a period of 10 days, with a few eggs being laid every day. These hatch in 14–20 days and the fry can be fed at first on infusorians★, later on *Artemia*★. They become adult in 6 months.

Aphyosemion australe (the yellow or lyretail or golden form, 5 cm or 2in)

Aphyosemion bivittatum (6 cm or 2¼ in)

Aphyosemion bivittatum

An active fish which occurs in a number of varieties or subspecies from different parts of western Africa.

Like *A. australe*, this species somewhat resembles a miniature pike. The ground coloration is a rich reddish-brown, with two dark longitudinal bands, and bright coloured fins, particularly in the male. This is possibly the best jumper in the group, so the tank must be properly covered.

Diet: small live food.

Sex differences: female smaller and less colourful than male, with the fins much more rounded.

Length: male 6 cm (2½ in), female 4 cm (1½ in).

Distribution: western Africa.

Compatibility: fairly good.

Temperature range: 19–25°C (66–77°F).

Breeding: as for *A. australe*.

Aphyosemion species (7.5 cm or 2¾ in)

Aphyosemion calliurum

A species from western Africa (Nigeria, Cameroon). Males reach a length of 7.5 cm (2⅞ in).

Aphyosemion sjoestedti

The male has greenish flanks changing to bluish towards the belly and the fins are bluish-green with some red. The female is dull green.

Diet: live food.

Sex differences: female less colourful.

Length: male 12 cm (4¾ in), female 8 cm (3 in).

Distribution: Africa (Nigeria, Cameroon).

Compatibility: doubtful.

Temperature range: 18–22°C (66–72°F).

Breeding: as for *A. australe*, but in a larger tank. The large, slightly adhesive eggs are laid on or near the bottom and they take several weeks to hatch.

Aphyosemion walkeri

The male is brown on the back, becoming

Aphyosemion sjoestedti (12 cm or 4¾ in)

somewhat paler towards the belly, with numerous red and maroon markings. The fins are yellowish, tinged with blue and red. The female is dull brownish.

Diet: live food.

Sex differences: the male is more brightly coloured than the female.

Length: male 6 cm (2¼ in), female 4 cm (1½ in).

Distribution: Africa (Ivory Coast and Ghana).

Compatibility: sometimes satisfactory, but is rather variable.

Temperature range: 20–24°C (68–75°F).

Breeding: as for *A. australe*.

Apistogramma

A genus of small fishes in the family Cichlidae* from South America. They are rather delicate, and particularly sensitive to some of the chemicals used to treat certain diseases. In addition to the species discussed below there are also *A. borelli*, from the Mato Grosso, *A. trifasciatum*, *A. ortmanni*, *A. cacatuoides* and others.

Apistogramma agassizi

A handsome dwarf cichlid with relatively large dorsal and caudal fins.

Diet: omnivorous.

Sex differences: tail pointed in the male, rounded in the female.

Length: male 8 cm (3 in), female 5 cm (2 in).

Distribution: Amazon Basin.

Compatibility: satisfactory, except during breeding periods.

Temperature range: 22–28°C (72–82°F).

Aphyosemion lujae (6 cm or 2¼ in)

Apistogramma agassizi female (5 cm or 2 in, the male measures 8 cm or 3 in)

Apistogramma ramirezi (5 cm or 2 in)

Breeding: as for substrate-spawning cichlids. The eggs are brownish, and the fry start to feed on infusorians★ 4–5 days after hatching.

Apistogramma ramirezi
An attractive greenish fish with a black band running through the eye. There is also a golden-orange variety.
Diet: omnivorous.
Sex differences: not obvious; the third ray of the dorsal fin is rather longer in the male.
Length: 5 cm (2 in).
Distribution: Venezuela.
Compatibility: very good; a rather shy species.
Temperature range: 24–29°C (75–83°F).

Breeding: difficult, although the conditions are similar to those of other cichlids: soft water, with hardness up to 10°DH, is recommended.

Aplocheilus
A genus of Asiatic Cyprinodontidae★, related to the African genus *Epiplatys*, with 7 species and numerous subspecies. The best known is probably *A. panchax*, the blue panchax. Others include the Ceylon killifish, *A. dayi*, 8 cm (3 in), and *A. lineatus*, southern India, 10 cm (3¾ in), both of which are hardy and easy to breed in the aquarium. The smaller green panchax, *A. blockii*, southern India, 5 cm (2 in), is very peaceful, but more delicate, being particularly prone to fish tuberculosis, which it may pick up in polluted water.

Apistogramma ramirezi, golden variety (5 cm or 2 in)

Aplocheilus panchax

With a wide distribution this species has several colour variants. Like related species, the shape is reminiscent of a miniature pike with a large mouth. The tank should be fairly long with areas of vegetation and of open water. This species jumps well.

Diet: omnivorous.

Sex differences: male slightly more colourful than female.

Length: 8 cm (3 in).

Distribution: India, south-east Asia and Indonesia.

Compatibility: doubtful when living with smaller fish.

Breeding: fairly easy in a well covered tank with almost any kind of water at 25°C (77°F). At each mating the female lays one or two eggs, which become attached by a short filament to the first object they encounter. The young hatch in about 12 days and may be attacked by the parents.

Aquariology

The maintenance and breeding of ornamental fishes is an art, and like other arts is dependent upon a certain number of techniques, often known collectively as aquariology. The subject was much studied in the Far East, particularly by the Chinese, but did not really start to find favour in Europe until the 18th century.

Since then progress has been rapid. Amateurs of the subject, usually known as aquarists, endeavour to establish an aquarium★ with several species of fish living in an aquatic environment that is aesthetically satisfying to the owner while completely fulfilling the requirements of the living occupants. Many aquarists are interested primarily in the habits★ and breeding★ in captivity of a wide range of species. They try to establish an environment that is relatively stable, with some measure of biological★ equilibrium between plants and animals so that a minimum of maintenance* is required. Some aquarists rapidly become competent specialists in the subject, who are afraid neither of the jargon of aquarium techniques nor of the sometimes difficult, but quite essential, scientific names of the living organisms concerned.

Certain amateur aquarists have also turned their attention to the maintenance in captivity of marine fishes. This is a subject with a set of rules rather different from those that are now current for the maintenance of a freshwater aquarium. Marine fishes are mostly rather aggressive and many do not tolerate companions of the same species in the tank. However, this is a subject that is not dealt with in the present book.

Aquarium

An aquarium may be a public institution exhibiting a large collection of living fishes and other aquatic animals, and there are several of these in many parts of the world; they are maintained by professional staffs. To the amateur aquarist, however, an aquarium is a large or small tank in which he maintains and usually tries to breed one or more species of ornamental fishes.

Leaving aside the unfortunate goldfish which ignorance often condemns to living in a spherical goldfish bowl, the majority of freshwater fishes are kept in rectangular aquarium tanks, with a length of at least 50 cm (20 in). These are, in fact, the only tanks usually suitable for fish-keeping.

Naturally, each fish will require a certain volume of water, depending upon its size and certain other factors. Within the limits of the pocket and the space available the amateur will normally want a tank that is as large as

Aplocheilus panchax, the blue panchax (8 cm or 3 in)

possible. With tanks of normal proportions (i.e., approximately a double cube) the total capacity can be regarded as a function of their length. Thus, a tank with a length of 50 cm (20 in) would hold 35 litres (c. $7\frac{3}{4}$ gallons)

60 cm (c. 24 in) would hold 50 litres (11 gallons)

80 cm (c. 32 in) would hold 85 litres (c. 18 gallons)

120 cm (48 in) would hold 200 litres (44 gallons)

150 cm (60 in) would hold 375 litres (c. 82 gallons)

However, one has to take into account the volume occupied by the rockwork* and the fact that the tank is never filled to the brim. In practice, an aquarium tank usually holds only 80 per cent of its total capacity.

Aquarium tanks can be made from a number of different materials and by various techniques.

Small tanks for special purposes, such as quarantine or rearing fry, can be made in plastic or in cast glass. Such tanks are not very transparent, but they are relatively cheap. The latter are fragile and costly. Both these types have the advantage that they do not rust as they have no metal parts, but visibility is poor.

The more usual type of tank is one with an angle-iron frame supporting the glass panes. The iron (or other metal) parts are soldered or brazed together and then painted. There are also more expensive models in which the frame is made of polished stainless steel or anodized aluminium. The bottom can be galvanized iron plate, stainless steel or glass. The panes are good quality plate glass, the thickness depending upon the depth of water and the corresponding pressure it exerts.

The glass panes are fixed to the frame with a special mastic compound or, in the case of anodized aluminium tanks, with a silicone glue.

In more recent years tanks have been constructed out of glass panes glued together with silicone glue and without any metal

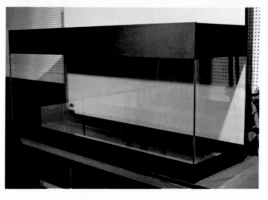

Various type of aquarium. From above: the highly unsuitable 'goldfish bowl'; an angle-iron tank in anodized aluminium; a tank with the panes sealed with silicone glue.

frame. These have great advantages over tanks with angle-iron frames which inevitably rust, however carefully they are painted.

An aquarium tank should always be fitted with a lid or cover. This will prevent dust settling on the water, avoid excess evaporation, stop the fish from jumping out of the

tank to die on the floor, and finally provide a support for the lighting*.
see Aeration, Setting up the tank, Heating, Positioning the aquarium, Maintenance, Filtration, Plants, Substrate, Transport.

ARCHER-FISH, see *Toxotes jaculator*.

Artemia

The brine shrimp, *Artemia salina*, is a small

A nauplius larva of *Artemia* seen under the microscope

crustacean from brackish waters which forms one of the best foods for aquarium fishes. The larva, known as a nauplius (plural nauplii), is a particularly valuable food for very young fishes.

The dried eggs can be bought at an aquarium dealer. When placed in salt water with aeration supplied through a diffuser these eggs will hatch in 24–28 hours into tiny nauplii. Small portions of such a culture can be transferred by pipette. Shut off the aeration for a few minutes beforehand so that the hatched eggshells can sink and any unhatched eggs can float; these could constipate or even kill the fry. Fill the pipette from the mid-depth of the water and transfer the nauplii to the tank of fry where they will rapidly be consumed.

The nauplii can be grown on until they reach adult size, which is about 1 cm ($\frac{1}{3}$ in). The successive stages can be fed to larger fishes. Some aquarists keep cultures of *Artemia* of various ages.
see Diet.

Astronotus ocellatus

Known popularly as the oscar or velvet

Astronotus ocellatus, the oscar (up to 30 cm or 12 in)

cichlid, this is a good fish for the amateur aquarist when it is young (up to 5 cm in length). It should then be maroon with yellowish markings. However, it grows fairly rapidly to more than 25 cm and is then velvety and almost black with orange markings.

Family: Cichlidae★.

Food: omnivorous.

Sex differences: the males sometimes have three round spots at the base of the dorsal fin.

Length: 15–30 cm (6–12 in), depending upon the volume of the tank.

Distribution: Amazon basin.

Compatibility: usually rather tame with the person feeding it, and generally tolerant towards other fish that are too large to be regarded as prey.

Temperature range: 22–28°C (72–82°F).

Breeding: in general, as for substrate-spawning Cichlidae★.

Astyanax mexicanus

Formerly known as *Anoptichthys jordani,* the subterranean form of this characin is completely blind. However, its other sense organs are very acute and this applies particularly to the lateral line (see Anatomy), which perceives vibrations in the water, and enables the fish to avoid obstacles and to seize its food with as much speed and precision as if it had eyes.

Family: Characidae★.

Diet: omnivorous.

Sex differences: none, except that the female has a more convex belly when ready to spawn.

Length: up to 8 cm (3 in) in the aquarium, more in the wild.

Distribution: caves in central Mexico.

Compatibility: satisfactory when young, doubtful when adult.

Temperature range: 22–28°C (72–82°F).

Breeding: rarely attempted by amateur aquarists, but can be done in a fairly large tank filled with hard water (over 15°DH) at 27°C (80°F). The eggs, which are laid by the female while swimming, are avidly hunted by both parents, which

Astyanax mexicanus, subterranean form, the blind cave characin (8 cm or 3 in)

should therefore be removed as soon as spawning is finished. The eggs hatch in 48 hours and the fry are free-swimming 4 days later, when they can be given infusorians★.

Atherinidae

A large family of tropical fishes known popularly as silversides or sand smelts. Most are marine but some live in fresh waters in Australia and Madagascar. They are characterized by having the dorsal fin in two parts, the first (front) part with spiny rays, the second with soft rays. The very small species *Pseudomugil signatus* from Queensland measures 4.5 cm ($1\frac{3}{4}$ in).

see *Bedotia geayi*, *Melanotaenia maccullochi*, *Telmatherina ladigesi*.

B

Badis badis

A small predatory fish that does not grow too large for the average tank.

Family: Nandidae★. Some recent authors place it in its own family, the Badidae.

Diet: large quantities of live food.

Sex differences: not very apparent. The female is usually smaller and more rounded.

Length: 6 cm ($2\frac{1}{4}$ in).

Distribution: India.

Compatibility: timid in the presence of other fishes too large to be devoured.

Temperature range: 25–30°C (77–86°F).

Breeding: possible, in conditions suitable for Cichlidae★. The male guards the eggs and fry★.

BARBODES, see *Barbus*.

Barbus

A genus of fishes in the family Cyprinidae★, distributed in Europe, Asia, and North Africa, known popularly as barbs. Sometimes divided into three separate genera according to the number of barbels in the mouth region: *Barbodes* (4 barbels), *Capoeta* (2 barbels), *Puntius* (no barbels). However, it is probably better to keep them all together under *Barbus*.

Barbus conchonius

A widely distributed hardy fish known in the aquarium world as the rosy barb, and a suitable subject for learning about the breeding of barbs in general.

Diet: omnivorous.

Sex differences: the male becomes red at spawning time.

Length: rarely more than 7 cm ($2\frac{3}{4}$ in) in the aquarium.

Distribution: India.

Compatibility: good.

Temperature range: 18–28°C (64–82°F).

Breeding: relatively easy, at an age of about 12 months. The water should be soft to medium-hard at about 25°C (77°F), and pH 6.5–7.2. The tank need not be longer than 50 cm (20 in), provided it has filtration, a substrate of sand, an area of open water and a clump of natural plants or of nylon wool. The ripe female should be introduced first, and then a few days later the male can be put in. Very often spawning takes place the following morning, the fish coming together flank to flank, and the male then wrapping his body and fins round the female. Spawning lasts for about two hours and both fish should then be removed to prevent them eating their eggs. The latter hatch in about three days, and the fry should start feeding on infusorians* 24 hours later.

Barbus cumingi
A barb from Sri Lanka which is rather similar to *B. conchonius* but more attractive, the orange-red dorsal fin being bordered with black.

Barbus conchonius, the rosy barb (7 cm or 2¾ in)

Barbus hexazona, the six-banded barb (6 cm or 2¼ in)

Barbus everetti

A brownish species with dark bluish markings and reddish fins. Known as the clown barb, it required a spacious tank as it grows quite large.

Diet: omnivorous.

Sex differences: the coloration of the male is slightly brighter.

Length: 13 cm (5 in).

Distribution: Malaysia, Borneo.

Compatibility: good with fish larger than 7 cm (2¾ in).

Temperature range: 23–28°C (73–82°F).

Breeding: not easy, and should only be attempted by those with plenty of space.

Barbus hexazona, B. pentazona, B. partipentazona and B. tetrazona

A group of barbs with red fins and a pinkish body marked with vertical black bands. Externally, the only difference between these four barbs is the arrangement and number of the black bands (six, five, four and a half or four). Most of the barbs of this type seen on the market are either *B. tetrazona* or hybrids between it and one of the other three.

They are all attractive, hardy, active and reasonable in size, and they thrive as well in a medium-sized tank as in a large one. Unfortunately, they tend to quarrel with their neighbours. So it is best to keep them in a group of at least six, without other species.

Diet: omnivorous and voracious.

Sex differences: scarcely detectable. The male is usually more brightly coloured, the female more rounded.

Length: 6 cm (2¼ in).

Distribution: Sumatra, Borneo.

Compatibility: doubtful.

Temperature range: 23–29°C (73–84°F).

Breeding: difficult. This should be attempted in the same conditions as for *B. conchonius,* but using slightly softer water and putting several males and females together as they seem to spawn better in groups. At 27°C (80°F) the eggs hatch in 60 hours and 2–3 days later feeding with infusorians should be started and continued for about a week.

Barbus lateristriga

A greyish barb, marked with two dark vertical bars and one equally prominent horizontal stripe. In spite of its attractive appearance this fish, known as the spanner barb, is not often kept on account of its size.

Diet: omnivorous.

Sex differences: the coloration of the male is slightly more intense.

Length: up to 14 cm (5½ in).

Distribution: Thailand, Malaysia, Indonesia.

Compatibility: good with fishes longer than 7 cm (2¾ in).

BELOW *Barbus tetrazona*, the Sumatra or tiger barb (6 cm or 2¼ in)

ABOVE *Barbus tetrazona*, the Sumatra or tiger barb (6 cm or 2¼ in)

Barbus lateristriga, the spanner barb (up to 14 cm or 5½ in)

Barbus nigrofasciatus, the black ruby (5 cm or 2 in)

Temperature range: 23–28°C (73–82°F).
Breeding: difficult, except in a very large
  tank.

Barbus nigrofasciatus
Known popularly as the black ruby. When
excited the male becomes almost unrecogniz-
able, the body and fins turning black and the
head bright red.
Diet: omnivorous.
Sex differences: the female is duller than
  the male.
Length: 5 cm (2 in).

Barbus oligolepis, the island barb (4 cm or 1½ in)

Distribution: Sri Lanka.
Compatibility: satisfactory.
Temperature range: 22–28°C (72–82°F).
Breeding: possible under the conditions
    recommended for *B. conchonius,* but not
    so easy. The water should be neutral or
    slightly acid and medium-hard. It is
    more difficult to get the fish to spawn
    than it is to rear the young.

Barbus oligolepis

The large scales on the body give this species,
often known as the island barb, a checkered
appearance. In the male the dorsal fin is red
with a black border. This barb is recom-
mended for a tank with small species.
Diet: omnivorous.
Sex differences: dorsal fin paler in the
    female.
Length: 4 cm (1½ in).
Distribution: Sumatra.
Compatibility: perfect.
Temperature range: 24–29°C (75–84°F).
Breeding: as for *B. conchonius,* but the
    water should have a hardness of
    10–15°DH. The parent fish are
    particularly prone to eating their eggs. At

27°C (80°F) the eggs should hatch in
about 60 hours and the fry will be ready
for their first infusorians* 2–3 days later.

Barbus 'schuberti'

The golden or Schubert's barb is a hardy
species that has never been properly described
scientifically and in some quarters there is
doubt whether it is a separate species or
merely a variety of *B. semifasciolatus.* How-
ever, from the aquarist's viewpoint this is an
attractive fish.
Diet: omnivorous, rather greedy.
Sex differences: scarcely detectable. The
    female is usually more rounded.
Length: 6 cm (2¼ in).
Distribution: unknown.
Compatibility: good.
Temperature range: 22–28°C (72–82°F).
Breeding: as for *B. conchonius,* but in old
    water. At 27°C (80°F) the eggs hatch in
    24 hours.

Barbus semifasciolatus

In this species the brown of the back shades to
yellow-green on the belly, and the flanks are
marked with several black bars. A hardy fish,
known as the green barb, but not commonly
kept, probably on account of its size.
Diet: omnivorous.
Sex differences: scarcely detectable. The
    female is slightly more rounded.
Length: 7 cm (2¾ in).
Distribution: south-eastern China.
Compatibility: satisfactory.
Temperature range: 18–27°C (64–80°F).
Breeding: as for *B. conchonius.*

Barbus ticto

Close to *B. conchonius,* this species from
Sri Lanka and India, known popularly as the
two-spot barb, has a black border to the dorsal
fin. *B. stoliczkanus* from Burma was long
thought to be a subspecies of *B. ticto* but it is
now regarded as a separate species.

Barbus titteya

A peaceful species, known as the cherry barb,

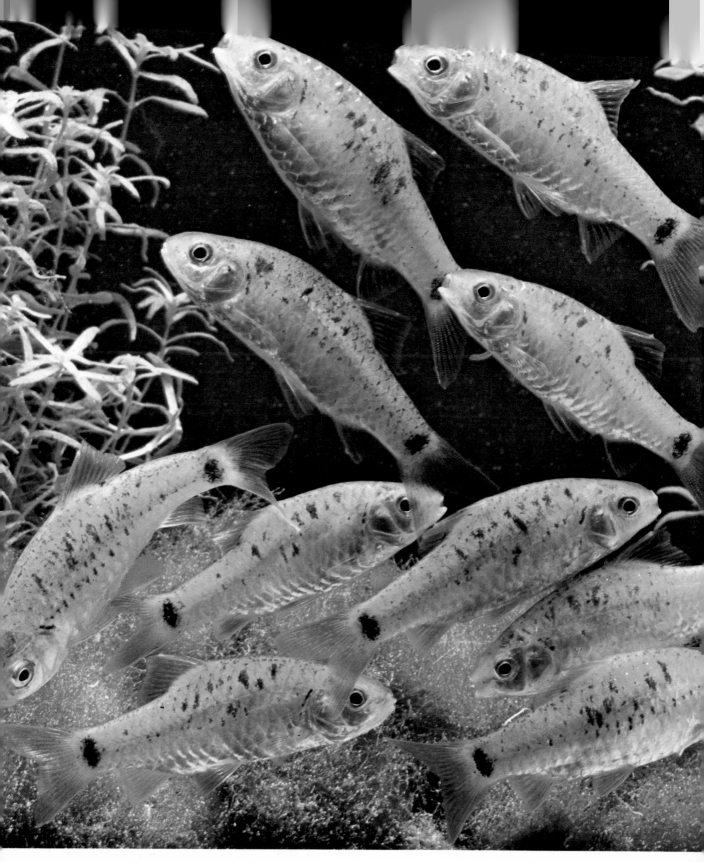

Barbus 'schuberti', the golden barb (6 cm or 2¼ in)

ABOVE *Barbus semifasciolatus*, the green barb (7 cm or 2¾ in)

BELOW *Barbus titteya*, the cherry barb (4.5 cm or 1¾ in)

which prefers to live in the shade among vegetation. The male becomes a beautiful blood-red when excited.

Diet: omnivorous.

Sex differences: male more slender and more brightly coloured.

Length: 4.5 cm (1¾ in).

Distribution: Sri Lanka.

Compatibility: very good. The species is rather timid.

Temperature range: 22–28°C (72–82°F).

Breeding: as for *B. conchonius*, but the water should be at 27°C (80°F) and medium-hard. The eggs hatch in 30 hours, and the tiny fry, which are not very numerous, will start to take infusorians★ after another 30 hours.

OTHER SPECIES OF BARBUS

These include *B. arulius* in which the male has the spiny rays of the dorsal fin elongated, *B.*

Bedotia geayi, the Madagascar rainbow fish (9 cm or 3½ in)

filamentosus which is somewhat similar but darker, *B. gelius* which can be kept at 18°C (64°F), and *B. schwanenfeldi* which is suitable when young, but the adults grow to a length of 40 cm (15½ in). The blind barb, *Caecobarbus geertsi,* from the Congo is no longer likely to be seen as its export is forbidden.

Bedotia geayi

An elegant, attractively coloured fish which lives gregariously in small shoals close to the water surface.
Family: Atherinidae★.
Diet: omnivorous.
Sex differences: the caudal fin of the male is edged with red.
Length: 9 cm (3½ in).
Distribution: Madagascar.
Compatibility: very good.
Temperature range: 22–28°C (72–82°F).
Breeding: not difficult. The eggs hatch in about 6 days and the fry★ start to feed on *Artemia*★ nauplii as soon as their yolk sac has been resorbed.

Betta splendens

Well known as the fighting fish on account of the aggressiveness of the males. Fights between males sometimes result in the death of one of the protagonists, but more often in injury, particularly to the fins which may be reduced to shreds. Fortunately these regenerate fairly rapidly.

Three varieties of *Betta splendens* known as the fighting fish because of the aggressive behaviour of the males, (above and overleaf). The fins of the males are highly developed and the coloration very brilliant

The males occur in several different colours with excessively developed fins. On account of their behaviour the males should always be kept separately. It is however quite possible to keep a pair in a community tank with other species, although it is best to provide hiding-places for the female. Outside the spawning periods these fish are relatively inactive, each remaining indolently in the vicinity of a plant.

The related species *B. brederi*, *B. picta* and *B. pugnax*, which have similar habits, are rare in captivity.

Family: Anabantidae★.

Diet: mainly live food, although some individuals accept dried foods.

Sex differences: in the females the coloration is duller and the fins much less developed.

Length: 12 cm (4¾ in) for the male, 6 cm (2¼ in) for the female.

Distribution: India, Malaysia, Thailand, Vietnam, Cambodia.

Betta splendens, the fighting fish

Compatibility: generally very good with other species, but quite intolerant of other members of their own species, and often even the females are quarrelsome.

Temperature range: 20–30°C (68–86°F).

Breeding: as for Anabantidae★. In *Betta splendens* the nest is composed exclusively of air bubbles, without any vegetable matter. The eggs hatch 30–40 hours after they are laid, and the fry★ start to take infusorians★ two days later.

Biological equilibrium

An aquarium can be considered to be in a state

of biological equilibrium when the water it contains remains clear. This equilibrium results from the natural sequence of vital processes involving the various organisms in the tank.

Under the action of light the plants produce oxygen, which is taken up by the fishes' gills. The fishes release carbon dioxide which is absorbed by the plants. The fish faeces and plant detritus are broken down by the microbial flora and transformed into mineral salts which are taken up by the plants.

The equilibrium of this small closed aquatic world is based on the carbon cycle, as it is in nature, and a deficiency in any one link will upset the whole chain of events.

An upset in the biological equilibrium may manifest itself in various subtle ways. The water, for instance, may not be crystal clear, or the plants may appear to be flagging. More usually, however, the trouble may be quite obvious, as in the examples given below.

Green water is due to an excess of light. Even though the tank glass and the rockwork are devoid of all algae the water itself is green. This is because of microscopic green algae, living in suspension in the water, which are of the same type which cause pond water to turn green when the natural light is intense. Such algae are not dangerous when present in small numbers but if they proliferate the fishes may die from asphyxia. The remedy in such cases is to change the water. The growth of these algae can usually be prevented by covering the sides of the tank exposed to the light. Alternatively, living *Daphnia*★ can be introduced, for algae in suspension form part of their natural food.

Brown water is normally due to other types of floating microscopic algae which thrive in poor light. This is a rare phenomenon which occurs in tanks receiving too little artificial light.

Greyish water is due to the presence of excess bacteria which are breaking down organic matter, usually excess fish food. The remedy is to reduce the amount of food and to renew half the polluted water. This trouble

39

only occurs in tanks that are badly maintained and overpopulated.

Milky water is also due to gross proliferation of bacteria and is the acute form of the previously mentioned trouble. This necessitates an immediate change of all the water. It sometimes occurs in newly installed tanks in which the biological equilibrium has not yet become fully established.

Cloudy water is a general, rather vague term sometimes used by aquarists. Apart from the phenomena mentioned above, it may be due to the proliferation of infusorians which remain in suspension. This sometimes happens in tanks containing voracious fishes that consume a large amount of oxygen. The remedy is to siphon off a proportion of the water at frequent intervals (e.g. one-fifth of the volume every 48 hours).

Yellowish water gives the aquarium a dejected appearance. It may occur when the tank has been going for a long time and is saturated with undesirable substances, particularly nitrates. This will entail cleaning out the tank and refilling with new water. Alternatively, yellowish water may be the result of

An aquarium is a microcosm, in which an equilibrium is established between plants and fishes

insufficient light and a pH that is too low. In this case it should be sufficient to increase the duration and the intensity of the lighting and to renew only part of the water.

The aquarium plants may also be affected by changes in the biological equilibrium. For instance, there may be too little light or, more rarely, too much. The water may be too hard or too soft, or the substrate may not be rich enough in nutrients. In some cases the plants suffer from the attention of the fishes, being either nibbled so that growth is affected or even uprooted, as happens when the tank contains some of the more boisterous Cichlidae★.

Only experience will enable the aquarist to select and cultivate those plants which are adapted to the environmental conditions in a given tank. Fortunately there are plenty of different aquarium plants★ to choose from.

BLACK MOLLY, see Mollies.

BLACK-BANDED SUNFISH, see *Enneacanthus chaetodon.*

BLACK TETRA, see *Gymnocorymbus ternetzi.*

BLEEDING HEART, see *Hyphessobrycon.*

BLIND CAVE CHARACIN, see *Astyanax mexicanus*

BLOODWORMS, see Diet.

Botia

A genus of tropical loaches characterized by the elongated snout surrounded by barbels, and by their bottom-living habits. They have evidently never been bred in captivity and it is possible that in the wild spawning is associated with certain migratory habits. The species most widely distributed in the aquarium is *Botia macracantha. B. hymenophysa, B. lohachata* and *B. modesta* are less often seen, probably because they are not so attractive.

Botia macracantha, the clown loach (15 cm or 6 in)

41

Botia macracantha

Known popularly as the clown loach on account of its amusing behaviour and bright colours, this is a very decorative orange fish with three black vertical bands, one of which traverses the eye. Unfortunately it has a tendency to hide away under stones and it is particularly susceptible to white-spot disease★ *(Ichthyophthirius)* which is difficult to cure in this species.

Family: Cobitidae★.

Diet: omnivorous.

Sex differences: not detectable.

Length: rarely more than 15 cm (6 in) in the aquarium, twice as long in the wild.

Distribution: Sumatra and Borneo.

Compatibility: generally very satisfactory.

Temperature range: 22–28°C (72–82°F).

Breeding: never recorded in captivity.

Brachydanio

A genus in the family Cyprinidae★ with a number of small species from southern Asia. Apart from *Brachydanio rerio,* which is the most popular, the species include the pearl danio, *B. albolineatus,* 5 cm (2 in), *B. frankei,* up to 4 cm (1½ in) which is more difficult to keep than its relatives, and the less hardy and more solitary *B. nigrofasciatus* from Burma, up to 4 cm (1½ in).

Brachydanio rerio, the zebra danio (4 cm or 1½ in)

Brachydanio rerio

A hardy fish, known as the zebra danio, which is particularly recommended for the beginner. It swims very actively and close to the water surface.

Diet: omnivorous.

Sex differences: the adult female has a more rounded belly.

Length: 4 cm (1½ in).

Distribution: eastern India.

Compatibility: excellent.

Temperature range: 18–27°C (64–80°F).

Breeding: one of the easiest of the oviparous fishes (see Breeding). All that is required is a small tank, about 12 cm (4¾ in) deep, filled with tap water at 26°C (79°F). The species of *Brachydanio* are prone to eating their own eggs and so these have to be protected. This can be done by covering the substrate with a layer of small glass balls (ballotini) or rounded gravel, so that the eggs can fall through into the interstices, or a piece of fine plastic mesh can be supported on a wooden frame about 3 cm (1¼ in) above the bottom. A single female, chosen for her rounded belly, is then introduced into the tank, and the following day two males are put in. The female spawns when the males chase her and press their flanks against hers. The eggs hatch in 30 hours, and the fry★ start to feed on infusorians★ about three days later. They grow rapidly and will soon take dried food★.

Brachygobius xanthozona

One of the bumblebee fishes, so called from the pattern on the body. It is separated from the very similar *B. nunus* and *B. aggregatus* by the number of scales, and by small differences in the colour pattern. These are nocturnal fish which spend the day attached to a rock or to the glass by the sucker formed by the fusion of the two ventral fins. They prefer water that is slightly brackish.

Family: Gobiidae★.

Diet: small live food.

Brachygobius xanthozona, the bumblebee fish (4 cm or 1½ in)

Sex differences: practically none.

Length: 4 cm (1½ in).

Distribution: Sumatra, Borneo, Java.

Compatibility: doubtful. Gobies have a tendency to nibble the fins of species that sleep during the night.

Temperature range: 20–28°C (68–82°F).

Breeding: not often successful, but has been achieved in slightly brackish water (1 g salt per litre: or 15 grains to every 1¾ pints) at pH 7.8 and a temperature of 26°C (79°F). The eggs hatch in about a week and the fry★ start to feed on infusorians★ 36 hours later, and subsequently on *Artemia*★ nauplii.

Breeding

Fishes can be grouped into two categories according to their method of reproduction, that is, whether they lay eggs (oviparity) or produce live young (viviparity). In both cases the female produces a number of ova which are fertilized by the male and become eggs. After incubation the eggs hatch into fry★.

Oviparous fishes In these the female liberates her ova into the water and the male then fertilizes them, either as they are laid, or all at once at the end of spawning, by releasing his sperm or milt over them.

This is by far the most widespread method of reproduction among aquarium fishes.

The simultaneous presence in the tank of the two partners is indispensable and sometimes these are not compatible. It is sometimes necessary to observe the fish over a long period before spawning in order to choose a male and female that appear to be compatible. In many cases this may be quite difficult as it is often not easy to distinguish the sexes. However, females ready to spawn will have a rounded belly, while the males which are more slender and often more brightly coloured, chase them for a few days or hours before spawning takes place.

The eggs are generally very numerous (sometimes several hundreds). In some species the eggs are adhesive and stick to the plants, while in others they fall to the bottom and slip into the substrate and this prevents them from being eaten by the parents. At about 26°C (79°F) the eggs of many species hatch in two days into tiny fry. At first the fry remain immobile for perhaps 2–3 days, living on the contents of the yolk sac. Then they start to swim and to feed on infusorians*.

Viviparous fishes These should really be known as ovoviviparous fishes. The fry hatch from an egg, but incubation and hatching do not take place in the water, as in oviparous fishes, but in the body of the female. Fertilization also occurs inside the female, the male having a special copulatory organ, the gonopodium, with which he introduces the sperm into the female's body. This organ, which is movable, is formed from rays of the anal fin. This enables the sexes to be distinguished, but quite apart from the gonopodium the distinction is usually easy for the males differ in shape, size and coloration from the females.

The vast majority of the viviparous aqua-rium fishes belong to the family Poeciliidae*, the best known being the guppy, *Poecilia* *reticulata*. Poeciliids are much easier to breed in the aquarium than the oviparous species. A single male can mate with several females, and a single mating often gives rise to successive broods. Gestation lasts some weeks, the period being shorter at higher temperatures. Before parturition the female's abdomen becomes inflated and in many species a black spot appears. This is the time to isolate the female to prevent the fry being eaten by other fishes. The fry are less numerous than those of oviparous fishes, but they are larger.

BUMBLEBEE FISH, see *Brachygobius xanthozona*.
BUTTERFLYFISH, see *Pantodon buchholzi*.

C

Callichthyidae

A family of catfishes from tropical South America. There are some two dozen families of catfishes, so called from the whisker-like barbels round the mouth. The Callichthyidae or armoured catfishes are characterized by the large head, the bony plates covering the body (instead of the usual scales) and the spiny fins which can inflict painful wounds in the hands of an unwary aquarist. They have an auxiliary method of respiration which involves the passage of atmospheric air through the intestine and this enables them to survive in waters that are deficient in oxygen. Apart from *Corydoras paleatus* which is particularly prolific the Callichthyidae are very difficult to breed in the aquarium.

see *Callichthys callichthys, Corydoras.*

Callichthys callichthys

One of the armoured catfishes in which the bony plates overlap like the slates on a roof. The large head has two mobile eyes and the mouth has four long barbels.

Family: Callichthyidae★.
Diet: omnivorous.
Sex differences: not detectable.
Length: up to 15 cm (6 in).
Distribution: Uruguay and eastern Brazil.
Compatibility: good, except with very small fish.

Callichthys callichthys, the mailed catfish (15 cm or 6 in)

Carassius auratus, the goldfish (up to 40 cm or 15½ in)

Temperature range: 22–30°C (72–86°F).
Breeding: rarely recorded. The male
  constructs a nest of air bubbles among
  the floating leaves and guards the eggs.
  The newly hatched fry feed immediately
  on *Artemia*★ nauplii.

CAPE LOPEZ, see *Aphyosemion*.
CAPOETA, see *Barbus*.

Carassius auratus

Known popularly as the goldfish, this member of the family Cyprinidae★ is the ancestor of a large number of domesticated forms known under such names as comets, shubunkins, veiltails and so on.

The original species from western China is olive-green, but over a period of perhaps 2,000 years the Chinese have selected fish that are golden or otherwise, and also forms with strange modifications of the fins and body shape. These include the veiltails with vastly exaggerated fins, the lion-heads with grotesque heads and the telescope-eyes with protruding eyes.

The more ordinary goldfish is a hardy animal suitable for outdoor water in temperate climates, where it breeds readily from an age of three years, and probably lives for up to 25 years, reaching a length of 40 cm (15½ in).

It can survive the winter at very low temperatures, providing the water does not freeze completely. When a fish pond freezes to a depth of 4–5 cm (1½–2 in), the best solution is to make a hole 10 cm (3¾ in) in diameter in the ice and to siphon out a few centimetres of water. This creates a cushion of air between the open water and the ice. The hole should be filled with a bunch of straw. If, however, the pond is very shallow it is better to transfer the fish to an unheated indoor tank.

Spherical bowls, the so-called goldfish bowls, are completely unsuitable and should be avoided at all costs. Goldfish kept indoors should be given a standard aquarium tank. They should never be fed more food than they can consume in one minute. From time to time a proportion of the water can be renewed

Carassius auratus, a veiltail variety of the goldfish (10–20 cm or 4–7¾ in)

Carnegiella strigata, the marbled hatchetfish (4–5 cm or 1½–2 in)

with water that has stood overnight in a glass or plastic container. This enables the new water to reach the same temperature as the original tank water and also to lose any chlorine it may contain.

Veiltails and the other odd varieties are more delicate and should be kept in a large tank, with plants, lighting, aeration and filtration. The water temperature need not, however, exceed 20°C (68°F), which is normal room temperature.

CARDINAL TETRA, see *Cheirodon axelrodi.*

Carnegiella strigata
This is one of the hatchetfishes, a family of surface-living tropical fishes closely related to the Characidae. They are characterized by the great development of the pectoral region and their ability to leap from the water and glide through the air to escape a predator. The related *Carnegiella marthae* is not often imported.
Family: Gasteropelecidae★.
Diet: omnivorous, with a preference for
    insects.

Sex differences: none.
Length: 4–5 cm (1½–2 in).
Distribution: Amazon basin and Guyana.
Compatibility: excellent.
Temperature range: 24–30°C (75–86°F).
Breeding: has occasionally been recorded.
    In soft, slightly acid water★.

CATFISH, see Callichthyidae, Loricariidae, Mochocidae, Siluridae.

Centrarchidae
A family of North American fishes from temperate waters, known as sunfishes. The dorsal and anal fins have spiny rays. Species kept in the aquarium include *Enneacanthus★ chaetodon, Elassoma evergladei,* c. 3.5 cm (1¼ in), and *Lepomis gibbosus,* up to 15 cm (6 in).

Centropomidae
A family of tropical fishes, also known as the Ambassidae. Most species come from the sea or brackish waters, but a few live in the fresh water of Asia. They are often called glassfishes

Gynochanda filamentosa (5 cm or 2 in)

on account of the transparency of the body. see *Chanda*.

Chanda

A genus of the family Centropomidae★, formerly known as *Ambassis*. The body is almost colourless, and so transparent that the bones can be discerned. In spite of its fragile appearance these are hardy fish which prefer to live in a small shoal in hard or slightly brackish water. The species usually seen in the aquarium are *Chanda ranga*, the Indian glassfish, *C. buruensis* which is more elongated, *C. wolfii*, a considerably larger fish, and in a neighbouring genus, *Gynochanda filamentosa*, in which the dorsal and anal fins of the male are extended into long filaments.

Chanda ranga

Family: Centropomidae★.
Diet: small live food.

Chanda, a glassfish (5 cm or 2 in)

Sex differences: the male shows slightly more colour.
Length: 5–7 cm (2–2¾ in).
Distribution: India, Burma, Thailand.
Compatibility: very good.
Temperature range: 20–28°C (68–82°F).
Breeding: possible in a planted tank with filtered water at 26°C (79°F). There may be 100 or more non-adhesive eggs which hatch in 24 hours. For four days the fry remain suspended from plants. The main difficulty is to get them to feed because they require microscopic organisms, which they snap at without actually swimming after them.

Characidae

A large family of fishes from the fresh waters of tropical Africa and America. They are mainly small, with well-developed dentition and often with an adipose (soft) fin between

Alestes longipinnis, a west African characin (13 cm or 5 in)

the dorsal and caudal fins. Most are peaceful, although the family does contain the ferocious piranhas★.

Characins, as they are known colloquially, do not all breed in the same way. Although they are never easy to breed in captivity, the difficulties involved vary considerably according to the species. The typical method is to rear several individuals and when they have reached sexual maturity to select a particularly active male and a female that is ready to spawn. A tank 50 cm (20 in) long is sufficient but it should preferably have no metal parts to avoid any chemical reaction with the acid waters that are often required. The eggs may either adhere to the plants or fall to the bottom. To prevent them being eaten by the parents it is best to have a layer of small glass balls or small round pebbles, or to fix a piece of fine plastic mesh a few centimetres above the bottom. If peat is required it should be well boiled, and in addition the tank and all accessories should have been carefully disinfected. Some species avoid the light, and in such cases the tank should be covered with brown paper or otherwise shaded. The very small fry★ should be given infusorians★ as soon as they have used up the contents of their yolk sac.

In addition to the numerous species indexed alphabetically, the family includes *Arnoldichthys spilopterus* and the species of *Alestes* from western Africa and of *Pyrrhulina* from the Amazon basin.

see *Astyanax mexicanus, Aphyocharax rubripinnis, Cheirodon axelrodi, Copeina arnoldi, Corynopoma riisei, Ctenobrycon spilurus, Gymnocorymbus ternetzi, Hasemania marginata, Hemigrammus, Hyphessobrycon, Megalamphodus megalopterus, Metynnis roosevelti, Moenkhausia oligolepis, Nematobrycon palmeri, Petitella, Phenacogrammus interruptus,* Piranha, *Pristella maxillaris, Thayeria obliqua.*

CHARACINS, see Characidae.

Cheirodon axelrodi

This is the cardinal tetra, one of the most beautiful aquarium fishes, with the body divided horizontally into an iridescent blue and a red area. In the wild these tetras live in

51

Cheirodon axelrodi, the cardinal tetra (5 cm or 2 in)

soft waters in places with subdued light, but they can become acclimatized to a life in hard water and fairly bright light.

Family: Characidae★.

Diet: omnivorous.

Sex differences: none, except that the female ready to spawn will have a rounded belly.

Length: up to 5 cm (2 in).

Distribution: Amazon basin, in the region of the Rio Negro.

Compatibility: excellent.

Temperature range: 24–28°C (75–82°F).

Breeding: as for Characidae★, although it is not often done. The water should have a pH of 6.1–6.5, and a hardness less than 10°DH. The eggs hatch in 24 hours and the fry will have used up the contents of their yolk sac in four days. The chances of successful breeding are greater with imported stock than with fish bred in the aquarium.

Chilodus punctatus

The popular name spotted headstander refers to the fish's habit of taking up an oblique position in the water with the head downwards. This is a characteristic which this fish shares with other members of its family.

Family: Anostomidae★.

Diet: live food and vegetable matter sufficiently small to be taken with the tiny mouth.

Sex differences: none.

Length: up to 9 cm (3½ in).

Distribution: north of Amazon basin and Guyana.

Compatibility: excellent. The species is rather timid.

Temperature range: 25–28°C (77–82°F).

Breeding: has been successful on some occasions.

CHIRONOMID LARVAE, see Diet.

Cichlasoma

A genus of American Cichlidae★ which are mostly easy to keep in the aquarium, although they often tend to be aggressive.

Cichlasoma festivum

A peaceful cichlid characterized by the green back, large belly and the black bar running from the rear part of the dorsal fin through the eye to the mouth. In the wild it is often seen in the company of angelfishes, *Pterophyllum★ scalare*.

Chilodus punctatus, the spotted headstander (up to 9 cm or 3½ in)

Cichlasoma meeki, the firemouth cichlid (15 cm or 6 in)

Diet: omnivorous, and including the shoots of tender plants.

Sex differences: not detectable.

Length: 15 cm (6 in).

Distribution: Amazon basin, among roots and vegetation.

Compatibility: good; this is a rather timid species.

Temperature range: 22–28°C (72–82°F).

Breeding: as for the Cichlidae*, but difficult in captivity.

Cichlasoma meeki

This is the firemouth cichlid, so called from the vivid red on the throat and belly, which contrasts with the grey-blue of the body. It is suitable for a community tank with other medium-sized fishes, and it does not destroy the plants.

Diet: omnivorous; very voracious.

Sex differences: dorsal and anal fins more pointed in the male.

Length: up to 15 cm (6 in).

Distribution: central America (Yucatan and Guatemala).

Compatibility: generally good with fishes of a certain size.

Temperature range: 22–28°C (72–82°F).

Breeding: easy. As for the Cichlidae*.

Cichlasoma nigrofasciatum

A hardy cichlid, with a slate-grey body and vertical black stripes.

Diet: omnivorous, with a preference for large live food.

Sex differences: the female, smaller and paler than the male, has slightly rounded fins.

Length: 11 cm (4 in).

Distribution: lakes of central America.

Compatibility: bad, even with members of its own species.

Temperature range: 20–27°C (68–80°F).

Breeding: sometimes difficult, the male only accepting a female chosen by himself.

Cichlasoma octofasciatum

A handsome fish with colours that change with age and mood. Known colloquially as the Jack Dempsey, on account of its pugnacious behaviour, this is essentially a fish for the larger tank (length over 1 m [3 feet]), with other largish fishes.

Diet: any live food.

Sex differences: difficult to detect. The male is usually more intensely coloured, with more pointed fins.

Length: 18 cm (7 in).

Distribution: Amazon basin.
Compatibility: bad.
Temperature range: 20–28°C (68–82°F).
Breeding: as for Cichlidae*.

Cichlasoma severum

Juveniles have the body marked with blackish bands, while the adults are mostly greenish or brownish, marked with small spots and a dark vertical line near the base of the tail, but the coloration is very variable.

Diet: omnivorous, with a preference for large prey.

Sex differences: not obvious, although the female is generally paler, with more rounded fins.

Length: up to 20 cm (7¾ in).

Distribution: north of the Amazon basin and Guyana.

Compatibility: good when young, bad when adult.

Temperature range: 20–27°C (68–80°F).

Breeding: relatively difficult.

Cichlidae

A large family of freshwater fishes widely distributed in Africa and America (southern U.S.A. to South America), with a few species in India and Sri Lanka.

Like the closely related perches, cichlids have spiny fins, but differ in having two nostrils, where the perches have four. Their lateral line is divided into two parts.

In the wild they live in lakes or flowing waters and vigorously defend their territory. In the aquarium, some cichlids are very aggressive and will change the tank decoration, displacing the rockwork and substrate and uprooting the plants. Others are less active in this respect, and some can even be described as very peaceful. These differences in behaviour are reflected in their sexual relations. In many species the male chooses his mate, and the pair often remain closely united and vigilantly guard their numerous offspring.

Cichlasoma octofasciatum, the Jack Dempsey (18 cm or 7 in)

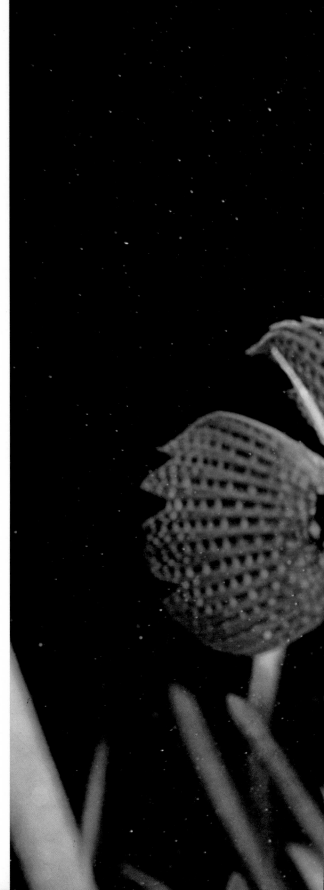

Cichlasoma severum, the banded cichlid (up to 20 cm or 7¾ in)

In most genera, a pair will start to prepare a suitable spawning site by digging a pit or by cleaning the surface of a rock. Their colours intensify, and from each a genital papilla begins to protrude, which is rounded in the female, small and conical in the male. Very soon the female starts to swim round above the chosen spawning site and then lays some eggs on it, which the male immediately fertilizes. This process is repeated until all the ripe eggs have been laid. The parents then start to guard the eggs and to fan them with their fins. When necessary they remove any unfertilized eggs which might start to decay and infect the others. Hatching takes place in 2–4 days. In some species the parents then take the fry* into their mouths and transfer them to a previously dug pit. Sometimes, if this place does not appear safe enough they will take the fry to another pit. After a further 4–8 days, having used up the contents of their yolk sac, the fry start to swim about but the parents still continue to guard them assiduously. The fry will soon take finely powdered food and *Artemia** nauplii.

In certain cichlids the female practises what is known as mouthbrooding. She takes the fertilized eggs into her mouth and holds them there until they hatch. She then guards the fry until the yolk sac is resorbed. The mouthbrooding cichlids of Africa include some of the brilliantly coloured but aggressive species from Lake Tanganyika and Malawi (formerly Nyasa).

Uaru amphiacanthoides, the triangle or chocolate cichlid, from South America (up to 25 cm or 10 in)

The Asiatic cichlids are not very brightly coloured outside the breeding period and are seldom imported. The one most likely to appear on the market is the orange chromide, *Etroplus maculatus*, which is about 8 cm (3 in) in length.

See *Aequidens, Apistogramma, Astronotus ocellatus, Cichlasoma, Hemichromis bimaculatus, Julidochromis ornatus, Labeotropheus, Melanochromis auratus, Nannacara anomala, Pelmatochromis, Pelvicachromis, Pseudocrenilabrus multicolor, Pseudotropheus, Pterophyllum scalare, Symphysodon.*

Citharinidae

A family of African fishes closely related to the Characidae★. Most are rather too large for the amateur aquarium. Those that are imported include a few species of *Nannaethiops*, of which the largest is *N. unitaeniatus* (6.5 cm: or $2\frac{1}{2}$ in), and also *Neolebias ansorgei* (up to 3.5 cm: or $1\frac{1}{4}$ in), which requires extremely soft water.

CLASSIFICATION, see Systematics.

Cobitidae

A family of bottom-living fishes, known as loaches, with representatives in Europe and Asia. A species has also been reported in Ethiopia. The mouth is ventral and surrounded by a number of barbels. There is an obliquely positioned, erectile spine below each eye. Loaches very rarely breed in the aquarium.

see *Acanthopthalmus Kuhlii, Botia*

Colisa

A genus in the family Anabantidae★. In addition to *C. lalia*, the genus includes *C. chuna* in which the male is orange and black, *C. fasciata* which reaches a length of 12 cm ($4\frac{3}{4}$ in), and *C. labiosa*, the thick-lipped gourami, a close relative of *C. lalia* but not so brightly coloured.

Colisa lalia

This is the dwarf gourami, an attractive

Cobitis taenia, the spined loach of Europe (5–10 cm or 2–$3\frac{3}{4}$ in)

Colisa fasciata, the giant gourami (up to 12 cm or 4¾ in)

species with alternate oblique bands of red and blue-green. It is a peaceful fish which does well in a sunlit tank with soft water and plenty of vegetation.

Diet: omnivorous.
Sex differences: the female is less brightly coloured, with more rounded fins.
Length: 6 cm (2¼ in).
Distribution: India (Bengal and Assam).
Compatibility: excellent.

Temperature range: 22–28°C (72–82°F).
Breeding: as for *Betta*★ *splendens*, but the female takes part in building the nest, in which some fragments of plants are incorporated.

COMET, see *Carassius auratus*.

Copella arnoldi
An elongated, surface-living fish with fine red

Colisa lalia, the dwarf gourami (6 cm or 2¼ in)

and black fins. It is a good jumper.
Family: Characidae★.
Diet: omnivorous, but small live food must
  be given regularly.
Sex differences: dorsal and caudal fins
  longer and more pointed in the male.
Length: 8 cm (3 in) for the male, 6 cm (2¼
  in) for the female.
Distribution: lower Amazon.

Compatibility: satisfactory.
Temperature range: 22–28°C (72–82°F).
Breeding: totally different from other
  Characidae★ and indeed from all other
  fishes. The species has been bred
  successfully in a large tank containing a
  depth of not more than 20 cm (7–8 in) of
  soft, acid water, filtered through peat. In
  the wild spawning takes place on leaves

or twigs just above the water surface. In the aquarium, the pair may spawn on a piece of rock or a leaf, or quite simply on the tank cover. The two fish jump out of the water to spawn and fertilize the eggs which adhere to the spawning site. When spawning is complete the male remains below and keeps the eggs damp by splashing water with his tail. The eggs hatch after 36–48 hours and the fry* drop into the water. At this point the parent fish should be removed and the fry can be fed on infusorians*.

Corydoras

A large genus of catfishes in the family Callichthyidae*. They are bottom-living fishes which occasionally come to the water surface to take in a little air. When not resting, which they sometimes do by balancing on a leaf, they spend their time searching for food in the form of small live prey or scraps left by the other fishes. In this way they remove excess food which would otherwise pollute the water. Unfortunately, in this active scavenging they stir up the substrate with their snouts and by the movements of the tail.

Apart from this slight inconvenience the species of Corydoras are perfect aquarium fishes which show no interest in other species, and are themselves ignored by the other occupants of the tank. The sexes are generally difficult to distinguish, although the fins of the male are often more pointed. Apart from Corydoras paleatus they rarely breed in captivity.

Corydoras aeneus
Diet: omnivorous.
Sex differences: the dorsal fin is rounded in the female, pointed in the male.
Length: up to 7 cm (2¾ in).
Distribution: eastern South America, from Venezuela to La Plata.
Compatibility: excellent.
Temperature range: 20–28°C (68–82°F).
Breeding: as for C. paleatus, but more difficult.

Copella arnoldi, the spraying characin (8 cm or 3 in)

Corydoras arcuatus
A brownish species with an arched black line running from the mouth to the base of the tail.
Diet: omnivorous.
Sex differences: female stouter and often longer.
Length: up to 5 cm (2 in).
Distribution: Amazon basin.
Compatibility: excellent.
Temperature range: 22–30°C (72–86°F).
Breeding: has been achieved from time to time.

Corydoras hastatus
A brown species marked with a horizontal black band. It often rises from the bottom and swims in the open water.
Diet: omnivorous.
Sex differences: female stouter and usually longer.
Length: less than 4 cm (1½ in).
Distribution: from Paraguay to the Amazon basin.
Compatibility: perfect.
Temperature range: 22–30°C (72–86°F).
Breeding: has been successful occasionally.

Corydoras julii

A very popular aquarium fish on account of the attractive dark markings on a beige background.

Diet: omnivorous.
Sex differences: female stouter.
Length: up to 6 cm (2¼ in).
Distribution: eastern Brazil.
Compatibility: almost perfect.
Temperature range: 22–30°C (72–86°F).
Breeding: has been achieved.

Corydoras melanistius

Darker than *C. julii* but with similar markings, including some below the head and at the base of the dorsal fin.

Diet: omnivorous.
Sex differences: female stouter and usually longer.
Length: up to 6 cm (2¼ in).
Distribution: Venezuela.
Compatibility: excellent.
Temperature range: 22–30°C (72–86°F).
Breeding: has been achieved.

Corydoras paleatus

A hardy, beige-coloured fish with brown markings, which has been known to live for as long as eight years.

Diet: omnivorous.
Sex differences: dorsal and pectoral fins pointed in the male, rounded in the female.
Length: up to 7 cm (2¾ in).
Distribution: south-eastern Brazil and La Plata region.
Compatibility: excellent.
Temperature range: 18–28°C (64–82°F).
Breeding: not so difficult as in the other *Corydoras* species. A tank 50 cm (20 in) long should be filled to a depth of 30 cm (12 in) with mature water at a pH of 7.0–7.2 and a temperature of 26°C (79°F). The tank should have a few plants★ with large leaves, slow substrate filtration★ and subdued lighting★. A female showing reddish spots on the belly should be chosen as these indicate that she is ready to spawn. She should be

Corydoras melanistius, the black-spotted catfish (up to 6 cm or 2¼ in)

put into the tank with one or two males. It is a good sign if the males chase the female and stroke her back with their barbels. If they appear indifferent, the temperature can be varied and a little new water added, in order to stimulate spawning. This occurs when a male and a female come together belly to belly. At each mating the female lays only a few eggs. These she collects with her ventral fins and then attaches them to the upper or lower surface of a leaf, sometimes to a rock or even to the aquarium glass. The male's sperm fertilizes the eggs, which are rather large, white and very adhesive. They hatch in about three days, and the fry*, which may number more than 200, can then be fed, first on infusorians*, later on *Artemia** nauplii.

Corydoras rabauti

This is a rarely imported species from the area of Manaus on the Amazon. It is remarkable for its small size, for it scarcely reaches a length of 3 cm (1¼ in).

Corynopoma riisei

A grey-green species, known as the swordtail characin. Each operculum has a long spine ending in a filament with a spoon-shaped tip. These filaments play an important part in mating behaviour. The related *Pseudocorynopoma doriae* does not have the opercular spines, but is otherwise very similar to *C. riisei*, and it breeds in the same way.
Family: Characidae*.
Diet: omnivorous, with a preference for live prey.
Sex differences: the lower lobe of the caudal fin is considerably more elongated in the male.
Length: 7 cm (2¾ in).
Distribution: Trinidad and Venezuela.
Compatibility: good.
Temperature range: 20–30°C (68–86°F).
Breeding: differs from other characins. In the course of the nuptial display the male extends the opercular spine towards the

female, quivers it and inserts a packet of sperm into the genital orifice of the female. Fertilization is thus internal and the female can spawn several times without any fresh contact with the male. She guards the eggs which hatch in 36 hours, and then continues to tend the fry*.

Ctenobrycon spilurus

A hardy but not very colourful characin which can even be kept at room temperature.
Family: Characidae*.
Diet: omnivorous, with an annoying tendency to nibble the plants.
Sex differences: none, except that the gravid female has a more rounded belly.
Length: 7 cm (2¾ in).
Distribution: coastal areas of northern South America.
Compatibility: doubtful with fishes smaller than itself.
Temperature range: 18–27°C (64–80°F).
Breeding: as for the Characidae*, but in a fairly large tank. Tap water is adequate provided it has stood for some time. The eggs hatch in 30 hours.

Cyclops

A small freshwater crustacean with a single eye. Smaller than *Daphnia**, it nevertheless forms a good nutritious food for fishes, and has the advantage that it is available throughout the year. It will attack any prey of its own size and should never be put into a tank with newly hatched fry*.
see Diet.

Cynolebias belottii

A blue-green fish with whitish spots, thus differing from the related *C. nigripinnis* which is blue-black with greenish spots and *C. whitei* which is maroon. The species of the genus *Cynolebias* are annual, that is the adults die after spawning when the waters in which they live dry up. The eggs then undergo a period of desiccation. On the return of the rains the eggs

Cynolebias nigripinnis, the Argentine pearl fish (5 cm or 2 in)

Diet: a marked preference for live food.

Sex differences: the female is much smaller than the male, and less colourful.

Length: up to 5 cm (2 in) for the male.

Distribution: Argentina.

Compatibility: doubtful, as all *Cynolebias* species are rather aggressive.

Temperature range: 18–30°C (64–86°F).

Breeding: has been achieved by amateur aquarists skilled in keeping *Aphyo-semion*★. The substrate should be covered with a layer of peat 5 cm (2 in) deep, into which the fish burrow before spawning. The eggs are then kept in the peat after the water has been drained off, usually for about five months. The eggs hatch some hours after they have been put back into the water.

hatch, the young grow rapidly to reach sexual maturity, and spawn before the next dry season, when they in their turn die as the waters recede.

Family: Cyprinodontidae★.

Cyprinidae

A large family with some 2,000 species, of which about 300 are kept as ornamental fishes. The species are distributed throughout the world, with the exception of Australia, South

Some varieties of *Carassius auratus,* the goldfish (up to 40 cm or 15½ in), the best known of the Cyprinidae

America, Greenland, Iceland and Madagascar. Most of them carry barbels in the mouth region and they all lack teeth on the jaws, although they have solid well-developed teeth in the pharynx, which are used for mastication.

The species most commonly kept in the aquarium are dealt with alphabetically. Others include *Epalzeorhynchus kallopterus* which has the merit of removing algae★ and planarians★ that infest the aquarium, and *Esomus danrica*, a fish with large pectoral fins which enable it to leap high out of the water. see *Barbus, Brachydanio, Carassius auratus, Danio malabaricus, Labeo bicolor, Rasbora, Tanichthys albonubes.*

Cyprinodontidae

A family of tropical and subtropical fishes with representatives in all the continents except Australia. In general characteristics they resemble the only distantly related Cyprinidae★, but they possess toothed jaws. Most are smaller or medium-sized and brightly coloured. All are oviparous but the details of breeding vary according to the genus.

Certain species with a restricted distribution are worth mentioning. These include *Aphanius iberus* from ponds along the coasts of Algeria and eastern Spain, *Chriopeops goodei* from Florida which can be bred provided the eggs are protected from the parents, and *Austrofundulus dolichopterus* from Venezuela, in which the male has remarkably long and pointed dorsal and anal fins. The species of *Pterolebias* from South America are very attractive and those of *Aplocheilichthys* from Africa are more peaceful than the majority of the Cyprinodontidae, but both are delicate and require much attention.

see *Aphyosemion, Aplocheilus, Cynolebias belottii, Epiplatys, Fundulus chrysotus, Jordanella floridae, Nothobranchius, Oryzias, Pachypanchax playfairi, Rivulus cylindraceus.*

Aphyosemion scheeli (5 cm or 2 in), one of the Cyprinodontidae

D

DANIO, see also *Brachydanio*.

Danio malabaricus

The genus *Danio* differs from *Brachydanio* in having a continuous lateral line and a greater number of dorsal and anal fin rays. *Danio malabaricus*, known as the giant danio, has 3–4 bluish longitudinal bands along the flanks. It is active and hardy but rather too large for a small aquarium.

Family: Cyprinidae*.

Diet: omnivorous.

Sex differences: apart from being more rounded when ready to spawn, the female has the middle blue band turned up at the base of the caudal fin, whereas in the male this band is straight.

Length: 12 cm ($4\frac{3}{4}$ in).

Distribution: Sri Lanka and the Malabar coast of India.

Compatibility: good.

Temperature range: 18–28°C (64–82°F).

Breeding: the tank should be at least 70 cm (28 in) long, but otherwise the conditions should be the same as for *Brachydanio* *rerio*.

Daphnia

A small freshwater crustacean varying in

Danio malabaricus, the giant danio (12 cm or $4\frac{3}{4}$ in)

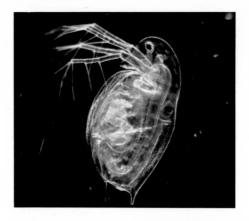

Daphnia seen under the microscope (1–3 mm $\frac{1}{25}$–$\frac{3}{25}$ in)

length from 1 to 3 mm (c. $\frac{1}{25}$ in to $\frac{3}{25}$ in), according to the species. When living it will be taken by most fishes and forms a good dietary supplement. If given alternately with other live food or with dried food it encourages growth. Dried *Daphnia* is available on the market but it has little food value and should only be used to feed goldfish *(Carassius* * *auratus)*.

DECORATION, see Setting up the tank.

Dermogenys pusillus

A surface-living fish from south-east Asia that is characterized by the very long lower jaw and the relatively short upper jaw. It lives in hard or even slightly brackish water with an abundance of vegetation.

Family: Hemiramphidae*.

Diet: insects in the wild, but dried food and small live prey at the surface when kept in an aquarium.

Sex differences. the male has the anal fin modified to form a pointed copulatory organ.

Length: male 6 cm ($2\frac{1}{4}$ in), female 8 cm (3 in).

Distribution: Thailand, Malaysia, Greater Sunda Islands.

Compatibility: good with other species, but the males fight savagely with one another; they are used for contests in Thailand, in the same way as *Betta**.

Temperature range: 23–28°C (73–82°F).

Dermogenys pusillus, one of the half-beaks (6 cm or 2¼ in)

Breeding: this is a viviparous species which can be bred in slightly brackish water. The period of gestation varies from 4–8 weeks depending upon the temperature. At birth the 15–30 young have jaws of equal length, and the adult type of snout does not develop until they are about two months old.

Diet

In the wild, apart from certain carnivorous species which devour a large prey animal once or twice a day, the majority of fish spend a considerable part of their life searching for food.

In the aquarium★ they do not have to do this and quickly learn their feeding time.

Fry★ should be fed very frequently and the regularity of their food has a considerable influence on their development. Thus, a fast of only a single day, particularly during the first days of active life, after resorption of the yolk sac, may result in an arrest of growth that is almost irreversible.

The adults, on the other hand, will be satisfied with a single daily feeding. With the exception of living *Daphnia★*, which continue to swim until eaten, the amount of food offered should be such that it is all eaten in a period of 15 minutes.

Overfeeding is one of the scourges of aquariology★, and must at all costs be avoided. It leads to various types of disease★, the pollution of the water★, and to an upset of the biological★ equilibrium.

The best food that could be offered to fishes living in captivity would be what they find in the wild. This is not always possible, but in general an effort should be made to provide some live food from time to time.

After resorption of the yolk sac, newly hatched fry★ which are tiny should be fed on infusorians★. Fry that are slightly larger can be given the nauplii (larvae) of *Artemia★*, the brine shrimp. Commercial powdered foods can also be given to those that will accept them–usually the hardier and more voracious species.

After the fry stage, the young fish can be given the same food as the adults. This consists of various dried foods and live food. The quality of the former has been greatly improved as a result of research on dried foods intended for fish farms, particularly those rearing trout. These products now have a balanced content of meat, fish and vegetable matter.

Dried foods are given in powdered form to fry, as pellets to older fish. Provided they are not crushed between the fingers, the pellets do not release the very tiny particles which are of no interest to larger fish which only serve to pollute the water and to nourish undesirable algae★.

In addition to pellets, manufacturers also offer freeze-dried products, mainly animal foods that cannot always be obtained in the living state, e.g. chironomid larvae, *Tubifex* and adult *Artemia*.

Chironomid larvae, often known as blood-worms, are actually the larval stage of certain midges which do not bite. *Tubifex* is the scientific name given to certain very thin worms, about 2 cm ($\frac{4}{5}$ in) long, which are rich in haemoglobin and have high nutritive value. These two live foods can be kept for 2–3 days in a bowl of water in the refrigerator, provided the water is changed daily. *Tubifex* can be kept for up to a week under a slowly dripping tap.

Brine shrimps *(Artemia★ salina)* are small marine crustaceans. The newly hatched larvae, known as nauplii (singular nauplius), are fed to fry, whereas the adults (about 1 cm [$\frac{1}{4}$ in] long when 5 weeks old) are fed to fish measuring more than 2.5 cm (1 in) long. These can be bought, or they can be reared.

Daphnia★ and *Cyclops★* are also small crustaceans, which live in fresh water ponds that are rich in organic matter. They can be netted from such ponds or bought from a dealer. When live they provide an excellent, very digestible food. Dried *Daphnia* have

A fuitfly, *Drosophila* (much enlarged)

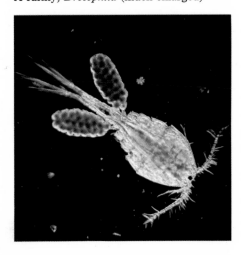

little nutritive value and are suitable only for feeding goldfish *(Carassius★ auratus)*.

Some amateurs raise their own live food, either because they live far from a dealer or because they keep and breed delicate species. Such foods include whiteworms or en-chytraeids (containing much fat and only to be fed sparingly), microworms and Grindal worms, which are also white but much smaller. Fruitflies *(Drosophila)* can also be bred for feeding to insectivorous fishes. Advice on methods of breeding these live foods and also on sources of supply is usually obtainable from a local aquarium society or club.

Cyclops, seen under the microscope

Holidays

Like most cold-blooded animals, fishes are accommodating as regards feeding schedule and can tolerate a prolonged fast, provided their general condition is satisfactory and that they have received a varied and abundant supply of food during the preceding weeks. However, the low diet should not be pro-longed for more than a month. In a well established tank the fish will also obtain some nourishment from the plants. The return to a normal diet should be gradual to prevent the rather hungry fish from gorging themselves and becoming ill.

Automatic dispensers of pelleted food are available on the market, but they are expen-sive.

There are also 'holiday blocks' which the fish slowly nibble. They have the disadvantage that they increase the calcium content of the water, which should therefore be at least partially renewed on return from holiday.

DISCUS, see *Symphysodon*.

Disease

Like all living organisms, fishes may become ill but the risk of this happening will be considerably reduced if certain common-sense rules of hygiene are observed:

Overpopulation will favour the spread of disease.

Under-feeding will lower resistance to disease.

Over-feeding is even more detrimental, as quite apart from its general effect on health it also rapidly leads to pollution of the water as the excess food starts to decompose.

Avoid sudden changes in the composition and temperature of the water.

Avoid the chance of introducing disease or a parasite by buying only from reputable dealers.

Try to keep only compatible species in a tank.

Keep the tank clean by regularly siphoning off any detritus that collects.

In spite of such elementary precautions, fishes do become ill. In practice their illnesses are of two kinds: those that can be treated and those that do not respond to treatment.

curable diseases or conditions Asphyxia, due to lack of oxygen in the water, causes the fish to come to the surface for air. If not very accentuated, lack of oxygen may result from a reduction in atmospheric pressure, as occurs in summer when the weather is thundery, for example before a storm. The remedy is to reduce the diet and increase the aeration*. Apart from such an exceptional case asphyxia may be due to insufficient access to air or to the presence of toxic substances (see below).

Constipation due to a poorly balanced diet occurs rather rarely, except perhaps in goldfish which appear to be predisposed to it on account of the very long intestine. Some aquarists take the fish out and give it a drop of oil, preferably castor oil, ensuring that it swallows twice before it is put back into the water.

Mycosis or fungal disease is caused by a microscopic fungus *(Saprolegnia)*. It appears round the mouth in the form of sticky white ulcerative matter, looking rather like cotton wool. This is a contagious disease, which can be cured by certain specialist drugs, but it is often better to treat it with salt. This method is particularly suitable in the case of livebearing fishes in which the fungus is normally inoffensive but may become pathogenic if the condition of the fish deteriorates as a result of bad living conditions. The sick fish should be placed for 12 hours in a separate tank containing 5 g of sea salt per litre of water (c. $\frac{1}{5}$ oz per $1\frac{3}{4}$ pints). After this the content of salt can be raised by adding 3 g ($\frac{1}{8}$ oz) of salt, and this addition can be repeated 12 hours later. The fish should be left in this bath, which now contains 11 g (almost $\frac{1}{2}$ oz) salt per litre ($1\frac{3}{4}$ pints), until the fungus has disappeared. It should then be moved every 12 hours through a series of tanks with decreasing concentrations of salt until the water has only 3 g ($\frac{1}{8}$ oz) of salt per litre ($1\frac{3}{4}$ pints). The fish can then be put back into clean fresh water.

The flatworm parasites *Gyrodactylus* and *Dactylogyrus* attack the gills and skin of fishes. Infected fish can be given a short bath in a solution of salt (as above).

Intoxication, or in more serious cases true poisoning, may be manifested in various ways: the fish seeks for air either at the surface or near the diffuser, its coloration becomes paler, it appears sleepy and loses its appetite. There may be several causes. The air may be polluted by paints, varnishes or various caustic substances, or by tobacco smoke, deodorants or insecticidal sprays. This is why it is always preferable to place the inlet of the air pump close to the open air, e.g. on a window sill, rather than right inside a building.

Apart from cases of overpopulation or overfeeding, toxicity in the water may be due to the presence of an unsuitable metal or to toxic substances leaching out of plastics. Metals to be avoided at all costs are copper and zinc, and all plastics should be of a quality used in the food and drink industry.

White-spot disease is caused by the microscopic protozoan known as *Ichthyophthirius*. This is the most persistent, the most contagious and the commonest of all the diseases that attack freshwater aquarium fishes. In former times it was a very serious scourge. Nowadays, the disease can be cured provided it is treated as soon as it is detected. The first sign is the appearance of two or three tiny stationary pearly spots on the body or more often on a fin. In bad cases the whole of the body and fins will appear as though covered with a fine white powder, and the fish will be clearly debilitated. If the powder is particularly dense, and the spots are very tiny and greyish rather than white and are seen to move slowly from place to place, the fish will be suffering from oodiniasis (see below).

Several drugs for the treatment of white-spot are available on the market; preparations containing malachite green are among the most effective. It is advisable always to have a bottle of one or other of these available, so that the fish can be treated without delay, using the dosage recommended. Whenever such drugs are used over any period of time it is essential to aerate through a diffuser so that the fish do not suffer from oxygen lack. However, the filter should be switched off as the filter medium would absorb some of the drug and thus reduce the effectiveness of the treatment.

After treatment, which usually takes a few days, half the water should be siphoned off and the remainder gradually diluted with fresh water. The filter can now be switched on to remove the last traces of the drug.

Oodiniasis, often confused with white-spot disease (see above), is caused by another microscopic organism, known as *Oodinium*. It appears as motile greyish-white spots, smaller and more densely packed than in white-spot. Here again there are now drugs on the market which cure this disease.

Abnormal swimming movements usually indicate that the fish have become chilled

A fish infected with white-spot (*Ichthyophthirius*)

owing to the water being too cold. In many cases this can be cured by raising the water temperature, at the rate of 2°C (c. 3°F) per day, until the maximum temperature for the species is attained. Take care to ensure adequate aeration, as warm water can hold less oxygen. Many aquarists also give the fish a salt bath, as recommended for fungus (see above). If the result is unsatisfactory, or if, after a cure, the condition returns, it is probable that the conditions in the tank are not suitable for the species concerned.

incurable diseases Certain rare, often non-contagious diseases are not curable in the present state of knowledge, although it is always worth checking that a new cure has not been found.

Worm cataract is caused by a trematode flatworm. The parasites are transmitted to the fish by snails* which serve as intermediate hosts.

Exophthalmia (bulging eyes) is a symptom of several diseases. It may disappear of its own accord, but in some cases it may be necessary to kill the fish.

Ascites is caused by an infestation of *Pseudomonas* type of bacteria. It is contagious and any fish suffering from it should be killed without delay.

Ichthyophonus disease is caused by a fungus. It is difficult to diagnose as the symptoms vary. External signs are sores, abscesses, lop-sided body, etc.

Plistophora is a micro-organism which almost exclusively attacks tetras, particularly the neon tetra, causing progressive discoloration. There is, at present, no known cure for this disease which is often known as neon disease.
see Accidents, Age.

DROSOPHILA, see Diet.
DWARF TOP MINNOW, see *Heterandria formosa*.

ELEPHANT-TRUNK FISH, see *Gnathonemus petersii*.

Enneacanthus chaetodon
The main point about this fish is that it can be kept in an unheated tank.
Family: Centrarchidae*.
Diet: omnivorous, with a preference for
    live food.
Sex differences: the female is slightly paler.
Length: 8 cm (3 in).
Distribution: eastern United States.
Compatibility: satisfactory with companions
    of its own size.
Temperature range: 10–20°C (50–68°F).
Breeding: possible, the eggs being guarded
    and fanned by the male.

Epiplatys
A genus in the family Cyprinodontidae*, with about 40 species from central and western Africa. The majority of these are not imported for the aquarium, either because they are not particularly decorative, or because, like *E. sheljuzhkoi*, they are too quarrelsome.

Epiplatys dageti
A small, hardy, surface-living fish shaped like a pike.
Diet: omnivorous.
Sex differences: the female is smaller and
    has smaller fins.
Length: 6 cm (2¼ in).
Distribution: Liberia, Ghana and Ivory
    Coast.
Compatibility: excellent.
Temperature range: 20–29°C (68–84°F).
Breeding: relatively easy in slightly acid
    water kept at 25°C (77°F), and with a
    hardness not exceeding 10°DH. The tank
    should have some vegetation, to which
    the very adhesive eggs will become
    attached. The plants and eggs can then

ABOVE *Epiplatys dageti*, the red-chinned panchax (6 cm or 2½)

BELOW *Enneacanthus chaetodon*, the black-banded sunfish (8 cm or 3 in)

be transferred to another tank, thus preventing the eggs being eaten by the parents. The eggs start to hatch after about 12 days. The water should not be deep and must be moderately lit from above, so that the fry can find the infusorians* which should be supplied in abundance.

Epiplatys sexfasciatus

A rather aggressive species marked with six vertical bars, which vary in prominence according to the mood of the fish.

Diet: omnivorous, and capable of eating any slender fish up to 6 cm (2¼ in) in length.

Sex differences: the female has a rounded anal fin, and her ventral fins are shorter than those of the male.

Length: 10 cm (3¾ in).

Distribution: Liberia to Zaire.

Compatibility: bad.

Temperature range: 22–30°C (72–86°F).

Breeding: as for *E. dageti*, but the plants can be replaced by nylon wool. The eggs hatch in 14 days, and the parents will not eat them or the fry*.

F

Feeding rings

These are small plastic gadgets with a mesh which are generally supplied with a suction cup to fix them to the side of the tank at the level of the water surface. The bottom is flat if it is to hold chironomid larvae (bloodworms) or conical with the point facing downwards if it is to hold *Tubifex*.

The mesh can sometimes be removed, leaving the ring, which can then be fixed at the water surface to prevent dry flake food from spreading and possibly adhering to the plants.

Although live food can be just dropped on

Food dispenser holding *Tubifex*

to the surface of the water a feeding ring prevents the worms, etc., from sinking too fast and thus escaping from timid fish that take time to make up their minds and never go down to feed on the bottom.

FIGHTING FISH, see *Betta splendens*.

Filtration

Aquarium fishes in a well maintained tank are living under conditions that are quite different from their natural environment. This is primarily due to the high density of fish per unit volume of water, and this is why filtration of the water is so often recommended. This operation can be done either by using the aquarium substrate as a filter medium or by having a special separate filter.

In the first method the water to be filtered passes through the substrate. The motive power is provided by air from the air pump, which pushes or sucks the water through a shallow box with numerous slits, usually known as a substrate filter, which is buried in the substrate. The water passes through the layers of substrate where it leaves its impurities which are subsequently broken down by bacteria and used by the plants. In fact, the area of substrate in the region of the filter acts as a kind of septic tank for the aquarium.

The advantages of this type of filter are relative invisibility, neatness, simplicity and efficiency, for the tank water clears very rapidly. The disadvantages are the speed with which organic matter is broken down into mineral salts and the leaching of the substrate which may affect the plants. In practice, the risk of an accumulation of mineral salts can be easily avoided by regularly siphoning off a proportion of the water and replacing with new water. The leaching effect can be limited by separating off the filtration area by an invisible barrier, such as a vertical strip of plastic buried in the substrate.

The second method of filtration involves the use of a filtration apparatus with a special filter medium, powered either by air from the air pump or by an electrically driven water pump.

For small or medium-sized tanks it is usually sufficient to bring the water to the filter medium by using an air-lift. This involves positioning a glass or rigid plastic tube vertically in the water in such a way that its lower end is about 2 cm ($\frac{1}{2}$ in) above the substrate and its upper end protrudes about 2

A high capacity external filter

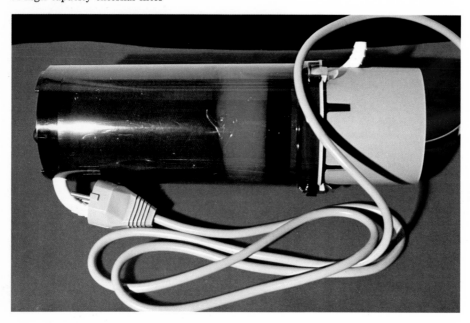

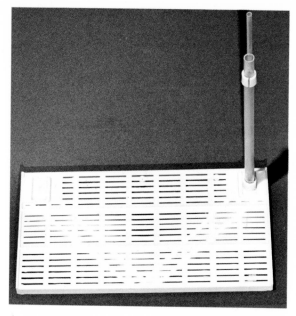

A substrate filter

and at the same time serve as a substrate for bacteria which break down the impurities.

Nylon wool which retains the waste matter but is a purely mechanical filter. Synthetic sponge can also be used, but glass wool is not recommended as it tends to shed fragments which may easily reach the fishes' gills and cause damage.

Activated charcoal also retains waste matter, and in addition it absorbs any gases produced during decomposition. It must, however, be renewed regularly (every 4–6 weeks) as it becomes clogged rather quickly and then ceases to function.
see Maintenance.

FOOD, see *Diet*.

Fry

Strictly speaking the term fry refers to young fish destined for the re-stocking of natural waters, but in the aquarium world it is applied to any young fish.

In egg-laying fishes the fry are mostly very

Fry of *Pelmatochromis* showing the yolk sac

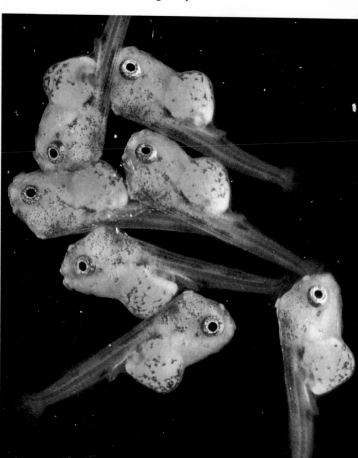

cm (½ in) above the water surface and is bent over at an angle. Air from the air pump is led into the lower end of the tube and as the bubbles of air rise they carry water with them. In this way a mixture of air and water reaches the top where it is expelled on to the filter medium. The actual container with the filter medium can be suspended either inside or outside the tank, the latter being the better alternative from the aesthetic viewpoint.

For larger filtration systems, involving the movement of 100 litres or more per hour, there are now several very efficient pumps on the market. These have to be positioned at a level below the water surface of the aquarium. The water is siphoned from the tank into a container filled with the filter medium. After passing through this the water is returned to the aquarium by the pump.

This type is used whenever intensive filtration is needed, e.g. for very large, over-populated tanks, or for those with large fishes or species which are constantly disturbing the substrate.

The filtration media used are:

Coarse gravel which retains large particles of waste matter.

Fine gravel and sand which clear the water

tiny. On hatching they look like an almost transparent comma and are only just visible to the naked eye.

The fry of viviparous or livebearing fishes, even those of small species such as the Guppy, measure at least 3 mm (c. $\frac{3}{25}$ in). Shortly after birth they swim in among the vegetation where they gain some protection from the attacks of predators, particularly of the mother fish. She often has a tendency to eat her own young, and she should be removed as soon as she has given birth.

Whether born or hatched the fry do not feed immediately. On the ventral side they carry a yolk sac which provides them with their first food. When this reserve has been consumed the young fish starts to look for its own food. It is at this moment that it must be given a plentiful supply of suitable food.
see Rearing, Breeding, Diet.

Fundulus chrysotus

Shaped somewhat like a small thick-set pike, this is an olive-green fish with red spots on the back, flanks and fins, and a paler belly. It lives mainly near the bottom, in spite of its general appearance which suggests that it is a surface-living species.

Family: Cyprinodontidae★.

Diet: mainly live food.

Sex differences: the female is less brightly coloured than the male.

Length: 8 cm (3 in).

Distribution: South-eastern United States.

Compatibility: bad, for it may attack fishes almost as large as itself.

Temperature range: 18–30°C (64–86°F).

Breeding: as for *Epiplatys★*, but natural plants★ should be replaced by some nylon wool and the water should be alkaline and very hard, or even slightly brackish.

G

Gambusia affinis

This fish is rarely seen in the aquarium as it is aggressive and not very colourful, but it is famous on account of its voracity, being capable of consuming its own weight of mosquito larvae every day. It has been introduced into many areas to keep down malaria, e.g. in central France where it is well established, being very hardy. The subspecies *G. affinis holbrooki* has black spots.

Gambusia affinis (3.5 cm or $1\frac{1}{4}$ in)

Family: Poeciliidae★.

Diet: all live foods.

Sex differences: the female is dull grey and larger than the male and has spots on the caudal fin.

Length: 3.5 cm ($1\frac{1}{3}$ in) for the male, 6 cm ($2\frac{1}{4}$ in) for the female.

Distribution: southern United States and northern Mexico.

Compatibility: bad, for it will even attack fishes larger than itself.

Temperature range: 6–30°C (43–86°F).

Breeding: viviparous and very easy, but the parents should be removed as soon as parturition has taken place, otherwise they will eat the fry★.

Gasteropelecidae

A family of South American fishes, generally known as hatchetfishes from the shape of the body when seen from the side. They live close to the surface where they catch insects and are able to make short flights out of the water, rapidly beating their pectoral fins like wings. see *Carnegiella strigata, Gasteropelecus levis.*

Gasteropelecus levis

A silvery hatchetfish with a dark stripe running from the operculum to the tail. It lives near the surface and sometimes leaps out of the water to fly for a short distance. The related species *G. sternicla* is slightly larger, but otherwise very similar.

Family: Gasteropelecidae★.

Diet: omnivorous, with a preference for insects.

Sex differences: none apparent.

Length: up to 5 cm (2 in).

Distribution: lower Amazon.

Compatibility: excellent.

Temperature range: 24–28°C (75–82°F).

Gasteropelecus levis, the silver hatchetfish (up to 5 cm or 2 in)

Breeding: has never been recorded in the aquarium.

GLASSFISH, see *Chanda, Kryptopterus bicirrhis*.

Gnathonemus petersii
This is one of the elephant-trunk fishes so called from the proboscis-like snout. This structure is actually situated just above the mouth and has a tactile function, helping the fish to detect prey as its vision is poor. These fish also have an electric organ which helps them to detect objects in their immediate vicinity, but not to stun their prey. The related species *Marcusenius schilthuisiae* has a much shorter trunk. Their colour ranges from dark brown to brownish violet.
Family: Mormyridae*.
Diet: small prey and any food particles found in the substrate.
Sex differences: none apparent.
Length: up to 18 cm (7 in) in the aquarium.
Distribution: western Africa (Congo).
Compatibility: good.

Temperature range: 24–28°C (75–82°F).
Breeding: never recorded in captivity.

Gobiidae
A family of over 600 species distributed throughout the world, in fresh, brackish and sea water. Few of them are of interest to the aquarist. They lack a lateral line and the ventral fins are fused to form a suction cup with which the fish fixes itself to rocks, a useful adaptation in places where the current is strong.
see *Brachygobius xanthozona*.

GOLDFISH, see *Carassius auratus*.
GOURAMI, see *Trichogaster, Colisa*.
GUPPY, see *Poecilia reticulata*.

Gymnocorymbus ternetzi
Often known as the black tetra from the sombre colour of the anal fin. In general the coloration is black in the young, turning to smoke-grey with age. This is a peaceful, hardy fish suitable for beginners, in spite of its susceptibility to white-spot disease*.
Family: Characidae*.

Gnathonemus petersii, an elephant-trunk fish (up to 18 cm (7 in) in the aquarium, 23 cm (9 in) in the wild)

Diet: omnivorous.

Sex differences: none, except that the female ready to spawn has a more rounded belly.

Length: up to 5 cm (2 in).

Distribution: Bolivia, Paraguay, Brazil.

Compatibility: good.

Temperature range: 22–26°C (72–79°F).

Breeding: as for Characidae, but in tap water that can be quite hard and alkaline, which is exceptional for members of this family. The eggs hatch in 36–50 hours.

Gyrinocheilidae

A family from swift streams in south-east Asia with one genus and three species, fairly closely related to the Cyprinidae★; indeed many authorities no longer separate them from the cyprinids. They are characterized by having a supplementary aperture above the ordinary gill opening, through which water can pass directly to the gills. This enables the fish to respire without releasing its sucker-like

Gymnocorymbus ternetzi, the black tetra (up to 5 cm or 2 in)

Gyrinocheilus aymonieri the sucker loach (15 cm or 6 in in the aquarium, 25 cm or 9¾ in in the wild)

mouth from the stones to which it clings as it feeds.

Gyrinocheilus aymonieri
A popular fish in the aquarium because it spends most of its time removing algal growths with its sucker-like mouth.
Family: Gyrinocheilidae★.
Diet: algae, or if there is an inadequate growth of them, boiled spinach, lettuce or cabbage.
Sex differences: none.
Length: rarely over 15 cm (6 in) in the aquarium, 25 cm (9¾ in) in the wild.
Distribution: Thailand.
Compatibility: good in the young, doubtful in older adults.
Temperature range: 23–28°C (73–82°F).
Breeding: not recorded in the aquarium.

Habits
Aquarium fishes do not all have the same habits. Some of them live a solitary life, except during the breeding season, while others live in pairs, but most live gregariously in shoals, like herring and mackerel in the sea.

Certain species get to know the person who looks after them, know their feeding time, and have a special place in which they spend the night. The members of some families, such as the Cichlidae★ have a very well-developed sense of territory, which they will defend vigorously. This is one of the main causes of aggressive behaviour. Omnivorous fishes are generally more sociable or compatible than those which feed on live prey and often attack their own young.

Gregarious species will normally accept very readily the presence of a newcomer in their tank, while others sometimes regard it as a more or less undesirable intruder, and may only accept its presence after a certain period of time.

HARLEQUIN FISH, see *Rasbora*.

Hasemania marginata
A yellowish-olive fish with deep brown fins, and no adipose fin. It is not difficult to keep and perfectly suitable for an aquarium tank with small species, though they require some time to acclimatise before looking their best.
Family: Characidae★.
Diet: omnivorous.
Sex differences: female paler and stockier.
Length: 4.5 cm (1¾ in).
Distribution: south-eastern Brazil.
Compatibility: excellent.
Temperature range: 20–26°C (68–79°F).
Breeding: as for Characidae. The water should be fairly soft and acid, and the tank should be in subdued light. The eggs hatch in 24 hours and the fry★ will

live on the contents of the yolk sac for 3–4 days.

HATCHETFISH, see *Carnegiella strigata, Gasteropelecus levis.*

Heating

The exotic fishes which can be successfully kept in the aquarium may be very roughly divided into two categories: those which come from mountainous country where the water is relatively cool and those which come from warmer regions. The former can be kept at about 20°C (68°F), but the latter require a higher temperature. These represent the majority of the ornamental fishes and they are also the most attractive in coloration and shape. They require a tank fitted with a heating system.

This is done with electric heaters which warm the water, thermostats which regulate the electric current, and thermometers which provide instant confirmation that the installation is functioning properly.

Unless intended for very large tanks the heaters are immersible, the outer covering being of Pyrex or similar glass. They are available with a voltage of 110 V or 230 V and a wattage of 15–200 W. A single heater is sufficient for a small tank, but over a certain size it is better to have two heaters, placed at opposite ends of the aquarium. This gives a better distribution of heat. As a rough guide it is reckoned that 1 W raises the temperature of 1 litre of water by 8°C (46°F).

Sometimes it happens that the room with the tank ceases to be heated, as when the owner goes away in winter. It will then be necessary to use more heaters in the tank.

The function of the thermostat is to cut off the current when the desired temperature is reached, and to switch it on again when the water temperature falls below a certain slightly lower reading. Most thermostats are made so that they can be fixed to the inside of the tank with only the top of the apparatus projecting above the water surface. This part, protected against humidity by a hood, has a

screw which allows the temperature to be regulated between 20 and 30°C (68 and 86°F). Some thermostats are designed to be fixed to the outside of the tank, and they control the temperature across the glass to which they are fixed.

The tank can also be heated by using a combined heater and thermostat, and some of these combinations are completely immersible.

There are also thermometers designed specially for the aquarium, and these are usually fixed to the inside of the glass by a suction cup.

If an entire room is given over to a large number of aquariums, it is often simpler and more economical to install a room heater.

Aquarium heater, thermostat and wiring

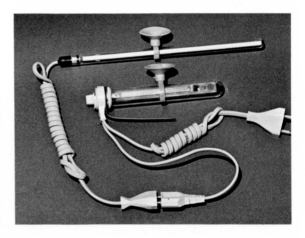

Hemichromis bimaculatus

A robust, prolific, bright red fish, known as the jewel cichlid. It is very aggressive towards other members of its own species.

Family: Cichlidae*.

Diet: omnivorous. A voracious fish which will attack the vegetation.

Sex differences: not detectable, but once a pair bond has been formed the behaviour of the male will differ from that of the female, whose belly becomes rounded when she is ready to spawn.

Length: up to 13 cm (5 in).

Distribution: Africa (Nile, Zaire, Niger).

Compatibility: bad.

Hemichromis bimaculatus, the jewel cichlid (13 cm or 5 in)

Temperature range: 20–28°C (68–82°F).
Breeding: as for those Cichlidae (substrate
   spawners) that do not incubate the
   eggs in the parent's mouth.

Hemigrammus

A genus of the family Characidae*, with
representatives only in tropical America.

They are much valued in the aquarium on
account of their small size and brilliant
colours. They are very similar to the species
of *Hyphessobrycon* with which they are often
confused. Many are widely distributed in the
aquarium world, others are less frequently
kept. The latter include *H. armstrongi,* the
golden tetra, which seems to lose its brilliant
coloration when bred in the aquarium, *H.
hyanuary,* recently rediscovered in the basin
of the Rio Negro, and *H. nanus,* in which the
male becomes red at spawning time.

Hemigrammus caudovittatus

The Buenos Aires tetra, which has a greenish
back, silvery flanks, a dark marking at the base
of the tail, and red fins. It can tolerate
relatively low temperatures.
Diet: omnivorous.
Sex differences: the fins of the female are
   almost colourless.
Length: up to 8 cm (3 in).
Distribution: Argentina, La Plata area.

Hemigrammus caudovittatus, the Buenos Aires tetra (up to 8 cm or 3 in)

Compatibility: rather mediocre.
Temperature range: 15–25°C (59–77°F).
Breeding: as for Characidae. Spawning is
more likely to occur if the tank is
exposed to the sun.

Hemigrammus gracilis

An attractive fish showing brilliant irides-
cence on the flanks, hence its popular name,
the glowlight tetra. It has been known as
Hemigrammus erythrozonus. This is an ideal
fish for a small community tank.
Diet: omnivorous.
Sex differences: females ready to spawn
have a rounded belly.
Length: 4 cm (1½ in).
Distribution: northern Amazon region and
Guyana.
Compatibility: excellent.
Temperature range: 23–27°C. (73–80°F).
Breeding: in general as for the Characidae,
with subdued lighting and very soft
water (hardness less than 5°DH), filtered
through peat.

Hemigrammus gracilis, the glowlight tetra (4 cm or 1½
in)

Hemigrammus ocellifer

Known as the beacon fish from the scintillat-
ing spots, red above the eye and yellow near
the base of the tail. This is an active, hardy
species but very susceptible to white-spot
disease*.

Diet: omnivorous.
Sex differences: none, except that females
ready to spawn have a more rounded
belly.
Length: 4 cm (1½ in).
Distribution: Amazon basin and Guyana.
Compatibility: excellent.
Temperature range: 22–28°C (72–82°F).
Breeding: as for Characidae*. Tap water
can be used if it has stood for some time
or been used in the aquarium.

Hemigrammus ocellifer, the beacon fish (4 cm or 1½ in)

Hemigrammus pulcher

Similar to *H. ocellifer,* from which it may be
distinguished by the dark horizontal marking
above the anal fin. Known as the pretty tetra.
Diet: omnivorous.
Sex differences: none, except that the
female is more rounded when ready to
spawn.
Length: 5 cm (2 in).
Distribution: central Amazon region.
Compatibility: excellent.

Hemigrammus pulcher, the pretty tetra (5 cm or 2 in)

Temperature range: 23–28°C (73–82°F).
Breeding: difficult, and only possible in soft water.

Hemiodontidae

A small family of South American fishes closely related to the Characidae*, of which they were formerly regarded as a subfamily. In fact they only differ from the Characidae in lacking teeth on the lower jaw. The mouth is much reduced in size and they can only eat small-sized food. They are difficult to breed in the aquarium, and when they do so the fry are tiny, and they grow slowly.
see *Hemiodus semitaeniatus, Nannostomus.*

Hemiodus semitaeniatus

An elegant, silvery fish, which swims and jumps well, and is characterized by a black spot in the middle of the body, which extends back as a black line to the lower lobe of the caudal fin.
Family: Hemiodontidae*.
Diet: omnivorous, with a marked preference for plant food.
Sex differences: none.
Length: 8 cm (3 in).
Distribution: Amazon region and Guyana.
Compatibility: satisfactory.
Temperature range: 23–28°C (73–82°F).
Breeding: never recorded in the aquarium.

Hemiramphidae

A small family of fishes from the fresh, brackish and salt waters of tropical Asia. They are characterized by the long lower jaw which is not movable and the short upper jaw which is movable. This unusual arrangement is reflected in the popular name: half-beaks.
see *Dermogenys pusillus.*

Heterandria formosa

A very small reddish-brown livebearing fish with a broad dark band along the flanks and a pale belly. It is easily bred in hard water, but can only be kept with other very small species.
Family: Poeciliidae*.
Diet: omnivorous.
Sex differences: the male has a gonopodium and is much smaller than the female.
Length: 2 cm ($\frac{3}{4}$ in) for the male, 3.5 cm ($1\frac{1}{4}$ in) for the female.
Distribution: Florida and North Carolina.
Compatibility: excellent.
Temperature range: 20–28°C (68–82°F).
Breeding: easy, the species being viviparous. The female produces about two young per day over a period of 6–10 days, and these are not attacked by the parents.

Hyphessobrycon

A genus in the family Characidae*, that is only distinguished from the related genus *Hemigrammus* by the absence of scales at the base of the caudal fin. Most of the species are known popularly as tetras. Certain species are only rarely imported and these include *H. eos* which has not yet been bred in captivity, *H. griemi,* very close to *H. flammeus* but smaller, and *H. metae* from Peru.

Hyphessobrycon flammeus

Known popularly as the flame tetra this is a hardy, inexpensive fish which can be kept in almost any kind of water. It is, however, rather susceptible to white-spot disease*.
Diet: omnivorous.
Sex differences: the male's anal and ventral fins have a black border.
Length: 3.5 cm ($1\frac{1}{4}$ in).
Distribution: Brazil, region of Rio de Janeiro.
Compatibility: good.

Temperature range: 20–26°C (68–79°F).
Breeding: relatively easy, using the method recommended for the Characidae. The water need not be very soft, nor need it be filtered through peat. The eggs hatch in three days.

Hyphessobrycon flammeus, the flame tetra (3.5 cm or 1¼ in)

Hyphessobrycon herbertaxelrodi
This is a small tetra with a wide horizontal dark band below a thinner iridescent whitish band.
Diet: omnivorous.
Sex differences: the female has rounded belly when ready to spawn.
Length: 4 cm (1 in).
Distribution: Brazil, in the Mato Grosso region.
Compatibility: excellent.
Temperature range: 23–28°C (73–82°F).
Breeding: as for Characidae, but the water must be soft, slightly acid and filtered through peat.

Hyphessobrycon innesi
This is the well-known neon tetra, first imported into Europe about 1930, which soon became very popular on account of its brilliant iridescent colours. It is a hardy fish that prefers soft water, subdued lighting and a dark substrate. Also known as *Paracheirodon innesi*.
Diet: omnivorous.
Sex differences: none, apart from the rounded belly of the female ready to spawn.

Length: 4 cm (1½ in).
Distribution: upper Amazon.
Compatibility: excellent.
Temperature range: 20–26°C (68–79°F).
Breeding: mainly achieved by professional aquarists, but still something of a problem for amateurs. The tank should be kept in subdued light and filled with very soft, slightly acid and peat-filtered water at 24°C (75°F). Successful breeding appears to depend upon having a good quality pair and keeping the water composition stable. The slightly adhesive eggs hatch in 24 hours and the fry★ use up the contents of the yolk sac in five days. They are very tiny and require an abundant supply of infusorians★.

Hyphessobrycon pulchripinnis
Known as the lemon tetra this is an active, peaceful species which when acclimatized becomes hardy and will not require any special type of water. It is characterized by the bright lemon-yellow coloration and the red eyes.
Diet: omnivorous.

Hyphessobrycon pulchripinnis, the lemon tetra (5 cm or 2 in)

Hyphessobrycon innesi, the neon tetra (4 cm or 1½ in)

Sex differences: in the male the anal fin has a broad black border.
Length: 5 cm (2 in).
Distribution: Amazon basin.
Compatibility: excellent.

Temperature range: 23–28°C (73–82°F).
Breeding: as for Characidae, but probably not often achieved. There is evidently no need to use specially soft water nor to filter it through peat.

Hyphessobrycon rubrostigma, the bleeding heart tetra (up to 8 cm or 3 in)

Hyphessobrycon rubrostigma

Known as the bleeding heart tetra from the blood-red marking in the middle of each flank.

Diet: omnivorous.

Sex differences: the dorsal fin of the male is elongated and sickle-shaped.

Length: up to 8 cm (3 in), which is very large for a tetra. It requires a spacious tank with peaceful companions.

Distribution: Colombia.

Compatibility: good.

Temperature range: 23–27°C (73–80°F).

Breeding: difficult, and probably not often attempted by amateur aquarists as this is a relatively recent importation.

Hyphessobrycon scholzei

A widely kept tetra with pale reddish fins and a horizontal black stripe along each flank. It is remarkably hardy and can even be kept at room temperature.

Diet: omnivorous.

Sex differences: none, except that the female has a more rounded belly when ready to spawn.

Length: 5 cm (2 in).

Distribution: Amazon basin.

Hyphessobrycon ornatus, the rosy tetra (4.5 cm or 1¾ in)

Hyphessobrycon scholzei, the black-line tetra (5 cm or 2 in)

Compatibility: good.
Temperature range: 20–27°C (68–80°F).
Breeding: as for Characidae, but very soft water and peat filtration are not necessary. The fry feed at first on infusorians★, later on *Artemia*★ nauplii.

Hyphessobrycon serpae
This is one of a group of small tetras, sometimes known as blood characins. They vary in colour and in the presence or absence of the black marking on each flank.
Diet: omnivorous.
Sex differences: none, except that the female becomes stouter when ready to spawn.
Length: 4 cm (1½ in).
Distribution: central Amazon.
Compatibility: satisfactory, although there is a tendency to nibble the dorsal and caudal fins of other fishes in the aquarium.
Temperature range: 23–28°C (73–82°F).
Breeding: as for Characidae, but not easy.

The water must be soft, slightly acid and filtered through peat.

HYPHESSOBRYCON CARDINALIS, see *Cheirodon axelrodi.*

Hyphessobrycon serpae (4 cm or 1½ in)

I

J

INDIAN GLASSFISH, see *Chanda*.

Infusorians

These are ciliated protozoans used for feeding the fry★ of oviparous fishes. They are microscopic and consist of a single cell. In the wild they form part of the freshwater plankton, the floating population of tiny plants and animals which provides the basic food of fishes and other animals.

In the aquarium, infusorians have to be cultured by the aquarist himself as they cannot be bought. They are, of course, present in all natural waters with vegetation, but it would not be practical to collect them from this source.

The simplest way to produce infusorians is to chop up a few lettuce leaves and allow them to macerate in water. Some aquarists use an infusion of hay. In 24–28 hours the water should be teeming with the tiny ciliates, which can then be separated off and fed to the fish fry, until the latter are ready to accept *Artemia*★ nauplii.

Jordanella floridae

A small brownish-green fish with blue, green and red spots, generally known as the American flagfish.

Family: Cyprinodontidae★.

Diet: omnivorous, but appears to require a regular supply of plant food.

Sex differences: the female is less colourful, and has dark markings on the flanks.

Length: 5 cm (2 in).

Distribution: southern North America (Florida) to Yucatan.

Compatibility: mediocre.

Temperature range: 20–26°C (68–79°F).

Breeding: unique for the Cyprinodontidae. The female is chased by the male. After a stormy courtship the female lays 50–70 eggs over a period of several days. At 25°C (77°F) the eggs hatch in about a week, during which they are guarded by the male. The fry thrive in a tank with plenty of algae.

Jordanella floridae, the American flagfish (5 cm or 2 in)

Julidochromis ornatus, one of the Lake Tanganyika cichlids (7 cm or 2¾ in)

Julidochromis ornatus

A yellow fish with horizontal black bands. It comes from the hard, alkaline waters of Lake Tanganyika.

Family: Cichlidae★.

Diet: omnivorous, but needs a regular supply of live prey.

Sex differences: practically none.

Length: 7 cm (2¾ in).

Distribution: only in Lake Tanganyika.

Compatibility: mediocre.

Temperature range: 24–27°C (75–80°F).

Breeding: in general as for the Cichlidae. The female lays eggs in a rock crevice and guards them. As the fry★ are very sensitive to changes in the composition of the water, any renewals should be frequent and in small amounts.

K

KNIFEFISH, see Notopteridae, *Xenomystus nigri.*

Kryptopterus bicirrhis

Known as the glass catfish because the body is so transparent that the spinal column is easily discernible. All the internal organs are in the region just below the head. This species should be kept as a group of 4–5 individuals in a well-planted tank.

Family: Siluridae★.

Diet: dried food regularly supplemented with small live prey.

Sex differences: none.

Length: up to 10 cm (3¾ in).

Distribution: Thailand, Java, Sumatra, Borneo.

Compatibility: excellent. A somewhat timid species that is not happy in a tank with boisterous companions.

Temperature range: 22–28°C (72–82°F).

Breeding: not yet recorded in captivity.

KUHLI, see Loach, *Acanthophthalmus kuhlii.*

(Overleaf) *Kryptopterus bicirrhis,* the glass catfish (up to 10 cm or 4 in)

L

Labeo bicolor

A rather large, velvety-black member of the barb family with a striking red tail and a white border to the dorsal and anal fins. This fish has a strongly developed territorial instinct, often regarding a large part of the tank as its own property and chasing away intruders, although without actually doing them any harm. Although it can become acclimatized to various conditions, it really prefers soft, acid water and fairly subdued lighting.

Family: Cyprinidae*.

Diet: omnivorous, including the algae growing on rocks and vegetation.

Sex differences: female usually stouter.

Length: up to 15 cm (6 in).

Distribution: Thailand.

Compatibility: acceptable, even with very small species.

Temperature range: 23–28°C (73–82°F).

Breeding: not yet recorded in the aquarium.

Labeotropheus

A genus of African Cichlidae* sometimes known as 'freshwater coralfishes', peculiar to Lake Malawi (formerly Nyasa), which has some 200 species of this family, including those in the genus *Pseudotropheus**.

Labeotropheus fuelleborni

A Malawi cichlid with an overhanging snout and very fine teeth which enable it to browse

Labeo bicolor, the red-tailed black shark (up to 15 cm or 6 in)

the algae* that grow on rocks. Most males and some of the females are blue with dark vertical bands, but other females, fewer in number, are ochre-yellow with black markings. Such polymorphism is rare in fishes. This species requires hard, alkaline water*, and does not like sudden fluctuations in pH or hardness.
Diet: omnivorous.
Sex differences: see above.
Length: 13 cm (5 in).
Distribution: only in Lake Malawi.
Compatibility: bad, with its own species and with others.
Temperature range: 23–27°C (73–80°F).
Breeding: as for Cichlidae in general, but the eggs are incubated in the female's mouth.

Labeotropheus trewavasae

As in the preceding species both sexes are polymorphic. Thus, some of them are yellowish-brown with dark markings, while others are like the males, being pale blue with darker vertical bands and a mainly red dorsal fin.
Diet: omnivorous, with a preference for plant food, and particularly algae.
Sex differences: see above.
Length: 10 cm (3¾ in).
Distribution: only in Lake Malawi.
Compatibility: bad.
Temperature range: 23–27°C (73–80°F).
Breeding: as for the Cichlidae in general, but a mouth brooder. The eggs are laid in a pit dug by the male who then fertilizes them. The female takes the eggs into her mouth and holds them there until they hatch after some days into fry* that measure 1.5 cm (½ in).

LABYRINTH FISHES, see Anabantidae.
LEAF-FISH, see Polycentridae.
LEBISTES RETICULATUS, see *Poecilia reticulata*.
LEERII, see *Trichogaster*.

Leporinus fasciatus

A handsome, cream-coloured fish with verti-

A pair of *Labeotropheus trewavasae* or red-finned cichlids (10 cm or 4 in)

cal black bars. Unfortunately it has three disadvantages: its feeding habits, its size and its price.
Family: Anostomidae*.
Diet: omnivorous with a preference for plant food, so it will browse on the decorative vegetation in the tank.
Sex differences: none apparent.
Length: up to 30 cm (12 in).
Distribution: Amazon basin.
Compatibility: satisfactory.
Temperature range: 22–30°C (72–86°F).
Breeding: not yet recorded in the aquarium.

Lighting

Light plays a very important part in the maintenance of biological* equilibrium in an aquarium, and it is therefore essential that its quantity and quality should be sufficient.

The quality of light is independent of its intensity. Light consists of a mixture of different wavelengths, of which our eyes can perceive only a part, those lying between the

Leporinus fasciatus (up to 30 cm or 12 in)

Lighting enhances the beauty of an aquarium and it is, of course, essential for the plants

violet and the red on the spectrum. Plants, on the other hand, also need ultraviolet and infra-red rays.

Natural light from the sun is insufficient in quantity for an aquarium tank situated at the back of a room, but may be excessive for one placed on the window-sill, at least in summer. Although its quality is excellent natural light cannot be regulated satisfactorily. It should not therefore be used as the sole source of illumination for an aquarium, but only as a supplement, used in moderation.

For a long time light from incandescent lamps was the only form of lighting employed in the aquarium. Its main advantage is that it is inexpensive to install and it can be produced by tubes which are available in various lengths. On the other hand, incandescent lamps produce too much heat—a disadvantage in the case of small tanks—and the quality of light produced is not ideal for plant growth.

Fluorescent lighting is the most suitable type for an aquarium, provided the correct type is chosen. Very white light is not suitable, and the best fluorescent tubes for an aquarium

are those designed for horticultural purposes, e.g. Plant-Gro (Westinghouse) or Gro-Lux (Sylvania). The mixture of red and blue rays emitted by these lamps stimulates plant growth.

This type of lighting tube produces no heat, but it requires a small starter lamp and a choke. Fluorescent lamps use very little current and they have a long life. Their installation should be carried out by an electrician.

duration of lighting In a normal aquarium tank with a suitable number of fishes and plants the lamps should be switched on for about eight hours a day during the first three months after the tank has been set up. At this stage it should be possible to check whether algae* are growing on the rocks and else-where. If there are none the lighting can be increased marginally, remembering that it is generally preferable to increase its duration rather than its intensity. If the aquarist has to be away for a time, it is not difficult to install a time clock which will switch the lighting on

Hemiancistrus vittatus, one of the Loricariidae (c. 13 cm or 5 in)

and off at the required time.

Finally, it should be remembered that although they have no eyelids and cannot therefore close their eyes, fishes still need to sleep. They should therefore have a period of at least eight hours darkness in the twenty-four, and care should be taken not to switch on the lighting too suddenly as this may cause a form of panic.

LION-HEAD, see *Carassius auratus*.
LIVEBEARING FISHES, see Poeciliidae, Breeding.
LOACHES, see Cobitidae.

Loricaria parva

A catfish with the mouth modified to form a sucker, with which it adheres to rocks, and so maintains position in fast-flowing rivers. It is not particularly colourful being olive-grey with darker markings. The similar *L. filamentosa* owes its name to the elongated filamentous upper ray of the caudal fin.
Family: Loricariidae★.
Diet: omnivorous, a preference for algae★.

Sex differences: none apparent.
Length: 14 cm (5½ in).
Distribution: southern Brazil and Paraguay.
Compatibility: excellent.
Temperature range: 22–28°C (72–82°F).
Breeding: probably has been achieved, but perhaps not by amateurs.

Loricariidae

A family of catfishes distributed in the fast-flowing waters of northern and central South America. In such conditions they manage to maintain position by reason of their stream-lined form and the suctorial mouth with which they attach themselves firmly to submerged rocks and browse on algae★ which form the principal part of their diet. This habit is appreciated by the aquarist as it helps to keep his tank glass clean.
see *Loricaria parva, Otocinclus flexilis, Plecostomus punctatus*.

M

Macrognathus aculeatus

A rather strange fish with an elongated brownish body with darker markings, a very long snout and small eyes. It lives mainly buried in the substrate with only the head protruding.

Family: Mactacembelidae*.
Diet: omnivorous, with a preference for live food.
Sex differences: none apparent.
Length: up to 20 cm (7¾ in) in the aquarium, 35 cm (13½ in) in the wild.
Distribution: India and Malaysia.
Compatibility: doubtful when over 15 cm (6 in) long.

Macrognathus aculeatus (up to 20 cm (7¾ in) in the aquarium, 35 cm (13½ in) in the wild)

Temperature range: 21–28°C (69–82°F).
Breeding: not recorded in the aquarium.

Macropodus opercularis

A brownish fish with vertical blue and red bands and long, elegant fins. This is said to be the first tropical fish to be imported into Europe, and was mentioned as early as 1665 by Samuel Pepys. It is a hardy species which can tolerate relatively low temperatures and a small volume of water. It has the reputation of removing planarians (free-living flatworms) from the aquarium.

Family: Anabantidae*.
Diet: live food with some dried food.
Sex differences: the female is paler and has shorter fins.
Length: 9 cm (3½ in).
Distribution: China, southern Vietnam, Taiwan, Korea.
Compatibility: fairly good, but often attacks small species.
Temperature range: 15–30°C (59–86°F).
Breeding: easy if the method recommended for *Betta* * *splendens* is followed. The quality of the water is not important and the eggs hatch in 30–40 hours.

Maintenance

An aquarium with a satisfactory biological* equilibrium should require very little maintenance, apart from topping up with water at the same temperature to make good losses due to evaporation and daily cleaning of the front glass. Even the latter task will be unnecessary if the tank contains efficient consumers of algae*, such as *Gyrinocheilus* * or *Plecostomus* *.

accessories These should include two scrapers, one fitted with felt for removing the oily film which forms on the glass, the other with a razor blade for removing green algae that settle on the glass. Another useful accessory would be an aspirator, worked by the air pump, for sucking detritus from the substrate. A long narrow tunnel trowel is useful for replacing any plants* that become

Macropodus opercularis, the paradisefish (9 cm or 3½ in)

loose. Finally, a relatively large net with a suitable mesh is essential for catching up fish that have to be moved to another tank. A net that is too small is quite useless for this job.

pests The destruction of any pests that may infect the aquarium is also part of maintenance.

These pests are relatively rare, but it is possible to introduce them accidentally, as for example when live food is collected from the wild, or if a new plant is introduced. They include leeches and a few undesirable snails★, but the only pests that may be really troublesome are hydras and planarians.

Hydras are almost transparent freshwater polyps, which measure less than 1 cm (⅓ in) when adult. They fix themselves to a plant and extend their tentacles which are armed with microscopic sting cells. Hydras are only dangerous to fry★ which they catch very easily. Fortunately, they are very sensitive to water containing a very small amount of copper. The best method of getting rid of hydras is, therefore, to put a piece of copper wire in the tank, and when the hydras have died to siphon off half the tank water and replace with fresh.

Planarians, looking somewhat like flat

A brown hydra (much enlarged)

A planarian (enlarged)

99

snails, are usually greyish or greenish and scarcely 2 cm (¾ in) long. They only cause trouble by eating the fish eggs in a breeding tank. There are two methods of destroying them. One is to get them eaten by certain fishes that are particularly fond of them, such as *Trichogaster*★, *Macropodus*★ *opercularis* and *Pelvicachromis*★. The other method is to remove the fishes and plants and then raise the water temperature to 30–40°C (86–104°F).

siphoning In the course of time a certain amount of detritus will accumulate on the floor of the tank and this must be removed periodically by siphoning. This requires a piece of flexible tubing about 1 m (a yard) in length. One end of this is placed in the tank and then the other end is sucked until it is full of water. This end is then placed in a bucket at a lower level than the tank out of which the

A siphon gadget, worked from the air pump, for removing detritus

water will then flow. The tank end of the tubing can be moved across the floor of the tank where it will suck up the detritus. The water siphoned out with the detritus can be kept and decanted, but it is more often replaced.

The frequency of siphoning will depend somewhat upon the size of the tank and the density of its fish population. On the average, it is best to replace about one-fifth of the water every month, though Cichlids benefit from more frequent changes. Lowering of the water level provides an opportunity to make any necessary adjustments to the plants★ and rockwork★.

renovation Even after this minor cleaning operation it sometimes happens that the water is not clear and the fishes appear somewhat inactive. This usually means that the tank needs a thorough cleaning. On average a tank with 50 litres (11 gallons) of water may need this to be done every eight months, whereas a tank with 150 litres (33 gallons) will usually only require such treatment every 18–20 months.

The method of cleaning out a tank is almost the same as that used when setting★ up the tank in the first place, except that the tank is now occupied and this entails a few modifications to the process.

First, make sure that all the necessary materials are to hand (e.g. a new diffuser, a selection of plants, suitable substrate, etc.). Then switch off and remove the heater, thermostat and thermometer, and siphon off some of the water into another container, which is to serve as a temporary home for the fishes.

Secondly, catch up the fishes and transfer them into this container. Remove the plants and rockwork from the aquarium.

Thirdly, stir up the water and substrate and siphon off the resulting cloudy water.

Fourthly, fill the tank with clean, clear water to a third of its depth. This water can be used to clean the sides of the tank. The substrate is then stirred up and once more the water becomes cloudy and is siphoned off.

Washing of the substrate in this way is continued until the water only has a pale beige tint, instead of the blackish colour it had when the substrate was first stirred up.

The replacement of the plants, rockwork and fishes should then be carried out according to the instructions given for the initial setting up of the tank.

Mastacembelidae

A small family of fishes living in the fresh and brackish waters of Asia and Africa. They have an elongated eel-like body.
see *Macrognathus aculeatus*.

Megalamphodus megalopterus

Although looking rather fragile this is a handsome, hardy fish. It somewhat resembles *Hyphessobrycon ornatus* in general appearance, but the ground coloration is greyish and there is an elongated, oval marking just behind the operculum (gill cover). In the male the dorsal fin is elongated and sickle-shaped, a feature which distinguishes this species from the smaller *Megalamphodus sweglesi* which has a straight dorsal fin.
Family: Characidae★.

Megalamphodus megalopterus the black phantom tetra (4.5 cm or 1¾ in)

Diet: omnivorous.
Sex differences: the female is smaller, with a short dorsal fin and a slightly reddish tinge.
Length: 4.5 cm (1¾ in).
Distribution: Brazil.
Compatibility: excellent.
Temperature range: 23–27°C (73–80°F).
Breeding: difficult, but can be done if conditions are those recommended for the most difficult characins★. They should have very soft, filtered water at 27°C (80°F). The eggs hatch in 24 hours, and the fry★ will have used up their yolk sac in six days. The species is not prolific.

Melanochromis auratus

The males of this fine cichlid are either bright blue, or they are yellow with longitudinal black markings, like the females. In addition there are differences of shade at spawning time and some adult females change colour to take on that of the dark males.
Family: Cichlidae★.
Diet: omnivorous, with a preference for large live food and algae★. In the absence of the latter they can be given a little lettuce or boiled spinach.
Sex differences: see above.
Length: 10 cm (3¾ in).
Distribution: Lake Malawi only.
Compatibility: often very bad. Very destructive towards plants.
Temperature: 22–28°C (72–82°F).
Breeding: possible. The eggs are incubated in the female's mouth, as in many other Cichlidae.

Melanotaenia maccullochi

An active hardy fish from Australia, known popularly as the dwarf rainbowfish. It likes a hard, slightly brackish water and being gregarious is best kept in a group. The related Australian red-tailed rainbowfish, *Melanotaenia nigrans,* is considerably larger.
Family: Atherinidae★.
Diet: omnivorous.

Melanotaenia maccullochi, the dwarf rainbowfish (8 cm or 3 in)

Sex differences: the female is less colourful and has a rounded second dorsal fin.
Length: 8 cm (3 in).
Distribution: northern Australia.
Compatibility: good.
Temperature range: 22–28°C (72–82°F).
Breeding: relatively easy in tap water. The

eggs, which are attached to leaves by a short filament, hatch in 6–10 days at 25°C (77°F). After the resorption of the yolk sac the fry*, of which there may be up to 200, can be fed directly on *Artemia**, without going through a period of feeding on infusorians*.

Metynnis roosevelti

A beautiful, much compressed fish without markings, but with an unfortunate tendency to browse on tender plants*. The related *M. maculatus* and *M. schreitmuelleri* are marked with spots.
Family: Characidae*.
Diet: omnivorous, with a preference for plant food.
Length: up to 15 cm (6 in).
Distribution: Amazon basin.
Compatibility: good.
Temperature range: 22–28°C (72–82°F).
Breeding: possible, but not often attempted, perhaps on account of their size and feeding habits.

MICRALESTES INTERRUPTUS, see *Phenacogrammus interruptus*.
MICROGEOPHAGUS RAMIREZI, see *Apistogramma*.

Metynnis roosevelti (up to 15 cm or 6 in)

Mochocidae

A small family of African catfishes lacking bony armour plates.
see *Synodontis nigriventris*.

Moenkhausia oligolepis

Characterized by the black marking at the tail base and the red eyes, this is a hardy fish which tends to become paler with age. It is frequently confused with the related *M. sanctaefilomenae* which also has a black marking at the tail base, but is smaller.

Family: Characidae★.

Diet: omnivorous.

Sex differences: not well defined. The fins of the female are slightly shorter.

Length: up to 10 cm (3¾ in).

Distribution: north-east of the Amazon basin and Guyana.

Compatibility: good with fish measuring at least 5 cm (2 in), doubtful with others.

Temperature range: 22–28°C (72–82°F).

Breeding: is done by professionals, but not much by amateurs, perhaps on account of the final size of the species.

MOLLIENESIA, see Mollies.

Mollies

The livebearing fishes popularly known as mollies belong to the family Poeciliidae★. They were formerly classified in the genus *Mollienesia*, but are now included in *Poecilia*★. Several species are characterized by a remarkably large dorsal fin, but this only develops to its full size in a large tank, with hard, slightly salt water.

Poecilia latipinna

Usually dark olive-green. In the male the dorsal fin is bluish with 6–7 dark transverse bars.

Diet: omnivorous, with a preference for plant food. Boiled spinach is a good substitute for the algae★ on which this fish feeds in the wild.

Sex differences: the male's anal fin is modified to form a gonopodium.

Length: up to 12 cm (4¾ in).

Distribution: south-eastern United States.

Compatibility: excellent, apart from a

Moenkhausia oligolepis, the glass tetra (up to 10 cm or 4 in)

One of the many varieties of black molly (10-14 cm or 4–5½ in according to the species)

certain amount of rivalry among the males.

Temperature range: 25–30°C (77–86°F).

Breeding: very easy. The parents do not attack their fry, which at birth are 1 cm (⅓ in) long and immediately capable of eating fine food. Rearing is more difficult, even in large tanks, and the fish never attain the size of imported specimens which are reared in outside tanks.

Poecilia sphenops

This species, often known as the pointed-mouth or sphenops molly, has several natural variants and artificially selected forms including completely black ones. This is probably the hardiest of the mollies, and it has the smallest dorsal fin. It has the same characteristics as *P. latipinna*, apart from the following:

Length: 10 cm (3¾ in).

Distribution: Mexico to Colombia.

Breeding: being a hardier species, they are easier to rear.

Poecilia velifera

This is the sail-fin molly with steel-blue coloration and an enormous dorsal fin, which may reach a height of 4 cm (1½ in). This fin has 18–19 rays, whereas in *P. latipinna* it has only 14 rays. Some specimens are completely black. The characteristics are the same as for *P. latipinna*, except for the following:

Length: up to 14 cm (5½ in).

Distribution: coastal, slightly brackish waters of Yucatan.

Monodactylus argenteus, the mono or fingerfish (10 cm or 4 in in the aquarium, 20 cm or 7¾ in in the wild)

Breeding: the rather large young are not produced in large numbers, Only the hardiest of the males develop the full dorsal fin.

Monodactylidae

A small but widely distributed family, extending from the Atlantic and Indian Ocean coasts of Africa to south-east Asia, Indonesia and northern Australia. At certain stages of their life they may occur in fresh, brackish or sea waters.
see *Monodactylus argenteus*.

Monodactylus argenteus

Known popularly as the fingerfish or mono, this is a brilliant silvery, lozenge-shaped species. When in good condition the two vertical black bands and the orange fin are particularly striking. These are gregarious fish which should be kept as a small shoal in a large tank. The composition of the water can be varied every three months or so, from fresh to slightly brackish (up to 5 g salt per litre; about ⅕ oz of salt for every 1¾ pints) and back

again. In the related *M. sebae* from west Africa the height of the body is greater than the length.

Family: Monodactylidae★.

Diet: live food.

Sex differences: none.

Length: 10 cm (3¾ in) in the aquarium, 20 cm (7¾ in) in the wild.

Distribution: East Africa to Indonesia.

Compatibility: good with other species and with members of its own species when kept in groups of five or more. If fewer individuals are kept, one will always become dominant.

Temperature range: 24–28°C (24–82°F).

Breeding: spawning occasionally takes place in the aquarium, but evidently the eggs have never hatched.

Mormyridae

A family with over a hundred species, living in the fresh waters of Africa. They are known popularly as elephant trunk fishes, partly on account of their general coloration, but more particularly from the elongated proboscis-like lower jaw found in some species. They have electric organs which are too weak to paralyze prey, but help in direction-finding and detecting food, and also serve to keep the individuals of the species in touch with one another.
see *Gnathonemus petersii*.

N

Nandidae

A small family with species living in the tropical fresh waters of South America, West Africa and South-east Asia. Certain authors confuse them with the related Polycentridae★, from which they differ in details of skeletal structure. Most are active predators and the only species peaceful enough for the aquarium is *Badis*★ *badis*.

Nannacara anomala

A brownish cichlid showing green on the flanks. The eyes are orange. This is a relatively peaceful species which will breed even in a small tank, provided there are numerous hiding-places and plenty of plants.
Family: Cichlidae★.
Diet: small live prey, with a little dried food.
Sex differences: the male's dorsal fin is more elongated and it has a blue and orange border.
Length: male 8 cm (3 in), female 6 cm (2¼ in).
Distribution: western Guyana.

Compatibility: good with other species, bad with members of its own species.
Temperature range: 22–28°C (72–82°F).
Breeding: in general as for substrate-spawning Cichlidae. The male should be removed as soon as he has fertilized the eggs, otherwise he may be attacked by the female.

Nannostomus

Known popularly as pencilfishes on account of the elongated body. They were formerly classified in the Characidae★, but are now included in the related Hemiodontidae★. They come from South America and are very easy to keep in a well planted aquarium with soft water (hardness less than 10°DH) and peaceful companions. They are not easy to breed in captivity.

Nannostomus anomalus, N. aripirangensis, N. beckfordi

Three forms that are rather difficult to distinguish. Most specimens on the market would appear to be hybrids between the first two, and some authorities regard these as subspecies of the third.
Diet: omnivorous.
Sex differences: male more slender, and with red on the anal fin and on the lower lobe of the caudal.

Nannacara anomala, the golden-eyed dwarf cichlid (8 cm or 3 in)

Length: up to 5 cm (2 in).
Distribution: north of the Amazon basin and Guyana.
Compatibility: excellent.
Temperature range: 23–28°C (73–82°F).
Breeding: very difficult, but has sometimes been achieved by using the methods advocated for the more demanding Characidae.

Nannostomus eques

Also known as *Poecilobrycon eques,* this fish swims obliquely, inclined at an angle of about 45°. A black band runs from the mouth to the lower lobe of the caudal fin. The characteristics of the species are the same as for the preceding species.

Nannostomus marginatus

This is one of the smallest of the *Nannostomus* species, and possibly the one most widely kept in the aquarium. The flanks have three dark longitudinal bands separated by areas of yellow. The characteristics are the same as those of the preceding species, except for the following points.
Sex differences: the anal fin is rounded in the male, truncated in the female.
Length: 3.5 cm (1¼ in).
Distribution: Guyana.

Nannostomus trifasciatus

This is one of the longest and most beautiful species in the genus, its fins carrying numerous red blotches. It comes from the centre of the Amazon basin and measures 6 cm (2¼ in). Otherwise its characteristics correspond with those of the other species of *Nannostomus.*

Nematobrycon palmeri

An extremely handsome characin that has only recently been imported. It requires very soft water and peaceful surroundings. It has been observed that the young tend to live in shoals, whereas the adults appear to be more territorial.
Family: Characidae★.
Diet: omnivorous.

Nannostomus trifasciatus, the pencil fish (6 cm or 2¼ in)

Sex differences: the male is larger and more brightly coloured than the female and the central rays of his caudal fin are much elongated.

Length: 5 cm (2 in).

Distribution: Colombia.

Compatibility: excellent.

Temperature range: 23–28°C (73–82°F).

Breeding: difficult, although some characin specialists have succeeded, but the species is evidently not very prolific.

NEON TETRA, see *Hyphessobrycon*.

Nothobranchius

A genus with about 20 species living in east Africa in conditions very similar to those experienced by the *Cynolebias* species of South America. In the wild, species of *Nothobranchius* lay their eggs in the substrate of a pond during the rainy season. Later on the water dries up and the adult fish die. The eggs remain in a state of suspended animation for up to a year and hatch when the rains return. In the aquarium these fish, of which the males are among the most beautiful of all ornamental fishes, may live for several years. The systematics★ of the genus is somewhat confused.

Nothobranchius guentheri

This species and the very similar *N. palmqvisti* are the ones most commonly imported In fact they may well be geographical variants of the same species, and they hybridize easily.

Family: Cyprinodontidae★.

Diet: live food.

Sex differences: the female is smaller and less brightly coloured than the male.

Length: 5 cm (2 in).

Distribution: Zanzibar and Kenya coast, East Africa, in pools and puddles.

Compatibility: mediocre, as this is a somewhat aggressive species.

Nematobrycon palmeri, the emperor tetra (5 cm or 2 in)

Nothobranchius guentheri (5 cm or 2 in)

Temperature range: 22–26°C (72–79°F). Breeding: as for *Cynolebias*★.

Nothobranchius rachovii
A species from the coastal areas of Mozambique, distinguished from the others by the blue dorsal and anal fins. In other respects it resembles *N. guentheri*.

A knife-fish (*Notopterus chitala*, up to 60 cm or 24 in)

Notopteridae

A small family from the tropical fresh waters of Africa and Asia, known popularly as knifefishes. They have very small scales, a mouth with teeth and soft fins which lack spiny rays. There are three genera: *Notopterus* and *Papyrocranus* with a small dorsal fin and *Xenomystus*★ with no dorsal fin.

Oryzias

Asiatic fishes which are only of limited importance in the aquarium, perhaps because they are seldom imported. The three species available from time to time on the market are *O. javanicus*, *O. latipes* and *O. minutillus*. They are known popularly as medakas and only differ in size and place of origin.

Family: Cyprinodontidae★.

Diet: small live food.

Sex differences: the dorsal and anal fins of the female are slightly rounded.

Length: 4 cm (1½ in) for *O. javanicus*, 5 cm (2 in) for *O. latipes*, and 2 cm (¾ in) for *O. minutillus*, one of the smallest fishes known.

Distribution: Java for *O. javanicus*, Japan for *O. latipes*, Thailand for *O. minutillus*.

Compatibility: good.

Temperature range: 23–28°C (73–82°F).

Breeding: possible, although these are rather delicate species. Pairing takes place at about 28°C (82°F). The eggs hatch in 10–12 days, and the young must be given infusorians★ for the first few days, followed later by powdered food and *Artemia*★ nauplii.

Oryzias latipes, the Japanese Medaka (5 cm or 2 in)

OSPHRONEMUS TRICHOPTERUS, see *Trichogaster*.

Otocinclus flexilis

A small catfish with greenish flanks, an almost black back and a whitish belly. It is popular in the aquarium as a consumer of algae★, but is rather delicate. It should be kept in a group of at least three individuals.

Family: Loricariidae★.

Diet: green algae★.

Sex differences: none.

Length: 6 cm (2¼ in).

Distribution: Rio de la Plata, Brazil.

Compatibility: perfect.

Temperature range: 23–28°C (73–82°F).

Breeding: has been achieved in the Exotarium at Frankfurt Zoo, but evidently not in amateurs' tanks.

Pachypanchax playfairi

A small pike-like fish with yellow-green flanks marked with red spots. The scales are slightly raised in the normal male, a condition which is a sign of illness in other fishes.

Family: Cyprinodontidae★.

Diet: live food.

Sex differences: the female is less brightly coloured and her caudal fin more rounded.

Length: up to 10 cm (4 in).

Distribution: Seychelles, Zanzibar and Madagascar.

Compatibility: very bad when hungry, but quite good with companions over 5 cm (2 in) long, when well fed.

Temperature range: 20–27°C (68–80°F).

Breeding: can be successful in a tank with floating plants★ or those with floating leaves. There should be three females to one male, as he is very active. The eggs, which are attached to the vegetation, hatch in about 12 days at 25°C (77°F). The fry★ hide away in dark corners and can be fed immediately on *Artemia*★ nauplii.

Pachypanchax playfairi (up to 10 cm or 4 in)

PANCHAX, see *Aplocheilus, Epiplatys, Pachypanchax playfairi*.

Pantodon buchholzi

A greyish-green to brownish species, known popularly as the butterflyfish, which spends its life at the surface of the water where it remains motionless among the vegetation and feeds on insects. It can jump out of the water to catch these, using the pectoral fins to perform a kind of glide.

Family: Pantodontidae*.

Diet: any live food that can be taken at the surface, preferably insects but also small fish up to 3 cm (1⅓ in) long; pellets of dried food are accepted.

Sex differences: the rays of the anal fin are longer in the male than in the female.

Length: 10 cm (3¾ in).

Distribution: forested areas of western Africa from Nigeria to Zaïre.

Compatibility: satisfactory with all fish that do not come up to the surface, or which are longer than 5 cm (2 in).

Temperature range: 24–30°C (75–86°F).

Breeding: has been achieved in soft, slightly acid water*. The eggs, which float at the surface, hatch in three days at 30°C (86°F), but the fry* are extremely difficult to rear.

Pantodontidae

A family containing only a single species, *Pantodon* * *buchholzi*, from western Africa.

PARADISE FISH, see *Macropodus opercularis*.

PARASITES, see Maintenance, Disease.

Pantodon buchholzi, the freshwater butterflyfish (10 cm or 4 in)

Pelmatochromis thomasi (9 cm or 3½ in)

Pelmatochromis thomasi
This rarely imported species from Sierra Leone is violet with blue dots and black markings.
see also *Pelvicachromis*.

Pelvicachromis
A genus of fairly small African Cichlidae★, related quite closely to the species of *Apistogramma*★ from South America. In the wild some of them live in slightly brackish water, and in the aquarium they can be kept in ordinary tap water, which is generally hard or sometimes very hard.

Pelvicachromis pulcher
Known formerly as *Pelmatochromis kribensis*, this is a peaceful attractive fish for the aquarium, although it sometimes attacks a plant or two.
Family: Cichlidae★.
Diet: omnivorous, but only develops fully when some live food is given.
Sex differences: contrary to the normal rule, the female is rather more brightly coloured than the male.
Length: 9 cm (3½ in).
Distribution: Africa, around the Niger delta.

Compatibility: satisfactory with other species, sometimes rather doubtful with members of its own species.
Temperature range: 24–29°C (75–84°F).
Breeding: easy, in a community tank, where spawning will usually take place in the shelter of a rock.

PENCILFISH, see *Nannostomus*.

Petitella georgiae
Known as the red-nosed tetra from the red snout. The tail has an attractive pattern of black and white. This is a somewhat rare and

Petitella georgiae, the red-nosed tetra (5 cm or 2 in)

Pelvicachromis pulcher (9 cm or 3½ in)

Phenacogrammus interruptus, the Congo tetra (8 cm or 3 in)

costly species that should be kept in a well-planted tank with soft, slightly acid water.
Family: Characidae★.
Diet: omnivorous.
Sex differences: none, except that the female has a rounded belly.
Length: 5 cm (2 in).
Distribution: lower Amazon.
Compatibility: excellent.
Temperature range: 23–28°C (73–82°F).
Breeding: very difficult.

Phenacogrammus interruptus

An African characin, sometimes known as *Micralestes interruptus,* which prefers soft, slightly acid water. The species is gregarious so several individuals should be kept together.
Family: Characidae★
Diet: omnivorous.
Sex differences: in the male the dorsal fin and the central part of the caudal fin are much elongated.
Length: 8 cm (3 in) for the male, a little less for the female.
Distribution: Zaïre basin.
Compatibility: excellent.
Temperature range: 23–28°C (73–82°F).
Breeding: has been achieved in the aquarium, but probably not very often.

Piranha

There are four species of piranha. Some authors classify them all in the genus *Serrasalmus,* others distinguish two genera: *Serrasalmus* and *Pygocentrus*. They are all silvery fish, some species having dark spots and a reddish throat. Piranhas are well known for their aggressive behaviour and incredible voracity. Living in very large shoals they are said to be capable of devouring within a few minutes an animal the size of an ox. This, of course, would only happen if they were hungry, as often happens in the wild. In the aquarium, where they are well fed, they can be kept with a minimum of precautions.
Family: Characidae★.
Diet: carnivorous.
Sex differences: none.
Length: up to 30 cm (12 in) in the wild, rarely more than 12 cm (4¾ in) in the aquarium.
Distribution: basins of the Amazon and Orinoco.
Compatibility: acceptable, provided the tank is sufficiently large and does not contain other species.
Temperature range: 22–30°C (72–86°F).
Breeding: achieved several times in large public aquaria. In the United States they

One of the piranhas (up to 12 cm or 4¾ in in the aquarium, 30 cm or 12 in in the wild)

are considered sufficiently dangerous for their importation to be forbidden.

PLANKTON, see Infusorians.

Planorbis

Gastropod molluscs, popularly known as ramshorn snails. Unlike so many other snails★, which have the habit of eating the plants★, ramshorns hardly touch the tank vegetation, for they feed almost exclusively on faeces and algae★. In this way the play a useful role in the aquarium. When conditions are suitable they breed freely, but usually die as soon as the biological★ equilibrium is disturbed. In this way they provide a valuable indication of the general health of the tank.

Unlike most other freshwater snails which have a spiral shell, the species of *Planorbis* have a flat one.

Plants

Aquatic plants living in the aquarium play several roles. First, their shapes and subtle shades of green are attractive to the eye. Secondly, they provide spawning sites for the

A ramshorn snail (*Planorbis*)

fishes and also a certain amount of supplementary food. Thirdly, and perhaps most important, they provide the fishes with shelter and hence a feeling of security. Finally, plants also play a part in maintaining the biological* equilibrium in the tank water.

Plants have to feed in order to grow and reproduce, and for this they require nutrient salts. These substances are produced as a result of the bacterial decomposition of faeces and unconsumed food, and they are taken in by the roots or in many cases by the leaves.

Under the influence of light, plants absorb the carbon dioxide given off by the fishes, use it to build up their own living organic matter, and at the same time give off oxygen.

The exchanges between aquatic animals and plants are mutually beneficial, and they can be summarized as follows:
a) carbon dioxide given off by the fishes is utilized by the plants,
b) oxygen given off by the plants is used in respiration by the fishes,
c) the waste products of the fishes are broken down into mineral salts which are absorbed by the plants.

Plants are, therefore, not only decorative but also beneficial. The following pages describe, in alphabetical order, some of the plants normally used in the aquarium, with notes on their requirements as regards water*, light, substrate* and temperature.

Acorus These plants do best in water at about

20°C (68°F), and they cannot be expected to survive in an aquarium tank kept at 25°C (77°F). They are not good oxygenators of the water, but they have the advantage that they are not eaten by herbivorous fishes.
Light: normal illumination.
Water and substrate: a large margin of tolerance.

Acorus gramineus somewhat resembles a tuft of grass. The smaller *A. pusillus,* up to 10 cm (4 in) in height, looks good when planted towards the front of the tank. The much larger *A. variegata,* up to 40 cm (15½ in) in height, has attractive variegated green and white foliage.

Anubias There are two species, *A. nana* which does not usually exceed a height of 15 cm (6 in), and *A. lanceolata* which grows to 30 cm (12 in) in the aquarium. These are slow-growing plants with long, thick leaves, and they are much in demand on account of their hardiness.
Water: all types tolerated, but preferably soft.
Light: weak to normal.
Substrate: all types.
Temperature: 22–30°C (72–86°F).

Left: *Acorus variegatus;* centre and right: *Acorus pusillus*

Aponogeton fenestralis, the Madagascar lace plant

Aponogeton Aquatic plants of tropical and subtropical Africa and Asia. The leaves are shed in winter. The tuberous rhizome should then be removed from the aquarium and stored for two months in a cool, humid atmosphere. It can then be replanted in spring. The systematics of the genus is somewhat confused.

A. crispus which grows to 25 cm (10 in), is very decorative, with laced edges to the leaves.
Water: all types tolerated.
Light: normal to intense.
Substrates: all types.
Temperature: 19–29°C (66–84°F).

A. madagascariensis, formerly *A. fenestralis,* is the Madagascar lace plant, so called because of the structure of the leaves, which are reduced to a lace-like network of ribs. It is a handsome but rather tender plant.
Water: avoid any excess calcium.
Light: moderate.
Substrate: preferably aerated.

Temperature: 19–26°C (66–79°F).

A. *ulvaceus,* which also comes from Madagascar, requires a large tank where it may grow to a height of 50 cm (20 in), with about 20 translucent, heavy leaves.
Water: avoid excess calcium.
Light: moderate to normal.
Substrate: any type.
Temperature: 20–28°C (68–82°F).

Bacopa A popular aquarium plant with small rounded leaves. When the base of the stem becomes bare it can be cut off and inserted as a cutting. Two species are used in the aquarium: *B. monniera* and *B. amplexicaulis.*
Water: almost any type.
Light: normal to intense.
Substrate: all types.
Temperature: 18–28°C (64–82°F).

Cabomba Plants with finely divided leaves,

resembling *Myriophyllum* and *Limnophila.* The species most commonly used in the aquarium are *C. caroliniana* from central America, and *C. aquatica* from Brazil. These are very tender, rapidly growing plants which should be frequently cut back.
Water: avoid calcium.
Light: normal.
Substrate: preferably rich.
Temperature: 17–27°C (63–80°F).

Ceratopteris thalictroides Commonly known as Sumatra fern, this plant grows very well when conditions are suitable, producing small plantlets which break off and float away.
These can be planted.
Water: large tolerance.
Light: normal to intense.
Substrate: any type, this fern takes in
    nutrients more through the 'leaves' (or

Cabomba

fronds) than through the roots.
Temperature: 20–28°C (68–82°F).

Cryptocoryne A genus with numerous species in tropical and subtropical Asia where they grow in marshland. Several species are used in the aquarium, but unfortunately they are rather sensitive to changes in their environment. The systematics of the genus, with more than 40 species, is rather confused.

C. affinis, often marketed as *C. haerteliana,* comes from Malaysia. It is a medium-sized plant which produces runners with offsets which can be removed and planted. The leaves are dark green above, purplish below.
Water: large tolerance.
Light: normal to moderate.
Substrate: preferably rich.

Temperature: 20–30°C (68–86°F).

C. balansae (formerly *C. somphongsii*) from Thailand may easily reach a height of 30 cm (a foot) in the aquarium. The attractive green leaves have wavy edges.
Water: fairly wide tolerance.
Light: normal.
Substrate: preferably rich.
Temperature: 20–30°C (68–86°F).

C. becketti, sometimes marketed as *C. ciliata,* comes from Sri Lanka. The smooth, lanceolate leaves are olive-green above, pink below. Growth is slow in the aquarium.
Water: fairly large tolerance.
Light: normal.
Substrate: preferably rich.
Temperature: 20–30°C (68–86°F).

C. blassii from Thailand may grow to a

One of the species of *Cryptocoryne*

height of 30 cm (a foot) in the aquarium. The large oval leaves, sometimes smooth, sometimes blistered, are a rather dull green above, and a beautiful wine-red below.

Water: fairly large tolerance.
Light: normal.
Substrate: preferably rich.
Temperature: 20–30°C (68–86°F).

C. griffithii from Malaysia grows to a height of about 25 cm (10 in) in the aquarium. The oval, pointed leaves vary in colour from green to brown. This peculiarity is partly responsible for the confusion which exists between this species and *C. cordata*, a related plant which is possibly not imported for the aquarium.

Water: fairly large tolerance.
Light: normal.
Substrate: preferably rich.
Temperature: 22–28°C (72–82°F).

C. nevillii, often marketed as *C. willisii*, comes from Sri Lanka. The oval, pointed leaves are a brilliant green. The plant grows only to a height of about 10 cm ($3\frac{3}{4}$ in), and is therefore suitable for the front of the tank.

Water: fairly large tolerance.
Light and substrate: with moderate light
    and poor soil the plant remains small. It
    attains its normal height when grown
    with reduced light in a rich substrate.
Temperature: 20–30°C (68–86°F).

Echinodorus This genus contains plants varying in height from 3 to 45 cm (1 to $17\frac{1}{2}$ in). In general, they are not fastidious as regards illumination, but very much so as regards the type of substrate. The systematics of the group is confused and there are numerous synonyms.

E. cordifolius from central and southern America is a fine plant with large, strongly ribbed leaves, suitable for a spacious aquarium tank.

Water: avoid calcium.
Light: weak to normal.
Substrate: rich, with a base of clay.
Temperature: 18–25°C (64–77°F).

E. grisebachii, also known as *E. intermedius*, comes from Cuba and Costa Rica, and has numerous varieties, with heights ranging from 3 to 15 cm (1–6 in). It has the same requirements as *E. cordifolius*.

E. paniculatus from South America grows to a height of at least 15 cm (6 in) in the aquarium and has bright green foliage. It has the same requirements as *E. cordifolius*.

E. tenellus, also known as *E. parvulus* and *E. subulatus*, is widely distributed from the southern United States to central South America. The leaves are pale green and the whole plant only grows to a height of about 10 cm (4 in). It has the same requirements as *E. cordifolius*.

Eleocharis Also known as *Scirpus*, these are rush-like plants with a wide distribution. Three main species are used in the aquarium: *E. parvula* (6–7 cm; or $2\frac{1}{4}$–$2\frac{3}{4}$ in), *E. acicularis* (18 cm; or 7 in) and *E. prolifera* (90 cm; or 35 in). These are useful plants for masking aquarium accessories.

Water: any type.
Light: normal.
Substrate: sand is quite suitable.
Temperature: 20–28°C (68–82°F).

Elodea densa An aquatic plant with small, recurved leaves, which does not tolerate high temperatures.

Water: large tolerance.
Light: normal to intense.
Substrate: sand is suitable. The plant
    should be cut back at frequent intervals.
Temperature: 15–22°C (59–72°F).

Heteranthera zosteraefolia An aquatic plant from northern and southern America, with fine, delicate leaves. It should be cut back periodically as it grows rather rapidly.

Water: avoid excess calcium.
Light: normal to intense.
Substrate: sand is suitable.
Temperature: 18–28°C (64–82°F).

Hygrophila polysperma A robust, bright green plant which can be cultivated so as to

Elodea densa

form small bushes. Growth is rapid so it must be severely pruned at regular intervals.
Water: large tolerance.
Light: normal.
Substrate: sand is suitable.
Temperature: 18–28°C (64–82°F).

Limnophila Also known as *Ambulia,* this plant, of which there are numerous varieties,

is widely distributed in southern Asia. It has fine, delicate pale green leaves, like those of *Cabomba* and *Myriophyllum.*
Water: should not be hard.
Light: intense.
Substrate: preferably rich.
Temperature: 24–30°C (75–86°F).

Ludwigia natans A sub-aquatic or

Hygrophila polysperma

marshland plant from the southern United States and Mexico, which grows rapidly and does not tolerate high temperatures. The small leaves are green above, red below.
Water: large tolerance.
Light: normal.
Substrate: sand is suitable. Frequent pruning is necessary.
Temperature: 15–22°C (59–72°F).

Lysimachia nummularia A plant, popularly known as creeping jenny, which is of limited use in the aquarium as it only grows in cold water. It can be planted in a tank with goldfish (*Carassius★ auratus*).

Myriophyllum A genus with species distributed throughout the world. Those from warmer parts are much used in the tropical

Limnophila

aquarium. Like *Limnophila* and *Cabomba* these are very decorative plants, but the delicate feathery leaves are often damaged by the fishes.
Water: large tolerance.
Light: normal to intense.
Substrate: sand is suitable.
Temperature: 18–27°C (64–80°F),
   according to the origin of the species.

Nomaphila stricta A marsh plant from Thailand, Malaysia and Indonesia, which can be grown underwater in the aquarium. The leaves are large and bright green.
Water: preferably medium-hard.
Light: normal to intense.
Substrate: sand is suitable.
Temperature: 20–28°C (68–82°F).

Nuphar pumilum A small water-lily from Europe and western Siberia with delicate green foliage. Unfortunately it is rather fragile.
Water: large tolerance.
Light: weak to normal.
Substrate: preferably rich.
Temperature: 15–23°C (59–73°F).

Riccia fluitans A widely distributed small floating plant with delicate green leaves. It is useful in the aquarium as it forms extensive carpets at the surface, beneath which fish fry★ can find shelter and infusorians★. With good light it should grow in any type of water.

Sagittaria A widely distributed genus of aquatic plants with long ribbon-like leaves. Most of the species used in the aquarium come from America. These include *S. chilensis* with leaves up to 50 cm (20 in) long and 2 cm ($\frac{3}{4}$ in) wide, *S. eatonii* up to 20 cm ($7\frac{3}{4}$ in) long, and *S. subulata*, up to 50 cm (20 in) with leaves which sometimes have spatulate tips.
Water: should not be too soft (i.e. not less than 5°DH).
Light: normal.
Substrate: sand is suitable.
Temperature: 20–28°C (68–82°F).

Synnema triflorum This plant somewhat resembles a fern, but is not closely related. It grows rapidly and will soon form a large clump but its delicate leaves are unfortunately much appreciated by certain fishes.
Water: soft or hard, even slightly brackish.
Light: normal illumination. If put under intense illumination it grows well but becomes pale and the fresh shoots are almost white.·
Substrate: it will tolerate a poor soil, but gives better results in a rich substrate.
Temperature: 23–30°C (73–86°F).

Vallisneria A genus of aquatic plants widely distributed throughout the world. They somewhat resemble *Sagittaria,* although they are not closely related botanically. The plants produce stolons which can be used for propagation.

Sagittaria

Water: large tolerance.
Light: normal to intense.
Substrate: preferably rich, but sand is acceptable.
Temperature: 18–28°C (64–82°F).

Vallisneria gigantea from New Guinea and the Philippines has leaves that grow up to 2 m (over 2 yards) in length, with a width of 2 cm (¾ in).

V. spiralis is a very widespread species in the tropics and subtropics, which grows to a height of c. 20 cm (7¾ in).

V. spiralis form *tortifolia* from America has twisted leaves. It reaches a height of up to 50 cm (20 in).

Vesicularia dubyana Known popularly as Java moss, this is a bright green aquatic moss from south-east Asia which forms tufts on the aquarium rockwork, which are often used as spawning sites. The plant is very tolerant as regards light, water composition and temperature.

PLATY, see *Xiphophorus*.

Plecostomus punctatus

A catfish which, like *Gyrinocheilus*★ *aymonieri*, is very useful in the aquarium as it removes green algae★ from the glass and rockwork. The mouth, which is in the form of a sucker, is situated on the ventral side of the large, flat head. The body is brownish with darker markings. This is a hardy fish which thrives in most types of water, but as it grows fairly large it is really only suitable for tanks with a length of 1 m (3 feet) or more. Being active at night it should be provided with a suitable hiding-place to which it can retire during the day.

Family: Loricariidae★.

Diet: exclusively algae when young. The adults will eat boiled spinach, cabbage or lettuce. Some old individuals become

Synnema

Vallisneria

omnivorous and then cease to clean the tank, and this diminishes their attraction to the aquarist.

Sex differences: none.

Length: up to 20 cm (7¾ in) in the aquarium, 30 cm (12 in) in the wild.

Distribution: Bolivia, Brazil, Paraguay, Uruguay.

Compatibility: excellent, with the exception of some old individuals which attach themselves by the mouth to the flanks of other fishes.

Temperature range: 22–28°C (72–82°F).

Breeding: has never been recorded in the aquarium.

Poecilia reticulata

Formerly known as *Lebistes reticulatus,* this is the well-known guppy, named after its discoverer the Reverend Robert John Lechmere Guppy who sent specimens from Trinidad to the British Museum (Natural History) in 1866. Since then the species has been introduced into several countries to take part in the fight against mosquitoes by eating their aquatic larvae. In the wild, guppies are small fish, the females a uniform beige colour, the males with short fins and coloured markings which vary from one individual to the next. In the hands of amateur and professional aquarists the species has been subjected to a vast amount of selection. The result is a large number of what are really domesticated fish. The females sometimes have coloured caudal and anal fins and the males appear in an incredible diversity of shapes and colours. The caudal fin, for instance, may be rounded or shaped like a spade, a fan, a flag, a spear, or a sword.

Family: Poeciliidae*.

Diet: omnivorous.

Sex differences: female larger and duller than male.

Length: female up to 6 cm (2¼ in), male 3.5 cm (1¼ in).

Distribution: north of the Amazon basin, Venezuela, Trinidad, Barbados.

Compatibility: excellent.

Temperature range: 22–28°C (72–82°F).

Breeding: very easy. The female produces 10–60 fry at a time, often at intervals of only 30 days.

Poeciliidae

A family of livebearing fishes living exclusively in America, and distributed from the southern United States to Argentina. The various species are among the most popular aquarium fishes, partly on account of their small size and rich colours, partly on account of their method of reproduction.

The eggs are fertilized within the ovarian cavity of the female by sperm introduced by the male's copulatory organ, known as a gonopodium, a complex tubular structure formed by the modification of the anal fin. The female can store the sperm in her oviduct for a long time, and may produce several batches of young from a single mating.

The young start to swim almost im-

Plecostomus (up to 20 cm or 7¾ in in the aquarium, 30 cm or 12 in in the wild)

mediately after birth, but in the aquarium they are, in most species, ruthlessly chased and eaten by both parents. This can be prevented by taking certain precautions. One can use a breeding trap to hold the gravid female; this is a small box-like gadget made of plastic mesh of a size that will contain the female but allow the fry to escape. Alternatively, the female can be placed in a large tank with plenty of vegetation to provide shelter for the brood. The young must be given an abundant and varied supply of food, starting with *Artemia*★ nauplii and powdered food, followed as they grow with dry flakes or small pellets and larger forms of live food. The aquarist should not hesitate to cull any young in which growth appears to be retarded

or those which are simply in surplus, because space is as necessary as food for rapid development. Finally, it is advisable to separate the sexes before the fish have reached the adult length, in order to prevent premature matings.

The systematics of the Poeciliidae has been the subject of considerable revision during recent years, and there have been frequent changes in nomenclature. Thus the genera *Limia*, *Lebistes* and *Mollienesia* are now included in the genus *Poecilia*. *Poecilia* (*Limia*) *melanogaster* from Jamaica has males measuring about 3–4 cm (1⅓–1½ in) and in the particularly prolific *Poecilia* (*Limia*) *nigrofasciata* from Haiti they may be slightly larger. Other species include *Girardinus metallicus*

Poecilia reticulata, the red veiltail guppy (3.5 cm or 1¼ in)

from Cuba, and the tiny and very decorative *Phalloceros caudimaculatus* from eastern South America which should be imported more often. The curious *Belonesox belizanus,* looking rather like a small pike, merits a mention, but its size (the female measures 20 cm [7¾ in]) and voracity render it a difficult subject for the amateur's aquarium.

see *Gambusia affinis, Heterandria formosa, Mollies, Poecilia reticulata, Xiphophorus.*

POECILOBRYCON, see *Nannostomus.*

Polycentridae

This family, closely related to the Nandidae★, has representatives in north-eastern South America and in western Africa. They are characterized by the completely transparent anal and caudal fins and by the remarkably extensile mouth which enables them to swallow very large prey.

Like the other species, *Monocirrhus polyacanthus* and *Polycentropsis abbreviata,* for example, they lie motionless in wait for their prey, often head down with the body at

129

Monocirrhus polyacanthus, the South American leaf-fish (8 cm or 3 in), one of the Polycentridae

an angle of 45°, looking like a dead leaf.
see *Polycentrus schomburgki.*

Polycentrus schomburgki

A well camouflaged fish, looking like a dead leaf, but actually a voracious predator. Like the related *Polycentropsis abbreviata* from Africa it lives in shady places.
Family: Polycentridae★.
Diet: carnivorous.
Sex differences: not marked, although the male is more brightly coloured than the female.
Length: 9 cm (3½ in).
Distribution: north-eastern South America and Trinidad.
Compatibility: good with fish of its own size, but it will devour smaller ones.
Temperature range: 22–28°C (72–82°F).

Breeding: difficult in the aquarium, although it has been successful on several occasions, using soft, acid water (pH 6.8 and hardness 8°DH). The eggs, which are laid on a flat stone or a large leaf, hatch in four days at 26°C (79°F). The female should be removed from the tank when spawning has finished and the male when the eggs have hatched.

POMPADOUR, see *Symphysodon discus.*

Positioning the aquarium

There are no fixed rules about the positioning of an aquarium tank. Some sites may well be more suitable from the viewpoint of establishing the biological★ equilibrium. However, even if the position chosen is not ideal, any deficiencies can usually be made up by technical means. Perhaps the only important factor in this context is the lighting*. Insufficient light, whether natural or artificial, can easily be dealt with by adding another lamp or two. On the other hand, excess light can be a great nuisance, and it is not always easy to provide shade without affecting the general appearance of the tank.

Depending upon the general layout and decoration of the room the tank can be positioned on a mantlepiece, on a table or other piece of furniture, or on a metal stand specially designed for it. Alternatively, a tank can be fixed against a wall or built into one, provided space is reserved for the accessories. Large aquaria must be given proper support, not only on a strong stand, but also over an adequately braced area of floor.

A large tank is heavy even when empty. see Setting up the aquarium.

Pristella maxillaris

A small, active and hardy fish formerly known as *Pristella riddlei,* that will live in almost any type of water and within a wide temperature range.

Family: Characidae*.
Diet: omnivorous.
Sex differences: scarcely any, but the belly is more rounded in the female.
Length: 4 cm (1½ in).
Distribution: Guyana and Amazon basin.
Compatibility: generally excellent.
Temperature range: 20–27°C (68–80°F).
Breeding: rather difficult. The eggs hatch in three days, and the fry* are tiny.

A well-positioned aquarium forms an excellent decorative feature

Pristella maxillaris, the X-ray fish (4 cm or 1½ in)

Pseudocrenilabrus multicolor

Known as the Egyptian mouthbrooder, this is an interesting fish as the female incubates the eggs in her mouth. In addition it is small enough to be very suitable for the amateur aquarist.

Family: Cichlidae★.

Diet: omnivorous.

Sex differences: dorsal and anal fins shorter in the female, which is also duller.

Length: up to 8 cm (3 in).

Distribution: Africa (Egypt to Tanzania).

Compatibility: good.

Temperature range: 18–27°C (64–80°F).

Breeding: as for mouthbrooding cichlids.

Pseudotropheus

The cichlids in this genus also those in the related genera *Melanochromis* and *Labeotropheus*★ come from the large African Lake Malawi (formerly Nyasa) which has an area of 26,000 sq km (c. 10,000 square miles). They are strongly territorial and very aggressive towards other members of their own species and towards other occupants of the tank. Nor do they respect the plants★ and tank decoration. In addition to the species described below, mention may be made of *P. elongatus* and of *P. tropheops* which grows to about 10 cm (3¾ in).

Pseudotropheus elongatus

Sex differences: in the usual form (there are other rare, poorly known forms) the male is grey-blue to bright blue, varying according to emotional state. The female is duller.

Length: 11 cm (4 in).

Other characteristics: as for *M. auratus.*

Pseudotropheus zebra

This is the largest of the Lake Malawi cichlids.

Sex differences: the male is usually blue, sometimes whitish, with dark vertical bars. The female is bluish or yellow, but also with markings that vary from orange to brown or almost black. There are other colour forms in which the fish lack dark bars and are entirely white, pale blue, or orange, or one of these colours overlaid with black blotches.

Length: up to 16 cm (6¼ in).

Breeding: possible, but often less successful than with other species in the genus. After laying her eggs and taking them into her mouth the female nibbles the bright markings, known as egg dummies, on the male's anal fin; they are so named because they strongly resemble the eggs. This action stimulates the male to release his sperm which then fertilize the eggs in the female's mouth.

Other characteristics: as for *M. auratus*.

Pterophyllum scalare

Since its introduction into Europe in 1909, this fish, known as the angelfish, has become one of the most popular of all ornamental tropical species. At one time it was rather costly, but now it appears on the market at very reasonable prices. It requires a tank that is at least 80 cm (32 in) long and 40 cm (15½ in) high, and the other occupants should be placid in temperament.

In addition to the usual form, a number of

Pseudotropheus elongatus (11 cm or 4¼ in)

133

Different varieties of *Pterophyllum scalare,* the angelfish (c. 10 cm or 4 in)

domesticated forms have been bred or selected. These include the veiltail angelfish, a very tall, rather delicate form with long filmy fins, the marbled veiltail with the vertical bands broken up, a smoky form in which the ground colour is smoky-grey instead of white, and the black angelfish in which the stripes can no longer be distinguished. There are also albino and other forms which are more curiosities than beautiful fish.

These domesticated forms, and particularly the black ones, are rather delicate.

Family: Cichlidae*.

Diet: omnivorous.

Sex differences: the only reliable method of distinguishing the sexes is to examine the genital papilla during the spawning period. This is short and turned backwards in the female, pointed and turned forwards in the male.

Length: rarely more than 10 cm (3¾ in) in the aquarium, with a height of 15 cm (6 in).

Distribution: Amazon basin.

Compatibility: generally perfect, but it is inadvisable to introduce fish the size of

Pterophyllum scalare (c. 10 cm or 4 in)

neon tetras into a tank with large adult angelfishes.

Breeding: perfectly possible for the normal form, less so for the selected forms. The eggs are laid on a large leaf which has been previously cleaned by the parents, who then guard them. If the parents appear to neglect the eggs the leaf can be cut off and placed in a small tank filled with water from the spawning tank, and given good aeration.

PUNTIUS, see *Barbus*.

R

Rasbora

This is a large genus belonging to the family Cyprinidae* and distributed throughout south-east Asia. *Rasbora* live gregariously in very soft waters with a low degree of hardness and an acid pH. Most of them are not difficult to keep in the aquarium but they do not breed readily. Certain species are regularly imported, others appear on the market at irregular intervals. These include *R. lateristriata,* a hardy, prolific species which reaches a length of 13 cm, *R. vaterifloris,* attractive but delicate, *R. urophthalma,* only 2.5 cm long, *R. borapetensis* from Thailand which does not appear to have bred in captivity and *R. pauciperforata* which is rather difficult to keep.

Rasbora dorsiocellata

An attractive silvery-white fish with a characteristic circular black spot on the dorsal fin.
Diet: omnivorous.

Sex differences: scarcely detectable, except that the female ready to spawn is more rounded.
Length: 5 cm (2 in).
Distribution: Malaysia and Sumatra.
Compatibility: excellent.
Temperature range: 23–28°C (73–82°F).
Breeding: possible. This is a very prolific species.

Rasbora heteromorpha

This is the popular harlequin fish distinguished by the striking dark marking on the rear of each flank. It can be kept satisfactorily with a group of small characins (Characidae*). In the related but slightly smaller *R. hengeli* the dark flank markings are smaller.
Diet: omnivorous.
Sex differences: very subtle. The base of the wedge-shaped flank marking is straight in the female, rounded in the male.
Length: 4 cm (1½ in).
Distribution: Malaysia, Thailand, Indonesia.
Compatibility: excellent.
Temperature range: 23–29°C (73–84°F).

Rasbora pauciperforata, the red-striped rasbora (7 cm or 2¾ in)

Rasbora heteromorpha, the harlequin fish (4 cm or 1½ in)

Breeding: for long thought to be impracticable, this has now been done in very soft, acid water (hardness less than 5°DH, and pH less than 6). Mating takes place briefly and repeatedly. The female spawns upside down under a leaf and the male wraps his body round hers. The species is somewhat shy of the light, so that the tank should be shaded. The eggs hatch in about 30 hours, and the fry* are free-swimming in about 5 days. They need a plentiful supply of infusorians*.

Rasbora maculata

This is a very small brick-red species marked with black dots. It is not often kept in aquaria and appears to be rather difficult to acclimatize.

Diet: omnivorous.

Sex differences: the males are slimmer and cherry-red, the females more rounded and yellowish.

Length: 2.5 cm (1 in) at the most.

Distribution: Malaysia, Sumatra.

Compatibility: excellent.

Temperature range: 23–28°C (73–82°F).

Rasbora trilineata, the scissortail (7 cm or 2¾ in)

Breeding: possible, using soft water and a
   dark substrate (peat).

Rasbora trilineata
Known popularly as the scissortail on account
of the scissoring movements of the caudal fin
lobes. This is particularly noticeable because
the tail has two black spots. The species is
hardy, even in hard water.
Diet: omnivorous.
Sex differences: practically none, except
   that a female ready to spawn has a more
   rounded body.
Length: up to 7 cm (2¾ in) in the aquarium,
   more than twice this in the wild.
Distribution: Indonesia, Malaya.
Compatibility: good.
Temperature range: 23–28°C (73–82°F).
Breeding: possible, using soft, neutral to
   slightly acid water.

Rearing
It has often been said that breeding★ is the
peak of the aquarist's art. It is not, however,
sufficient for the fishes to mate and spawn, for
the fry have to be reared and this is often
difficult for the amateur.

Losses may be due to pollution caused by
overfeeding. The fry★ must at all times have a
plentiful supply of available food. This may
mean that the tank water contains excess food
which at tropical temperatures soon starts to
decay and cause pollution which kills the fry.
This can be largely avoided by siphoning off
excess food and detritus at frequent intervals.

Overcrowding is one of the main causes of
deformation and stunted growth. Even after a
few days the fry may show considerable
variation in growth, some being twice the size
of others. If this happens it is essential to cull
the deformed and stunted specimens.

Lack of space can impede growth, even though the fry are being properly fed and their number in relation to the water volume appears to be correct. For instance, ten young fish in 10 litres (2¼ gallons) of water will develop normally, whereas two in 2 litres (3½ pints) of water will be endangered.

Lack of food at the start of life is responsible for growth checks in many cases. As soon as they have resorbed their yolk sac, the fry must be able to find suitable food immediately. If there is a delay of 24 hours growth will be irreversibly retarded.

Fry of different sizes should not be kept together, as the larger individuals will consume a disproportionate amount of the available food. Smaller fry should either be culled or transferred to another tank.

The young of livebearing fishes should not be kept together, as they will never develop fully if they mate prematurely.

RED-NOSED TETRA, see *Petitella georgiae*.

Rivulus cylindraceus

Like related species, *R. milesi*, *R. langesi* and *R. urophthalmus*, this is a good jumper, so the tank must be securely covered.

Family: Cyprinodontidae*.

Diet: almost omnivorous, with a preference for live food.

Sex difference: as in all the *Rivulus* species the female is duller than the male, and has a dark marking near the base of the caudal fin.

Length: 5 cm (2 in).

Distribution: Cuba.

Compatibility: satisfactory.

Temperature range: 20–26°C (68–79°F).

Breeding: is not very often done perhaps because being less brightly coloured than other Cyprinodontidae, the species of *Rivulus* are not very widely distributed in

Rivulus cylindraceus, the Cuban rivulus (5 cm or 2 in)

Slate is very suitable for the decoration of an aquarium tank

the aquarium world. They can, however, be bred in relatively soft water at 24°C (75°F). The female spawns near the surface on the leaf of a floating plant. The large adhesive eggs hatch in 10–15 days. The parents can be left in the tank even after the fry★ have hatched. The fry are sufficiently large to take *Artemia*★ nauplii as their first food.

Rockwork

In the aquarium, rockwork is used for decorative purposes, for it is pleasing to the eye and it also helps hide the tubing and other accessories. It also serves to hold the plants★ in position.

Although all rocks can perform these functions they are not all suitable. Those with sharp edges and angles should be avoided as these might injure the fish, and care should be taken to exclude any with a chemical composition that is harmful.

Thus, one should proscribe those which are too calcareous as under acid conditions they will gradually dissolve and alter the character of the water★. Similarly, rocks with a high metal content must be avoided. There are also certain rocks with numerous small cavities in which detritus accumulates and this quickly leads to pollution.

There are, however, several different kinds of rock which are quite safe to use, and these include all the schists, which have an extensive range of colours. For aesthetic reasons it is best to place the darker rocks at the rear of the tank and the paler ones in front. It is also best not to mix colours, by having, for instance, red and green rocks close to one another. Slate is one of the most suitable materials, and it has the advantage that it is very easy to work. It can be cut with metal shears or split with an old chisel.

Fluorspar can also be used, and so can all rocks with a base of silica. One of the most beautiful materials for aquarium rockwork is petrified wood.

Willow roots can be used to give the effect of a mangrove swamp, but they must be carefully boiled before being put into the tank.

Opinions vary but many aquarists use a considerable amount of rockwork in the tanks. In a tank 1 m (a yard) long, for instance, it would not be unusual to use about 30 kg (66 lb) of rock. On average one can reckon that the rockwork and substrate of an aquarium will occupy about 20 per cent of the total tank volume.

ROLOFFIA, see *Aphyosemion*.
ROSY BARB, see *Hyphessobrycon*.

Scatophagidae

A small family with members living along the coasts of south-east Asia, Australia, east Africa and Madagascar, often in brackish and much polluted waters. They mainly frequent estuaries, ports, and sewage outlets where there is plenty of faecal and other wastes which form their diet. They also enter fresh water, and sometimes the sea, mainly in order to spawn in rock crevices.
see *Scatophagus argus*.

Scatophagus argus

This is the scat or argus fish. It has a tall, compressed and flat body, normally yellowish with black spots. There is an orange variety, formerly regarded as a distinct species under the name *S. rubrifrons*. This is not always an easy fish to keep in the aquarium. Specimens bought from a dealer should neither be thin nor show a tendency to swim with irregular movements. When young they can be kept in very hard fresh water (over 25°DH) or better, in slightly brackish water. When adult (length 10 cm [4 in] or more), they are probably best kept in brackish water, the salinity of which is varied every few months, say in the specific gravity range 1002–1010.

Family: Scatophagidae★.

Diet: omnivorous. This fish requires plenty to eat and substantial live prey animals, such as chironomid larvae, are practically indispensable for the young. When they have reached a length of 7–8 cm (2¾–3 in) they should be given a supplement of vegetable matter in the form of raw lettuce.

Sex differences: none apparent.

Length: up to 30 cm (12 in) in the wild, rarely more than 15 cm (6 in) in the aquarium.

Distribution: Australia, Indonesia, south-east Asia.

Scatophagus argus, the scat or argusfish (c. 15 cm or 6 in)

Compatibility: good with other species, bad with members of its own species if living in groups of less than four individuals, as the strongest then becomes tyrannical.
Temperature range: 22–28°C (72–82°F).
Breeding: not yet recorded in captivity.

SCISSORTAIL, see *Rasbora.*

Selection
The selection of ornamental fishes is partly a matter of taste, but it also depends upon the type of tank accommodation. If the tank is

Scatophagus argus, another variety

with a few specimens of a few species, and to find out which will thrive in the conditions offered.

It is rather more difficult to select suitable fishes. With some exceptions these should be gregarious species that are compatible with their companions. It is always better to have a few specimens (say 6–8) of each of a smaller number of species than to put into the tank a great variety of species, each represented by only one or two specimens.

When a tank is used to accommodate more than one species it is always essential to ensure that these are compatible with one another and that the water composition is suitable for them.

Finally, care should be taken to buy only from a recognized, reliable dealer who sells healthy fishes acclimatized to the local water. The cheapest is not always the best.

SERPAE, see *Hyphessobrycon.*

Setting up the tank

The establishment of an aquarium tank must be carried out methodically.

The first operation is to wash the inside of the tank, using only clean, clear water. The outer face of the rear glass pane, which eventually becomes inaccessible, should also be thoroughly cleaned. Before installing the tank in its final position, it is a good idea to cover this pane externally with a black or blue background, perhaps just a simple sheet of paper fixed in position by adhesive tape. This will avoid the rather ugly reflections produced by a sheet of transparent glass.

The second operation is to install the filter if this is to be a substrate filter. In tanks with a metal bottom plate, care should be taken to interpose a sheet of transparent plastic between the latter and the bottom of the filter.

The third operation is to put in the substrate*, and in so doing bury the plastic tubing leading to the diffuser or airstone, which should itself rest on the surface of the sand.

The fourth operation is to install the rockwork, mostly round the sides and rear of

unheated and merely kept at ordinary room temperature the choice will be somewhat limited. Apart from goldfish it could be used for such tropical species as *Danio* * *malabaricus,Pristella* * *maxillaris* and *Tanichthys* * *albonubes.* If, on the other hand, it has heating* then it can accommodate any of the numerous tropical fishes available on the market.

The tank itself should not be too small and a minimum length of 50 cm (20 in) is recommended. The maintenance of an aquarium does, of course, depend upon having a suitable biological* equilibrium, and this is easier in a large volume of water than a small one. A few grams of pollutant material (e.g. food remains) will be ten times more concentrated in a volume of 10 litres (2¼ gallons) than in 100 (22 gallons). In the first case there will be a risk of upsetting the equilibrium, in the second the consequences would not be serious.

The choice of rockwork* to decorate the aquarium will depend partly upon taste, partly on the necessity to avoid any materials that might injure the fishes, whether physically or chemically.

In the case of plants* it is better to start

144

the tank, and arranged to form an attractive composition. The centre and front of the tank should, in most cases, be free of rocks, and the substrate arranged so that there is a depression where detritus can collect, so that it can be removed more efficiently. The rocks must be brushed and washed in advance, and care should be taken that they are firmly embedded in the substrate so that they do not become loosened when the tank is filled with water. The rocks should be positioned so that the fish can swim in between them, or between them and the glass.

The fifth operation is to install the heating* equipment. The heater can be hidden behind a rock, with the thermostat positioned so that its top projects above the water surface, and the thermometer placed so that it is unobtrusive but still visible.

The sixth operation is to introduce the plants*, and there are two ways of doing this. The first is partially to fill the tank with water in order to obtain some idea of the final result. It is not very easy to plant underwater, and this method is generally used only for very large tanks where the time taken for the whole process would be too long for the plants to survive the risk of desiccation, as might occur with the second method.

In the second method the plants are put into the damp substrate before the water is added. Small pits can be made with a finger or with a small trowel and the plants carefully put into these, spreading the roots where necessary, and then firming the substrate round them.

It is a good idea to separate the plants into three groups: small ones for the front of the tank, medium-sized ones for the centre and larger ones, or those which will become large, for the back. If the plants show signs of drying out their leaves should be sprayed with a little water.

In the wild one would never see a water lily, an iris and a rush growing side by side. In order that the tank should look as natural as possible it is, in fact, best to plant in fairly large groups, each of one species, and to avoid having single specimen plants.

When planting has been completed the tank bottom (with the plants) should be carefully covered with a sheet of thin plastic. This will prevent damage to the plants and substrate when the water is introduced.

For the seventh operation is, in fact, to fill the tank with water. Small tanks can be filled using a jug, but for those containing more than 100 litres (22 gallons), it is simpler to use a length of tubing to bring the water from tap to tank.

The temperature of the water should be in the range of 17-27°C (63–80°F), remembering that plants are more readily damaged by heat than by cold. The rate of filling should be slow at first, to allow the substrate to become impregnated quite slowly, as any sudden change in its consistency might cause the displacement of the rockwork.

The eighth and last operation is the installation of the lighting* and of the tubing leading to the air pump.

On the following day the lighting can be switched on and any dead leaves carefully removed. Two days later the tank should have settled down sufficiently and the first fish can be introduced.
see Positioning the aquarium, Maintenance.

SHUBUNKIN, see *Carassius auratus*.

Siluridae
A family of catfishes with representatives in Europe, northern Africa, Asia and Australia. Like the Callichthyidae* and Mochocidae* they are known as catfishes from the whisker-like barbels in the mouth region. These are sometimes short and rigid, sometimes long and filamentous. The skin of these catfishes is scaleless.
see *Kryptopterus bicirrhis*.

SLEEP, see Lighting.

Snails
These are gastropod molluscs of which some species live in fresh water. For a long time it was considered that they fulfilled a useful

function in the aquarium, by scavenging. It is true that they do graze algae off the aquarium glass, but they do so very unsystematically, and of course they add to the waste products in the tank by their own faeces. Apart from ramshorn snails (*Planorbis*★) it is probably best not to have any snails in the tank. Pond snails of the genus *Limnaea* should certainly not be used, for not only do they attack certain plants, but there is always a risk that they may bring parasites into the aquarium. Finally, snails are extremely prolific and once established in a tank they are sometimes very difficult to eradicate.

Substrate

The substrate of an aquarium should satisfy four requirements: it should be pleasing to the eye, help to hold the rockwork in position, provide a footing for the plants and take part in the filtration★ of the tank water. River sand and quartz are the materials which best satisfy these requirements. Quartz in particular provides an absolutely neutral substrate, but it is very poor in nutrient. Some gravels may have pebbles that are large enough to block a siphon tube when the tank is being cleaned.

It is quite essential that all substrate materials should be very thoroughly washed,

LEFT, installation of heating equipment. RIGHT, the plants are put into position. BELOW LEFT, plastic film is used to protect the plants before (below right) the tank is filled with water.

A pond snail (*Limnaea*), once popular in the aquarium, but now to be avoided

until the washing water is absolutely clear, before they are introduced into the tank. Sand is sometimes regarded as unsatisfactory for growing plants as it lacks nutrients (nitrates, phosphates). However, this view is only partly justified as many submerged aquarium plants obtain their nutrients through their leaves rather than through their roots. Furthermore, waste products produced by the fishes soon break down to produce nitrates and other substances which plants, such as *Cryptocoryne* and *Echinodorus,* can assimilate through their roots.

It is possible to make a compost based on soil, but this should only be attempted by the experienced amateur aquarist as it can easily lead to upsets in the biological* equilibrium. A good compost of this type should be neither too alkaline nor too acid. It could be made by mixing four parts sieved moorland soil with one part of clay soil and two parts of wood charcoal, the latter serving to absorb the gases produced during fermentation and also helping to render the compost less compact. This rich soil can be used as a substrate in areas where there are plants that need it.

Whatever the material used for the substrate, the quantities required will vary somewhat, but can be reckoned broadly speaking as 10 kg (22 lb) for a tank 50 cm (20 in)

long, 20 kg (44 lb) for a length of 80 cm (32 in), and 40 kg (88 lb) for 1.20 m (48 in).
see Biological equilibrium, Setting up the tank.

SWORDTAIL, see *Xiphophorus*.
SWORDTAIL CHARACIN, see *Corynopoma riisei*.

Symphysodon

A genus containing what are perhaps the most beautiful of the tropical freshwater fishes suitable for the aquarium. After a long period of confusion, it is now generally agreed that there are two species. The first species is *S. discus,* the discus or pompadour fish which has a brown ground colour with irregular horizontal blue markings and dark vertical bands. The other species is *S. aequifasciata* which has three subspecies, namely *S. aequifasciata aequifasciata,* the green discus, with a brownish-green ground colour, wavy horizontal blue markings and dark vertical bands, *S. aequifasciata axelrodi,* the brown discus,

The substrate of an aquarium should be clean, decorative and functional

Symphysodon aequifasciata aequifasciata, the green discus (15 cm or 6 in)

with a deep maroon ground colour and distinct dark vertical bars and *S. aequifasciata haraldi*, the blue discus, also brown, but with blue horizontal stripes only at the top and bottom of the body. The latter subspecies has the reputation of being the hardiest form in a very delicate genus.

These fish live in very soft, clear, slightly acid waters. They require a large tank, filled with water at about pH 6.5 and with a hardness less than 10°DH. It is best not to keep other fish species in the tank.
Family: Cichlidae*.
Diet: small live food in variety. Some

individuals will take dried and freeze-dried foods.

Sex differences: none detectable.

Length: 12–20 cm (4¾–7¾ in), depending on the variety.

Distribution: Amazon basin.

Compatibility: good with other species. When kept in groups of four individuals or less there is a tendency for one fish to become dominant and tyrannical.

Temperature range: 25–30°C (77–86°F).

Breeding: has been successfully achieved by some amateur aquarists. It requires a compatible pair, sufficient space, very strict hygiene and very soft water. The hardness should not exceed 6°DH. The eggs are laid, often in the evening, on a plant with large leaves or on a vertical rock. At 29°C (84°F) they hatch in about three days and the fry* then remain attached to this support for four days. As soon as they have used up the contents of their yolk sac and are free-swimming, they attach themselves to the flank of the parents where they feed on mucus secreted by the skin—a phenomenon that appears to be unique in the world of fishes.

Symphysodon discus, the discus (20 cm or 7¾ in)

The species of *Symphysodon* are the only aquarium fishes which feed their young on a mucus secreted by their own flanks

Synodontis nigriventris

A brownish catfish with dark markings, but peculiar in having a pale back and a darker belly, the reverse of what is normal in fishes. This is an adaptation to the fish's habit of living upside down. The same habit occurs in the more brightly coloured but rarely imported *S. angelicus*.

Family: Mochocidae*.

Diet: omnivorous.

Sex differences: none detectable.

Length: 6 cm (2¼ in).

Distribution: Zaïre basin.

Compatibility: good.

Temperature range: 22–28°C (72–82°F).

Breeding: has not yet been achieved in the aquarium, although eggs have been laid.

Systematics

This is the term used for the method of classifying all organisms according to their evolutionary relationship to each other, so that they can be recognized internationally. There are about 25,000 different kinds or species of fishes living in the world today.

These are grouped into classes, orders and families. Each family (e.g. Cyprinidae) contains a number of genera (singular: genus) and each genus has one or more species. Each species is given two names. The first of these is the generic name, e.g. *Tanichthys*, the second the name of the particular species, e.g. *albonubes*. In technical monographs on fishes it is usual to add the name of the author who first described the species and the date of description. Thus the White Cloud Mountain minnow would be *Tanichthys albonubes* Lin, 1932. From time to time the systematics of a group of fishes may be revised and this may lead to adjustments or changes in the names. Such revisions are generally carried out when new investigations have revealed fresh information on the structure of the fishes concerned, e.g. their dentition, scale arrangement, fin structure and so on.

Vernacular or popular names are more or less useless in scientific circles as they are not understood internationally, and often lead to confusion.

T

Tanichthys albonubes

This is the White Cloud Mountain minnow, so called from its place of discovery, the White Cloud Mountain near Canton. It is a hardy species that can tolerate relatively low temperatures.

Family: Cyprinidae★.

Diet: omnivorous.

Sex differences: male more colourful, female with a rounded belly.

Length: 4 cm (1½ in).

Distribution: China, near Canton.

Compatibility: excellent.

Temperature range: 18–25°C (64–77°F).

Breeding: as for *Brachydanio★ rerio*. This is often successful in water kept at 24°C (75°F). The slightly adhesive eggs hatch in about 60 hours, and both they and the fry★ are respected by the parents, provided the latter have been properly fed.

Tanichthys albonubes, the White Cloud Mountain minnow (4 cm or 1½ in)

TANK, see Aquarium.

TELESCOPE EYE, see *Carassius auratus*.

Telmatherina ladigesi

An attractive fish with brilliant iridescence and long, elegant fins. It can be kept in a tank with hard neutral water and some vegetation. The addition of a little sea salt to the water is often recommended.

Family: Atherinidae★.

Diet: dried foods are not appreciated.

Sex differences: in the males the first rays of the anal fin and of the second dorsal fin are much elongated.

Length: 7 cm ($2\frac{3}{4}$ in).

Distribution: Celebes.

Compatibility: good.

Temperature range: 23–28°C (73–82°F).

Breeding: the yellow eggs, laid on the leaves of plants, hatch in 8–11 days. The fry★ should be fed on fine powdered foods and infusorians★.

Telmatherina ladigesi, the Celebes sailfish (7 cm or $2\frac{3}{4}$ in)

TEMPERATURE, see Heating.

TETRA, see *Cheirodon axelrodi, Gymnocorymbus ternetzi, Hemigrammus, Hyphessobrycon, Phenacogrammus interruptus*.

Tetraodon fluviatilis

A pufferfish with numerous black markings

Tetraodon fluviatilis, the green pufferfish (up to 17 cm or $6\frac{3}{4}$ in)

on a greenish ground colour which, like the related *T. palembangensis* from Thailand and Indonesia, lives in fresh or preferably brackish water.

Family: Tetraodontidae★.

Diet: any live prey, particularly freshwater snails, and from time to time a little lettuce.

Sex differences: none detectable.

Length: up to 17 cm ($6\frac{1}{2}$ in) in the wild.

Distribution: fresh and brackish waters of southern Asia and Indonesia.

Compatibility: mediocre.

Temperature range: 22–28°C (72–82°F).

Breeding: has been achieved in some public aquaria.

Tetraodontidae

A family of mainly marine fishes, with a few representatives in fresh and brackish waters of the Old World tropics and subtropics. Known popularly as pufferfishes, they have pectoral, dorsal and anal fins capable of carrying out helicoid movements, rather like sculling.

Carinotetraodon somphongsi, one of the pufferfishes (6 cm or 2¼ in)

These enable the fish to rotate while remaining in one place and also to move up and down, rather like a helicopter. Four powerful teeth form a sturdy beak which can even crush the shells of some molluscs. The skin lacks scales, but in some species such as *Carinotet-*

raodon somphongsi (6 cm or 2¼ in long) from Thailand, it has erectile spines. Finally, the Tetraodontidae have the ability to inflate themselves with water or air when threatened, thus transforming themselves into little balloons that are too large for many predators. They can deflate themselves when the danger has passed.

see *Tetradon fluviatilis.*

Thayeria obliqua

A hardy, gregarious fish characterized by the striking black lower lobe of the caudal fin, and the oblique position of the body when swimming. There is some confusion in the naming of the species in this genus.

Family: Characidae*.
Diet: omnivorous.
Sex differences: none, except that the
   gravid female has a more rounded belly.
Length: 7 cm (2¾ in).
Distribution: Amazon basin.
Compatibility: satisfactory.
Temperature range: 23–28°C (73–82°F).
Breeding: as for most of the less demanding

Thayeria obliqua, the penguin fish (7 cm or 2¾ in)

Characidae★, in relatively soft, old water. The yellow-brown eggs hatch in two days and the fry will have resorbed their yolk sac four days later and can then be fed on infusorians★.

Toxotes jaculator
An attractive silvery-green species with black markings. Known as the archerfish from its unusual method of catching prey. When it sees an insect alight on a plant above the water surface the fish ejects from its mouth a fine jet of water at the prey. The aim is remarkably good over distances of at least 1 m (3 feet). This is done by forming a kind of compression barrel between the tongue and a groove in the roof of the mouth, and then expelling through this the water held in the gill chamber.

This species must be kept in a large tank with hard or brackish water.
Family: Toxotidae★.

Diet: omnivorous, with a distinct preference for insects.
Sex differences: none apparent.
Length: up to 20 cm (7¾ in) in the wild.
Distribution: Australia, south-east Asia, Philippines, western Pacific.
Compatibility: satisfactory with all fish measuring at least half its own length.
Temperature range: 24–29°C (75–84°F).
Breeding: not recorded in captivity.

Toxotidae
A small family with about five species distributed from the Red Sea to the western Pacific. They live primarily in brackish waters, and do not move far, either towards the sea or into fresh water. They can tolerate fluctuations in the salinity of the water.
see *Toxotes jaculator*.

Transport
transporting an aquarium tank When it is

Toxotes jaculator, the archerfish (up to 20 cm or 7¾ in)

necessary to move a tank it must be emptied, not only of the water★ and rockwork★, but also of the very heavy substrate★. Even when empty it should not be lifted by the sides, but slid along until it can be lifted from below.

transporting fishes Fishes require the water in which they are living to have a sufficient content of dissolved oxygen to satisfy their respiratory needs, and it is quite useless merely to pierce a few holes in their transport container.

A well-sealed plastic bag, filled with one-third water and two-thirds air, or better oxygen, provides the most efficient method of transporting fishes

A couple of fish each not over 5 cm (2 in) long can be transported over a period of a few hours in a one-litre (one-quart) glass or plastic jar filled with water to within 2–3 cm (¾–1 in) of the top and well closed. If the journey is longer or if there are more fish the best method is to use a transparent plastic bag. This should be filled to a quarter of its capacity with some of the tank water and then gently inflated with oxygen from an oxygen cylinder. The bag is sealed with a rubber band and placed in an insulated carton to conserve the heat. This is the method by which all tropical aquarium fishes are transported (e.g. by air from Singapore and Sri Lanka to Europe and North America).

On arrival at its destination the bag is first placed for some minutes in the tank of water prepared for the fish. This allows the temperature of the two waters to equalize.

For species with spiny fin rays it is best to use two plastic bags, one inside the other.

Trichogaster

A genus of the family Anabantidae★ with species from south-east Asia. Some of the species are bred in aquaria and have become widely distributed, while others such as *T. microlepis* from Thailand and *T. pectoralis* from south-east Asia (up to 25 cm [9¾ in] long) are less frequently seen in the aquarium.

Trichogaster leerii

The pearl gourami, an attractive anabantid with a laterally compressed body and a brilliant spotted pattern. It is a rather delicate and somewhat timid fish which requires soft water and a relatively high temperature.

Diet: omnivorous, with a marked liking for the young shoots of tender plants★.

Sex differences: in the female the fins, particularly the dorsal, are shorter and more rounded.

Length: up to 12 cm (4¾ in).

Distribution: Indonesia, Malaysia, Thailand.

Compatibility: very good, except that the males are somewhat aggressive towards one another at spawning time.

Temperature range: 24–30°C (75–86°F).

Breeding: not difficult. The male builds a large nest of air bubbles, as is typical of many Anabantidae★, and he guards the eggs and fry★. There are records of over a thousand eggs from a single spawning, but the losses are often considerable, particularly during the period when the labyrinth is being formed.

Trichogaster trichopterus

A widely distributed blue fish marked with a dark spot on the flank and a similar one on the base of the tail. The species has a tendency to become aggressive with age. A selected variety, also blue but with a dark marbled pattern, is sold as the Cosby gourami.

T. trichopterus is very susceptible to flat

154

Trichogaster microlepsis, the moonlight gourami (up to 15 cm or 6 in)

Trichogaster leerii, the pearl gourami (up to 12 cm or $4\frac{3}{4}$ in)

abscesses on the skin; these seem to occur rather commonly in the Anabantidae.

Diet: omnivorous and very voracious.

Sex differences: in the female the fins, particularly the dorsal, are shorter and more rounded.

Length: up to 15 cm (6 in).

Distribution: Thailand, Vietnam, Malaysia, Indonesia.

Compatibility: good when small, doubtful when they reach a length of 8 cm (3 in).

Temperature range: 23–28°C (73–82°F).

Breeding: quite easy, as for the Anabantidae in general.

TUBIFEX, see Diet.

Trichogaster trichopterus, the blue gourami (up to 15 cm or 6 in)

VEGETATION, see Plants.

VEILTAIL, see *Carassius auratus.*

Water

Fresh waters vary considerably in composition in different parts of the world, and even in a single country or region there may be great variation. The waters of a mountain stream, for instance, will be quite different from those in a small pool fed with rain water, and this in turn will not be the same as the water of a coastal lagoon receiving small quantities of sea water from time to time.

For all these reasons the water of an aquarium presents the aquarist with some of his major problems.

It would be wrong, however, to exaggerate the difficulties involved. In many cases ordinary tap water is quite adequate for a community tank with plants and a few fish species. Generally speaking, tap water is clear, with a neutral pH, and it contains neither algae*, parasites nor pathogenic microbes.

Natural waters vary in hardness and in pH, and it is essential that these two characteristics should be understood by the aquarist.

The hardness of a water is due to the presence of varying amounts of calcium and magnesium compounds held in solution. Hard water is rich in such compounds, soft water poor. The total hardness of a water is expressed in degrees of hardness, and there are various different ways of calculating this. For the aquarist the most suitable is the German method, in which the hardness is expressed in parts per million of calcium oxide (CaO). Thus one German degree of hardness equals 17.9 parts per million of CaO, and this is usually written as 1°DH.

The hardness of fresh waters can be tabulated as follows:

Very soft water	= 0– 4° DH
Soft water	= 5– 8° DH
Medium-hard water	= 9–12°DH
Fairly hard water	=13–18°DH
Hard water	=19–30°DH
Very hard water	=over 30°DH

Water hardness can be measured with one of the numerous kits available on the market.

The letters pH stand for 'pondus Hydrogenii' or the weight of hydrogen and they indicate the degree of acidity or alkalinity of a water. Thus, waters with a pH of 7 are neutral, those with a lower figure are acid, those with a higher figure are alkaline. This is a universally used scale.

In an aquarium the pH should normally be in the range 6–8. In theory there is no link between the pH and the DH of a water. In practice, however, there is no natural water which is very soft (e.g. 2°DH) and at the same time alkaline (e.g. pH 8). Soft waters, in fact, tend to be acid, hard waters alkaline.

The following table is intended to provide a guide to the pH of waters used in the aquarium:

Very acid	pH 6.4 or less
Acid	6.7
Neutral	7.0
Alkaline	7.3
Very alkaline	7.5 or more

Most aquarists are not fastidious about pH, partly because tap water is generally neutral or slightly alkaline and partly because the pH fluctuates, being subject to certain factors which tend to raise or lower it. Thus, in an aquarium the pH after a night of darkness will not be the same as after a day of sunlight.

On the contrary, the degree of hardness of a water is quite constant. A water is either hard or it is not. In many cases it is rather too hard for the majority of tropical fishes which come from slightly acid waters which are poor in calcium.

Some aquarists do, in fact, modify the water to make it accord with the water from which the fishes originally came. Here are some examples of how this can be done.

1. You have a soft water, but want to keep fishes requiring a hard water. Place a piece of plaster in the tank and leave it there until a check shows that the desired degree of hardness has been reached.

2. The water is acid and you want to raise its pH so that it becomes alkaline. Here you can add small amounts of previously dissolved sodium carbonate, carefully measuring the result obtained after each addition, and continuing until the desired pH is reached.

3. The water is alkaline and you want to make it acid. So, add small amounts of acid sodium phosphate measuring the result after each addition, and continuing until the required acid pH is obtained. However, if the original water is hard as well as alkaline, this process will give an unnatural water that is acid and hard. (This method is not recommended unless the aquarist has an understanding of chemistry.)

4. The water is neutral but it has a DH of 25°, and you want a water that is softer (about 10°DH) and preferably slightly acid. This is the most frequent situation encountered, and there are three methods of dealing with the problem:

a) Do not use tap water, but look for a source, possibly an artesian well, providing water of the required type.

b) Add a special resin to the filter medium. These substances should lower the DH, but probably only by a few points.

c) Mix tap water at 30°DH and two-thirds soft water with little or no hardness to give a water with about 10°DH.

The problem of finding a soft water is not insoluble. For example, the following sources may be useful:

i) the melted water obtained when a refrigerator is defrosted.

ii) rain water, collected in a plastic container. In towns with polluted air this should not be collected until the rain has had time to wash down the toxic vapours.

iii) melted snow is suitable if collected in a clean area and filtered.

iv) distilled water is very suitable, but costly.

v) mineral waters, provided the label on the bottle states that the water has a low degree of hardness.

In addition to these more general cases it is sometimes necessary to keep the water of a particular tank at a constant pH, usually when keeping and breeding certain delicate species. The best method is to put some boiled peat in the filter, taking care not to use horticultural peat with chemical additives.

Finally, there are occasions when the water should be slightly brackish. This is often recommended for species that live in coastal lagoons or for those which move from fresh to sea water at certain periods. Kitchen salt is not really suitable, but unrefined sea salt can be used to make a brackish water. The best method, however, is to add a certain proportion of natural or synthetic sea water to the tank water. Synthetic sea water is made up from salts obtainable from an aquarium dealer.

WHITE-SPOT, see Disease.
WHITEWORMS, see Diet.

X

Xenomystus nigri
A brownish knifefish, lacking a dorsal fin which distinguishes it from the related genera *Notopterus* and *Papyrocranus*. Undulatory movements of the very long anal fin can move the fish backwards as well as forwards. This is a nocturnal species which should be kept in a shaded tank filled with slightly acid water.
Family: Notopteridae★.
Diet: live food, including fish small enough to be swallowed.
Sex differences: none.
Length: up to 20 cm (7¾ in) in the aquarium.
Distribution: tropical Africa (upper Nile to Liberia).
Compatibility: doubtful, particularly with small species that may well be asleep when the knifefish is most active.
Temperature range: 22–28°C (72–82°F).
Breeding: never recorded in captivity.

Xiphophorus
A genus of viviparous fishes in the family Poeciliidae★, that are very popular for the aquarium, partly on account of the bright coloration, partly because they breed very readily and have produced numerous attractive varieties. They are gregarious and best kept as a group in a large tank with hard water.

Xiphophorus helleri
This is the well known swordtail, which in the wild is olive-green. It was first imported into Europe in 1909 and has since then given rise to various coloured varieties, including:

1. the green swordtail with a reddish zigzag line running along the green body at the level of the lateral line,

2. the red swordtail, which is more or less scarlet,

3. the wagtail swordtail, which is green or red and characterized by black lips and fins,

Xiphophorus helleri, the swordtail (red variety, up to 12 cm or 4¾ in excluding the sword)

4. the black swordtail with greenish iridescence, which is the result of a cross between *X. helleri* and *X. maculatus*.

In many of these varieties the dorsal fin may be tall or the tail may be forked (lyretail).

In this species changes of sex occur quite frequently, the females changing into males. The usual explanation is that the determination of sex is not solely under the control of the chromosomes, and that if there is a decrease in the amount of female hormone secreted by the ovaries then the male hormones start to predominate.

Diet: omnivorous, including algae* and boiled spinach.

Sex differences: in the male the anal fin is modified to form a gonopodium, and the much elongated rays of the lower caudal fin lobe form a beautiful sword, bordered with black.

Length: up to 12 cm (4¾ in), excluding the sword.

Distribution: south-eastern Mexico and Guatemala.

Compatibility: satisfactory, apart from some rivalry among the males.

Temperature range: 22–28°C (72–82°F).

Breeding: very easy, as in most viviparous aquarium fishes. The conditions should be the same as for the guppy *(Poecilia**

reticulata). The interval between the broods varies according to the temperature, but is usually about 40 days.

Xiphophorus maculatus

Widely known as the platy this species is sufficiently close to *X. helleri* for the two to hybridize quite readily. This is partly, at least, because their gonopodia are very similar. The present species is, however, smaller, with a more rounded and relatively taller body, and the male lacks the sword. The platy can be kept in quite a small tank and does not require such hard water as *X. helleri*. The numerous varieties include:

1. the blue platy with the uncoloured fins and the flanks showing green reflections,
2. the moon platy, which is orange-yellow with a dark marking on the base of the tail,
3. the red platy, sometimes with blue eyes,
4. the tuxedo platy, spotted with prominent black markings,
5. the wagtail platy in which the fins and the tip of the snout are black.

Diet: omnivorous.

Sex differences: the male's anal fin is modified to form a gonopodium.

Length: up to 6 cm (2¼ in).

Distribution: Mexico to Guatemala.

Xiphophorus maculatus, the platy (up to 6 cm or 2¼ in)

Temperature range: 23–29°C (73–84°F).
Breeding: similar to the guppy and
    swordtail, but the small fry are delicate
    during their first month.

Xiphophorus variatus
The body is rather more slender and the fins
more fully developed than in *X. maculatus*.
The coloration is grey-green with spots
above, yellowish-orange below, the caudal fin

generally reddish, the dorsal orange.
Diet: omnivorous.
Sex differences: the male is more colourful
    and his anal fin is modified to form a
    gonopodium.
Length: 6 cm (2¼ in).
Compatibility: good.
Temperature range: 23–28°C (73–82°F).
Breeding: easy, but the young grow rather
    slowly.

Macramé

By the Editors of Sunset Books
and Sunset Magazine

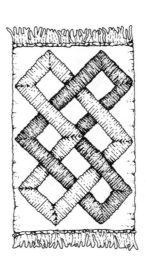

Lane Publishing Co. • Menlo Park, California

Acknowledgments

We would like to thank the following individuals for their suggestions and advice regarding the contents of this book: Helene Bress, Helen Freeman, Barbara Jee, Dona Meilach, Gertrude Reagan, and Ginger Summit.

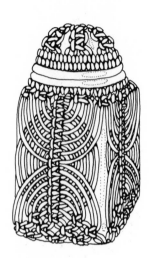

Edited by
Alyson Smith Gonsalves

Design: Tonya Carpenter

Illustrations: Nancy Lawton

Cover: Nubby Textured Rug (page 56) designed by Ginger Summit, and Sculptural Plant Hanger (page 59) designed by Joy Coshigano of Hidden House. Photo by Norman A. Plate.

Editor, Sunset Books: David E. Clark

Seventh Printing January 1979

Contents

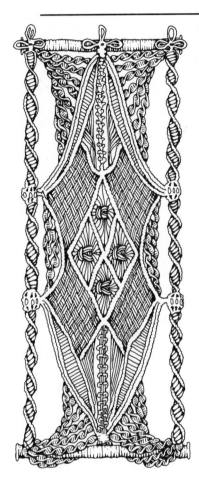

Loose macramé netting *from ancient Egypt, courtesy Museum of Fine Arts, Boston.*

Introducing Macramé

Macramé (pronounced mak′ra•mā) comes either from a 19th century Arabic term, *miqramah,* which meant veil, or from the Turkish word for towel, *maqramah.* Both the veil and the towel were adorned with a knotted fringe.

The handcraft known as macramé probably developed when man first needed to attach two lengths of cord or to bind two objects together in a permanent or semipermanent manner. The square and hitch knots may date back to Paleolithic or Neolithic man, who undoubtedly used these knots in his daily life.

As time passed, knots were used for a variety of utilitarian, mnemonic, and superstitious purposes. However, once the beauty of the knots themselves was recognized, a new art form emerged.

History Repeats Itself

Existing examples of knotting date back to early Egyptian culture, when knots were used in fishnets and in decorative fringes (see facing page). The Incas of Peru used a *quipu,* a length of knotted rope constructed of mnemonic knots, to aid them in keeping mathematical records and other important information. In classical Greece, knots were used in medicine (as slings for broken bones) and in games (the Gordian knot was one such puzzle). Both the early Egyptians and Greeks used the Hercules knot (square knot), which had magical or religious connotations, on their clothing, jewelry, and pottery.

Knotting techniques were probably spread far and wide by sailors who, in their spare time, would create a multitude of knotted items to decorate their ships, to trade, or to give as gifts. The sailors on ancient sailing ships sometimes carried a knotted cord which, claimed legend, witches had tied. The knotted cord supposedly bound the winds and therefore controlled the destiny of the sailing ship.

Macramé in the sailors' vocabulary was better known as "McNamara's Lace" or "square knotting" because the square knot predominated in their work.

Evidence of macramé reaching North America can be seen in the work of the Northern California Indians after contact with Europeans. In the Victorian era, the

Want something special in the way of techniques? This chapter has them. Learn how to make a good start and a photo-perfect finish to your work. We've also added notes on shaping macrame, adding and subtracting extra cords, and special working techniques to give you some of that "edge" the experts possess.

stylish gowns and cloaks of the gentry in European society were adorned with macramé knots. Some craftsmen of that period, having even greater ambitions, created larger pieces, such as whole tablecloths, bedspreads, piano drapes, and even doorway curtains.

Today, macramé is enjoying a 20th century renaissance. As people find that they have more spare time, men as well as women are turning to such handwork, creating pieces that are both utilitarian and esthetic.

Great pleasure can be derived from evolving a seemingly intricate textile design through the use of only two basic macramé knots: the half hitch and the square knot. Since the combinations and variations of these two knots seem to be endless, they lend themselves to a vast array of two-and three-dimensional designs. And macramé is an individualistic craft—each person's style of knotting adds a unique touch to his work.

Macramé the Easy Way

A craft for all ages and capabilities, macramé is really an international concept found just about anywhere today from the United States to the People's Republic of China. Equipment and materials are available everywhere; all that's needed are cords or yarns for the knots themselves, a few pins, and a working surface large enough to accommodate the project you're creating. Most macramé can be carried with you and comfortably worked on any time.

Macramé projects have few limitations. For an idea of some of the possibilities open to you, take a look at the projects offered in this book, starting on page 34.

If you're a beginner, start out with the knotting instructions beginning on page 10. Then look over the section on color, texture, and design on page 30 for information on planning your work to avoid mistakes and to achieve maximum results.

Have you had previous experience with macramé? Then check out the section on general techniques (page 24) and the gallery of advanced work (starting on page 74) or go directly to the projects. You're sure to find something of interest.

Equipment You'll Need

Minimal equipment is needed for macramé—just a support for the work, pins to hold the work in place, and a few accessories to measure, cut, and bundle the working cord ends. Dime stores, craft shops, and lumber supply yards carry just about everything you'll need. Macramé equipment can be divided into three categories: working surfaces, pins, and miscellaneous materials.

Choosing Working Surfaces

The type of working surface you'll need will depend to a great extent on the size of your project, the materials you'll use, and the amount of working space you have available. Some surfaces are made specifically for macramé work; others can be temporarily adapted to your needs from furnishings already in your home.

Specifically for macramé

Fiber board and foam rubber slabs—lightweight and portable, with firm surfaces easily adaptable to most macramé work —are inexpensive and can be purchased in almost any size. Felt can be stapled to the fiberboard or pinned to the foam rubber to create an improved working surface (see facing page). Foam rubber comes in a number of shapes; the most useful and most easily located are flat slabs, pillow fillers, or bolster rolls.

Many Victorian macramé pieces were worked on heavy, sand-filled cushions, an idea that can be put to use today. Sew a pillow liner of heavy muslin, stuff it firmly with dry sand, and whip the edge shut; then cover it with a snugly fitting "sleeve" of felt.

The lap board (shown on facing page) is an easily made clamp and board frame for small macramé projects, such as belts and jewelry. Cut an 18-inch-long 1-by-4 board into 12-inch and 6-inch sections. With screws, attach paper clamps at one end of each board, in the center. Then join the two board lengths with a pair of offset hinges as shown in the photograph on the facing page. This frame can be folded flat for storage.

Some adaptations

Picture frames, purchased wooden or metal hoops, even a dress form or wig stand can serve for special macramé projects. Use the frames and hoops when you want your macramé to have a built-in

setting. Try the dress form or wig stand for such macramé pieces as hats, necklaces, or even entire garments that need to be shaped to fit.

Other adaptations can include ladder-back chairs, clipboards, or padded ironing boards. A mounting cord can be tied between the knobs of the chair; small pieces can be mounted on the clip board for a portable working surface or pinned down on the ironing board surface for working at home.

Pins for Macramé

You use pins to secure a macramé project to a working surface and to hold the shape of the piece while it is worked on. Use pins, too, wherever an area needs reinforcing or securing. A selection of pins suitable for macramé work is shown on the facing page. Push pins, card pins, and T-pins are available in stationery stores. Look for hat pins, plastic-headed sewing pins (only for small projects), or upholstery pins in sewing centers.

Miscellaneous Materials

You'll need some basic tools for measuring, cutting, and bundling cord lengths. Keep a scissors, tape measure, and yardstick on hand, as well as rubber bands, twist-ties, and plastic or cardboard bobbins (see page 35 for bobbin making). Use paper clamps to hold cords out of the way while you work. To measure off cord lengths, use a pair of C-clamps set at a distance equal to the length needed and attached upside down on a table edge.

For planning out your work ahead of time, make use of the varied graph papers sold in stationery stores. You can lay out the project design in terms of color and overall pattern, averting the chance of making mistakes later on.

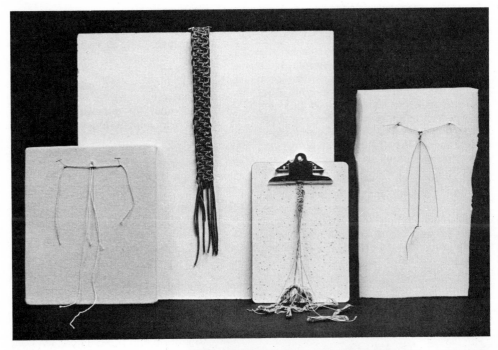

Conventional working surfaces *are shown here (left to right): felt-covered fiberboard, plain fiberboard, a clipboard, a thick foam slab.*

Unusual macramé supports *include (top to bottom): the stretcher bar frame, wig stand, homemade lap board.*

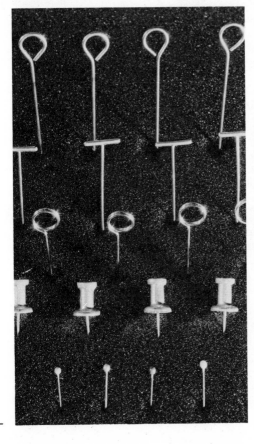

A selection of pins *for macramé (top to bottom): upholstery pins, T-pins, card pins, push pins, glass-headed pins.*

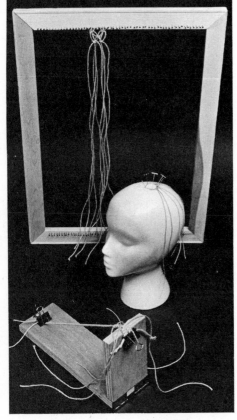

Materials for Macramé

Any pliable materials available in great lengths are suitable for macramé work. These can be comprised of anything from kite string or sisal rope to surgical tubing or fine wire. Some very unusual materials have been used for macramé; they include bed sheet strips, leather thong, paper twine, and rolls of plastic grocery bags.

The only absolute requirements are pliability and strength without undue stretchiness, suitability for the ultimate use to which a project will be put, and a surface quality that will enhance the design and the individual macramé knots. Knotting materials can be divided into three categories: vegetable fibers, synthetic fibers, and animal fibers.

Vegetable Fibers

The most popular of all macramé materials, vegetable fibers include jute, linen, and cotton. All are readily available, knot easily, come in a variety of weights and colors, and can be dyed. Most of these cords can be purchased in their natural finish, as well as with protective coatings like wax, creosote, or sizing.

Cotton. Found in many forms, cotton can be soft or stiff and comes in varied sizes, textures, and finishes. It is exceptionally strong and long-wearing. Naval and clothesline rope, as well as package string and perle cotton, fall into this category.

Jute. A brightly colored, prickly surface characterizes jute cord. But this material doesn't wear well; it can fade or rot, unless chemically treated, and it sheds during knotting.

Linen. Strong, smooth-surfaced, and lint-free—linen cord has these qualities. More expensive than most materials, linen nevertheless gives good knot definition and a soft, smooth overall texture.

Synthetic Fibers

Chemically produced fibers such as acrylic, polyester, nylon, rayon, and plastic metallics are considered synthetics. They are often combined with natural fibers, such as cotton or wool, to give added elasticity.

Acrylic and polyester. Soft, weather resistant, and warm, these two materials are excellent for use in clothing or projects for outdoor use. They dye well and usually come in bright colors.

Nylon and rayon. Available in silky, shiny braid or cord, these materials are beautiful but not easy to work with. Both tend to unravel and slip during knotting.

Metallic cord. This has a pliable rayon core wrapped with a thin strip of gold or silver-colored, plastic-coated metal. Metallic cord is used for clothing detailing and for jewelry work.

Animal Fibers

Wool, silk, and hair fibers are contributions from the animal kingdom. Of all types of yarns, these have the greatest color range; however, they have a tendency to stretch and break under tension, as well as to shed during knotting.

Wool. Soft, lightweight, and warm, wool comes in two different forms: wool worsted, a smooth strong yarn; and woolen, which has a fuzzy, soft appearance. Of the two, worsted is better suited to the pulling and stretching that occur during knotting.

Silk. A beautiful, strong yarn, silk is somewhat expensive for large macramé projects. It has a soft, slippery surface in its most common form and a rough texture when spun from tussah, or wild silk.

Hair. Taken from horses, goats, dogs, and other animals, spun hair has a prickly, coarse texture suitable for sculptural work or rugs.

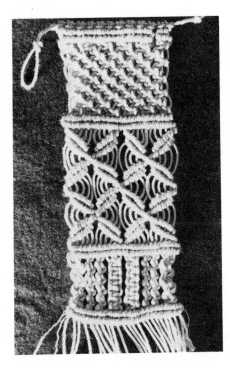

Linen produces a beautiful surface effect when knotted; it is soft and supple yet well defined. An elegant material to work with, linen is relatively expensive, and its color range is limited.

Jute is a colorful vegetable fiber that works up into a fuzzy, prickly-textured surface. In spite of a tendency to shed and fade, jute enjoys great popularity.

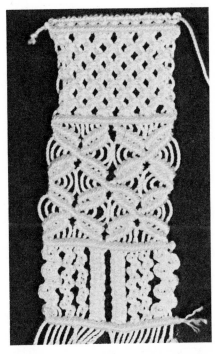

Nylon cord has a silklike surface quality and a beautiful appearance when knotted, though it's slippery to work with and tends to unravel unless the ends are sealed with glue or melted.

Wool enjoys a tremendous color range **(right).** It is the most versatile of knotting materials but not necessarily the strongest. A tendency to stretch and break under tension limits its use in macramé projects that must support weight.

Cotton cord **(left)** comes in a variety of sizes, textures, and colors. A strong, durable material, cotton cord produces well-defined macramé knots.

Basic Macramé Knots

It's a pleasant surprise to find that most macramé patterns, though complicated in appearance, generally employ only two knots: the square knot and the double half hitch. You can work out an endless number of variations by using multiples or combinations of these two knots tied in different directions or at different angles.

To add occasional decorative elements to these variations, combine them with Josephine and Turk's-head knots, wrapping, plaiting, or picots.

Taking the Mystery Out of Macramé

When taken as a whole, a macramé piece can appear as an undecipherable maze of knots and cord ends. This is not the least bit encouraging to the beginner; it can even be intimidating—but it doesn't have to happen to you.

First, learn the knots on the following 13 pages. Then you'll be able to zero in on specific areas of any macramé work by asking yourself these questions: "How was it started? What groups of knots do I recognize, and how were they combined? Is there a repeat or an overall plan to the pattern? How was this piece finished?" Memorizing the knots is the key to breaking the code.

Two approaches

You'll find there are two ways to master the basic macramé knots: 1) Explore each knot individually (this is the simplest method) or 2) Make a knotting sampler by working all of the knots with the same cords. The yarn and cord samplers on page 9 were formed in a similar manner. Making a sampler will help you to understand how knots interrelate with one another and also to compare the differences between knotted areas made with square knots and those made with double half hitches.

If you plan to work with each knot individually, cut as many 1-yard lengths of cord as the individual knotting directions call for; also cut a 10-inch length of cord to use as a mounting cord.

But if the idea of making a sampler appeals to you, different preparations are in order. Cut 12 cords, each 288 inches long, as well as a 20-inch length to use as a mounting cord. Fold the long cords in half and mount them at their midpoints

onto the mounting cord (see the instructions for mounting knots on the facing page).

Since long cord ends tend to tangle easily, it's best to wrap each end into a bobbin after your working cords have been mounted. Instructions for wrapping bobbins may be found on page 35.

Before you begin the sampler, pin the mounting cord to the working surface by tying an overhand knot at each end and pinning through each knot. From this point on, work all knots in their proper order from page 11. Picot headings are the only exceptions: there won't be room on the sampler for all the variations. Choose those you'd like to learn first for your sampler; then cut shorter lengths of cord to practice the remaining picots individually.

Using the Instructions

Instructions and their accompanying illustrations have been kept as simple as possible in order to avoid confusion. The knots themselves have been arranged in the order in which they are normally used: mounting knots first, followed by the double half hitch and the square knot, as well as by a number of their basic variations. Decorative techniques and knots (including picots) come last.

Use cord, rather than yarn, for learning the knots; it remains strong in spite of the great amount of friction, stretching, and tension it undergoes. The smooth surface qualities of most cords are ideal for macramé because they form clean-lined, well-defined knots.

Knots can be tied from left to right or vice versa. If you want to reverse the directions given, simply hold a small pocket mirror at a 90° angle to the illustrations to see the image backward.

Mounting Knots and Overhand Knot

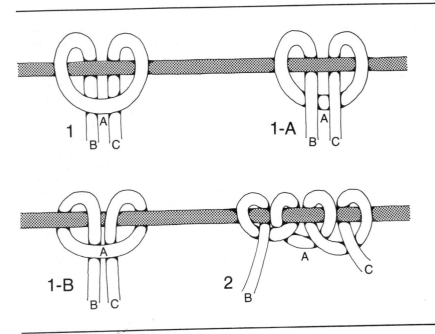

Mounting knots are used to secure working cords onto a support at the starting point of a piece or at an area where cords are being added. The two knots shown at left are those most often used.

1. Fold the working cord in half and place loop A under the mounting cord; then bring A down in front of the mounting cord (1). Pull ends B and C down through loop A (1-A). Pull knot tight. To reverse this mounting knot, work from front to back (1-B).

2. To form the double half hitch mounting knot, mount the cords as shown in 1-A. Then bring each end over and behind the mounting cord and out through the loops formed (2). Pull the cords tight.

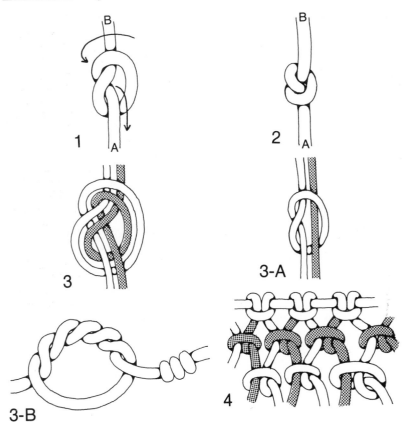

Simplest of all macramé knots, the overhand knot itself requires only one cord yet has several interesting variations. Use it for finishes or filler or in chains.

1. Make a loop with the cord by placing end A over end B; then bring end A from behind B and out through the loop (1).

2. Pull the knot tight (2). Several knots in a row will form a chain.

3. Basic variations of this knot include the use of 2 cords to form a single knot (3); the use of 2 cords, 1 knotted around the other (3-A); and the Monk's Belt knot, in which end A is brought around and through the existing loop several times, then pulled tight to form a barrel-like knot (3-B).

The overhand knot variation shown in figure 4 can be adapted to an overall pattern by tying knots across an entire area, then moving one cord over (to the right or to the left of the knot above) in the next row of knots. Repeat this sequence until the pattern area is complete.

Half Hitch and
Double Half Hitch

The half hitch is the first step to forming a double half hitch, one of the two basic macramé knots. A loose, looplike "knot," the half hitch is rarely used by itself; instead, this "knot" can be added to a basic double half hitch to form triple and quadruple half hitches.

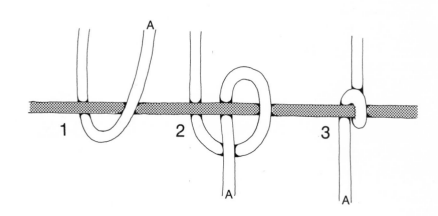

1. Place the midpoint of the working cord behind the holding cord; then bring end A up over the holding cord (1).

2. Pull end A down behind the holding cord and out through the loop that is formed (2); then pull the "knot" tight (3). The half hitch is not secure by itself; it must be repeated to form a snug, somewhat permanent knot.

The double half hitch is just two half hitches knotted in succession, using the same tying cord. Very versatile, this knot can be used to create a variety of special effects.

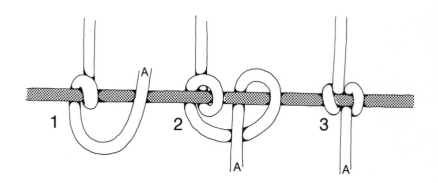

1. To form a double half hitch, follow the steps given for the half hitch; then bring end A back up over the holding cord (1).

2. Pull end A down behind the holding cord and out through the loop formed by the 2 half hitches (2).

3. Pull the end tight to form a completed knot (3).

The placement of the holding cord and the angle at which it is held makes it possible to create many different effects with a succession of double half hitch knots. Horizontal, diagonal, and free-form rows of double half hitches are the basic ingredients for a wide range of macramé patterns.

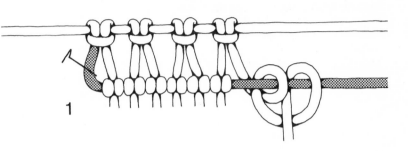

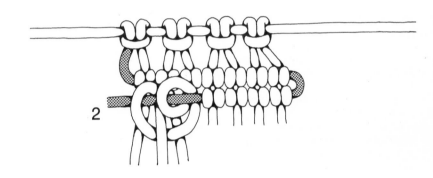

1. Mount the midpoints of 4 cords to form 8 working cords; then, using the far left-hand cord as a holding cord, tie a double half hitch over it with each of the remaining working cords (1).

2. When the last cord has been knotted, turn the holding cord in the opposite direction and knot a row of double half hitches from right to left (2).

3. The first variation possible is the diagonal bar. Either outside working cord may be used as a holding cord if pinned to the working surface just under the mounting knot. When this holding cord is pulled taut at a 45° angle across the other cords and double half hitches are knotted over it, a diagonal row is formed (3).

4. Double half hitch bars are really quite flexible—they'll take on any shape you desire. Just pull the holding cord across the working cords and knot away, varying the direction of the holding cord as you tie (4).

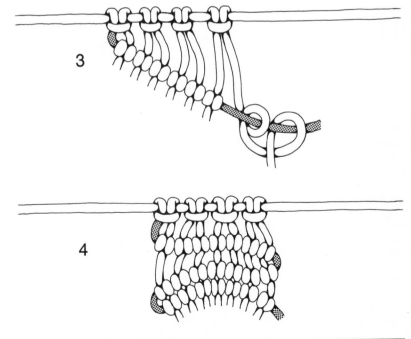

Double Half Hitch Patterns

Double half hitch bars can be combined in a variety of ways to form patterns. The diamond is a basic pattern shape with infinite possibilities.

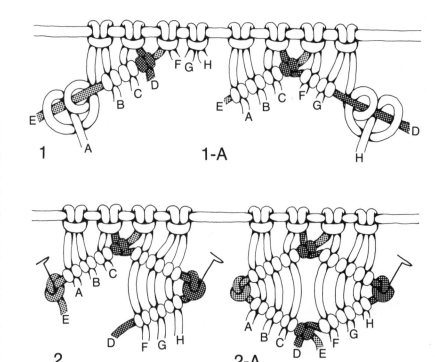

1. Mount 4 (or more) cords at their midpoints to form 8 working cords. Hold cord E at a 45° angle to the left over cords A, B, C, and D, using them to tie a diagonal row of double half hitches over E (1). Leaving cord E, hold cord D at a 45° angle to the right over cords F, G, and H. Use these cords to tie a diagonal row of double half hitches over D (1-A).

2. At the end of each diagonal row, tie an overhand knot, pinning each securely to the working surface. Hold cord D at a 45° angle to the left over cords F, G, and H; then tie a diagonal row of double half hitches with these cords (2).

Next, hold cord E at a 45° angle to the right over cords A, B, C, and D and tie a diagonal row of double half hitches with these cords to complete the diamond (2-A).

A diagonal cross pattern is formed by using the two outside cords of the pattern unit (comprised of four or more cords) as holding cords for two crossing diagonal rows of double half hitches.

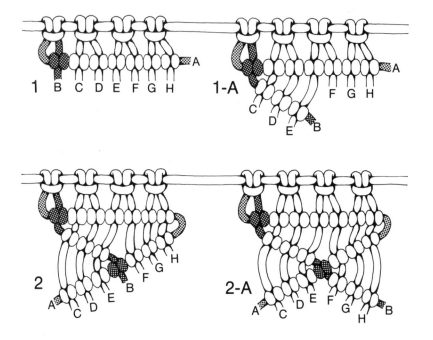

1. Mount 4 cords at their midpoints to make 8 working cords. Tie a row of double half hitches from left to right, using cord A as the holding cord (1); then pin cord B to the working surface and hold it at a 45° angle to the right. With cords C, D, and E, tie a diagonal row of double half hitches (1-A).

2. Pin cord A to the working surface and hold it at a 45° angle to the left; with cords H through C, tie a diagonal row of double half hitches, using cord B at the crossing point (2).

3. Complete the cross by tying the remainder of the diagonal row to the right with cords F, G, and H (2-A).

Half Hitch and
Double Half Hitch Chains

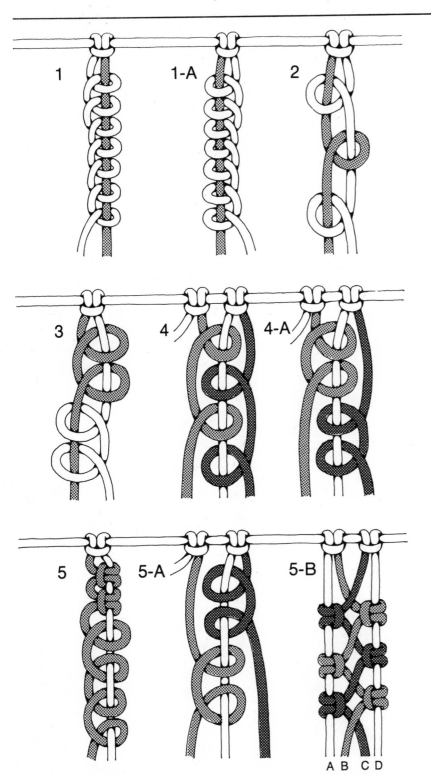

Chains are decorative fillers made by tying variations of the same knot down two or more working cords. The basic half hitch chain and a number of variations appear at left.

1. Mount 2 cords at their midpoints to form 4 working cords to be used as needed. Put the left cord over and around the right cord and out through the loop that is formed. Repeat several times to form a chain that twists to the right (1). For a twist to the left, loop the right cord around the left (1-A).

2. This variation uses 2 cords alternately looping around each other in half hitch knots (2).

3. Based on variation 2, this 2-cord chain is formed by looping the left cord around the right cord in 2 half hitch knots and then using the right cord to loop 2 half hitch knots around the left cord (3).

4. Three working cords are needed for this pair of half hitch chains. The 1st chain is formed when the left cord is looped around a center cord alternately with the right cord (4). For the 2nd chain (4-A), the left cord is looped twice around the center cord, followed by the right cord looped twice around the center cord.

5. Similar to the mounting knot, the Lark's Head chain can use from 2 to 8 working cords. The basic chain is formed when 1 cord is tied in a series of Lark's Head knots over a 2nd cord (5). The 3-cord version of this knot utilizes a center cord over which Lark's Head knots are tied alternately by the left and by the right cords (5-A).

Four cords are used for a latticework effect, the 2 outside cords (A and D) acting as anchors or holding cords for Lark's Head knots tied first with cord C over cord A, then with cord B over cord D (5-B). Chains with more cords than this are variations on these 3 basic chains.

Shaping with Double Half Hitches

You can go beyond the limitations of parallel borders in macramé by using these methods for making color changes, sharp angles, or three-dimensional shapes.

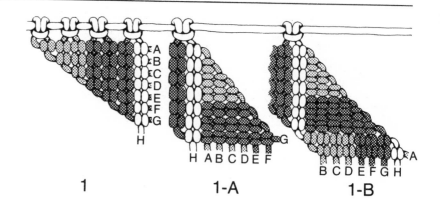

These instructions can be reversed and the number of cords changed to alter shapes, spirals, angles, and color changes.

1. For an example of how color changes can be made, at their midpoints mount 2 cords of 1 color and 2 cords of a contrasting color to make 8 working cords. Make 7 horizontal rows of double half hitches, working from left to right and moving over 1 holding cord at a time, to form a triangular shape (1).

At that point begin working double half hitches downward along the right edge, starting with cord A as a vertical holding cord; also use cords B through F as holding cords to form a shape as in 1-A. To continue the angle of the pattern, begin to use the bottom cords as holding cords (1-B). To reverse the angle, work back in the opposite direction (1-C).

2. Other color changes are possible when the vertical double half hitch is introduced (2).

3. To form a sharp-angled zigzag shape (multiples of which can be interlocked), start with 4 working cords and knot them as in 1 and 1-A; but continue to use this method until all 4 working cords have been used as tying cords to form a shape as in 3. Then change directions and angle back as in 1-C until all 4 cords have been returned to their original locations (3-A). Repeat for zigzag.

4. Three-dimensional shapes, such as the pagoda bell pull project shown on page 47, are made possible by starting with working cords knotted to the point shown in illustration 1. Then the entire shape is turned on its side (4) and again knotted from left to right until a 2nd triangular shape, or side, is formed (4-A). Continue to turn the piece and knot triangles to form a spiral.

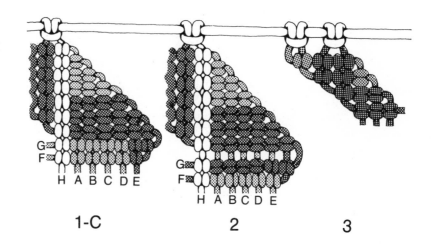

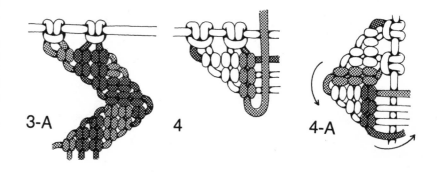

Vertical Double Half Hitch and Alternate Diagonal Double Half Hitch

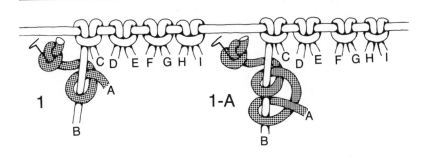

For textural variation, shaping, and color changes, the vertical double half hitch is an important knotting variation. The holding cord becomes the tying cord, and all working cords become holding cords.

1. Mount 4 cords at their midpoints and pin cord A to the working surface. Bring cord B over cord A and knot a double half hitch over B with cord A (1 and 1-A).

2. Pull the knot tight; then complete a row of vertical double half hitches, beginning each knot with the horizontal tying cord A under each vertical holding cord (2).

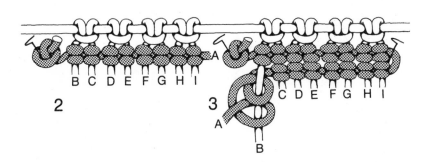

3. For a 2nd row of knots, pin cord A to the working surface and place it behind cord I. Pull cord A around behind cord I and through the loop formed. Bring end A down, around, and behind I again; then pull A out through the loop formed. Repeat this procedure until all knots in the 2nd row are formed (3).

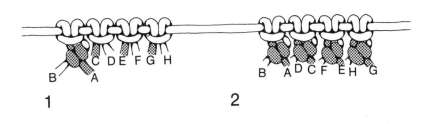

A seemingly random, nubby pattern emerges when the directions of rows of diagonally tied double half hitches alternate from left to right.

1. Mount 4 cords at their midpoints to form 8 working cords. To begin the first row of diagonal double half hitches, hold B at a 45° angle to the left over cord A and tie a double half hitch diagonally angled to the right on cord B with cord A (1).

2. Using pairs of cords as in step 1 work from left to right, tying 4 diagonal double half hitch knots in all (2).

3. For the 2nd row, work from left to right again, but this time leave the far left cord (B) free. With cord D, tie a double half hitch diagonally angled to the left over cord A. Complete the row by tying 2 more knots in the same manner (3).

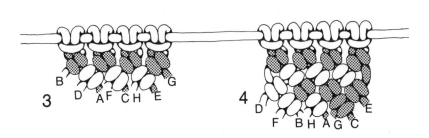

4. For an overall pattern, continue to alternate rows in this way. Eventually a nubby, random appearance will become visible throughout the area (4).

Square Knot and Alternate Square Knot

The square knot is one of the two basic macramé knots (the double half hitch is the other). Variations and patterns occur when you add tying and holding cords and combine this knot with other knots.

1. Mount 2 cords at their midpoints to make 4 working cords. Keep the 2 middle cords stationary and work with cords A and D. Pull cord A across cords B and C and under cord D (1).

2. Then bring cord D under cords C and B and over cord A, coming up through the loop formed between cord B and cord A (2).

3. Next, bring cord A over cords C and B and under cord D (3). To complete the knot, pull cord D under cords B and C, then up behind cord A and out through the loop formed by A (4).

4. Pull the knot tight. If you want to reverse the direction of the knot, start with cord D.

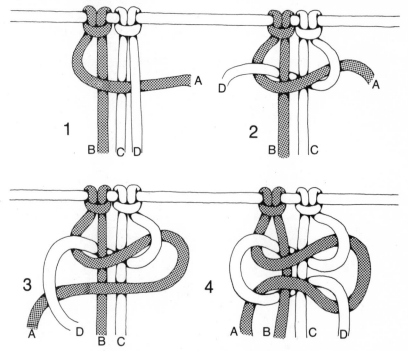

The alternate square knot pattern is formed when holding cords and tying cords are exchanged in succeeding rows of knots. This knot can have a lacy appearance or a weavelike texture, depending on how tightly it is knotted.

1. Mount 6 cords at their midpoints to make 12 working cords; then tie 3 square knots, using 4 cords for each knot (1).

2. Pull aside cords A and B, as well as cords K and L; then divide the remaining 8 cords into 2 groups of 4 cords each. Tie a square knot with each group of 4 cords (2). In this row, working cords from row 1 become holding cords and holding cords from row 1 become working cords.

3. Bring down cords A, B, K, and L, incorporating them again into the knotting. As in row 1, knot 3 square knots, using 4 cords for each knot (3) to create an overall pattern.

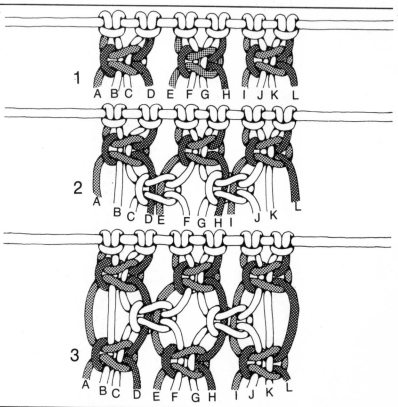

Half Knot and Square Knot Chains

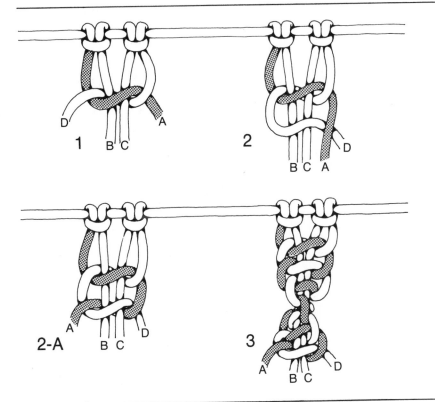

A basic variation on the square knot chain, the half knot chain has a natural twist to the right or to the left, depending on which working cord is used first.

1. Mount 2 cords at their midpoints to form 4 working cords. Tie a half knot as in figure 1, starting with cord A going over cords B and C and under D. Cord D goes under cords C and B and over A.

2. To continue, again start from the left, which is now cord D, and place D *over* cords B and C, then under A (2). Bring cord A under D, behind C and B and out between B and D (2-A).

3. Repeat steps 1 and 2 in order several times, and you will notice a definite twist to the right in the chain (3). Don't let the twisting chain confuse you about which cord to start with; always use the cord closest to the side from which you originally began the chain.

4. For a twist to the left, start with the right-hand cord.

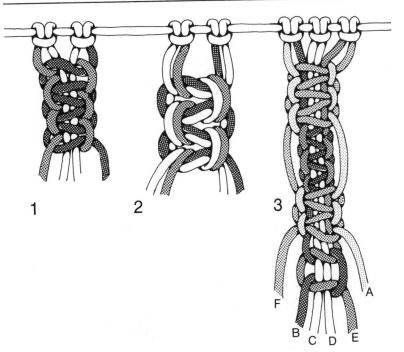

The square knot can be used for chains, as well as for an overall pattern. You can vary this basic chain design by adding or subtracting holding cords or tying cords from original chain design.

1. Create the basic square knot chain by tying a series of square knots with the same 4 cords (as in figure 1).

2. A basic variation of this chain is the use of 4 working cords and no holding cords (2).

3. Another variation uses 6 cords; the 2 outside cords (A and F) are used to tie a series of square knots over the 4 center cords. Then cords A and F are pinned to the side while cords B and E are used as working cords to tie a series of square knots over cords C and D. These knots are followed by a repeat of the 1st element, cords A and F tying square knots over cords B, C, D, and E (3).

Bobble Knot
and Berry Pattern

Three-dimensional sculptural forms add textural interest to macraméd surfaces. The bobble (or popcorn) knot is a simple means of forming a knobby surface. It's comprised of a square knot chain pulled up and back into itself to form a ball (or bobble) shape.

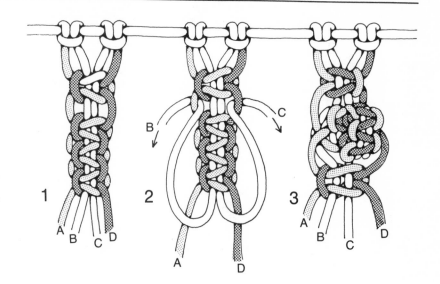

1. Mount 2 cords at their midpoints to form 4 working cords. Tie 1 square knot, leave a small space; then tie a series of 3 (or more if the bobble is to be large) closely spaced square knots (1).

2. Pass cords B and C up and back through the space made by separating the 1st square knot from those that follow (2).

3. To form a tight ball, pull down on cords B and C until the square knot chain doubles back on itself and forms a loop-like bobble. With A and D, tie a firm square knot directly under the bobble (3).

Another knoblike pattern used for surface detail work, the berry pattern (also called "hobnail") is slightly more complicated than the bobble but has a more definitively shaped appearance.

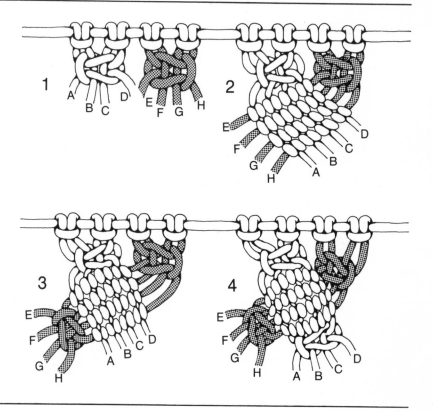

1. Mount 4 cords at their midpoints to form 8 working cords. Divide them into 2 sets of 4 cords each and tie 2 square knots (1).

2. Use cords E, F, G, and H as holding cords to tie 4 diagonal rows of double half hitches from upper right to lower left (2) with cords A, B, C, and D.

3. Using cords E, F, G, and H, tie a square knot at the left side of the berry, using cords F and G as holding cords and cords E and H as working cords. Push up against the square knot and tie it firmly to round out the berry shape (3).

4. To complete the pattern, tie a 2nd square knot at the right side of the berry with cords B and C as holding cords and cords A and D as working cords (4). Firm up the shape as in step 3 to complete.

Josephine Knot and Turk's-head Knot

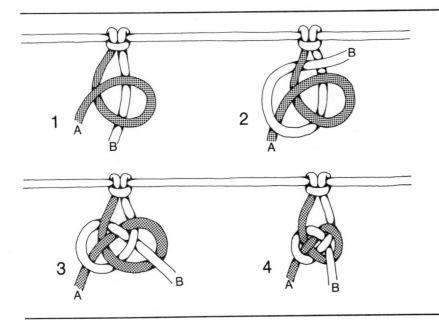

A decorative knot used quite often in belts and jewelry, the Josephine knot can be a small, delicate filler or a bold, almost graphic statement, depending upon the number of cords used to tie the knot.

1. Mount 1 cord at its midpoint to form 2 working cords. Loop cord A and place this loop over cord B (1).

2. Pull the end of cord B over, then under, cord A (2).

3. Bring cord end B down over the top of the looped portion of cord A, under cord B itself, and out over the outside of the looped portion of cord A (3).

4. Pull both cord ends to tighten the knot (4). To make a larger, more dramatic knot, use groups of 2 or more cords for A and for B.

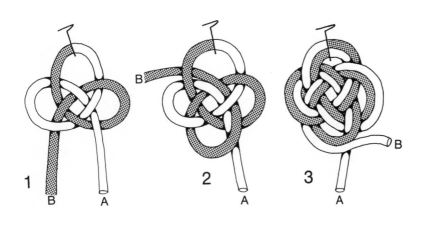

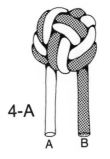

Use the Turk's-head knot to make buttons, closures, or rings. Or use it as a decorative ending for hanging cords.

1. Cut one 30-inch-long cord and pin it to the working surface 10 inches from end A and 20 inches from end B, allowing both cord ends to hang free. (If cord end A is attached to your macramé piece, work with this page turned upside down and pin down the cord 10 inches below the point of attachment.) Tie a Josephine knot (see above) near the pinned fold of the cord so that the fold forms a 3rd loop (1).

2. Bring end B over end A and up parallel to cord A; then begin to follow A with end B around the flat Josephine knot (2).

3. Continue to follow along the original loops in the knot until every part of the knot has 2 cords and end B is again over end A (3). Repeat this process as many times as you wish; each repeat will enlarge the knot.

4. To form a ring, place your index fingers through the center opening of the flat knot and pull outward (4). For a tight ball, place a small marble or bead in the center of the ring and pull on all cords in the ring until they close snugly around the bead core (4-A).

Picots

Picots—lacelike decorative elements added to the starting point of a macramé piece—are formed before or during the mounting of working cords. Directions for several styles are given at right.

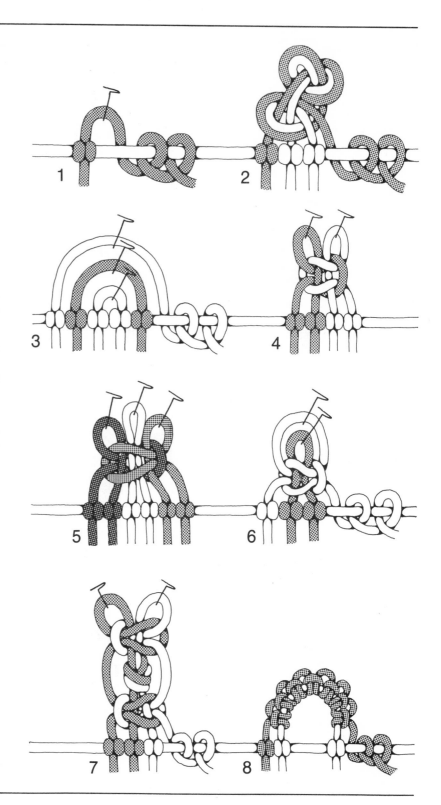

1. Form this picot by double half hitching both ends of a working cord slightly below its midpoint to the mounting cord (1).

2. Make this picot by mounting 2 cords, then looping them as 1 and remounting them as shown in figure 2.

3. The midpoints of 3 successive cords are pinned just above the mounting cord, then mounted from the center out to form this rainbow-shaped picot (3).

4. Begin this picot by pinning the midpoints of 2 cords next to each other above the mounting cord. Using the two central ends as an anchor, tie a square knot with the outer ends; then pull the knot tight and mount all 4 cords (4).

5. Arrange the midpoints of 3 separate cords in a pyramid, the center midpoint pinned above the outer midpoints. Tie a square knot over the central cords with the 2 outer cords; then mount all 6 ends (5).

6. Pin the midpoints of 2 cords, 1 above the other, to the working surface. Use the lower cord as an anchor for a square knot tied with the ends of the upper cord; then mount all 4 cords (6).

7. Make picot 4 but, before mounting it, tie an overhand knot with the 2 central cords; then tie a 2nd square knot below the overhand knot (7). Mount ends.

8. Mount the midpoints of 2 cords; then use the left-hand cord to tie a series of 6 or more Lark's Head knots over the right-hand cord (8). Mount the 2 remaining ends.

Wrapping and Plaiting

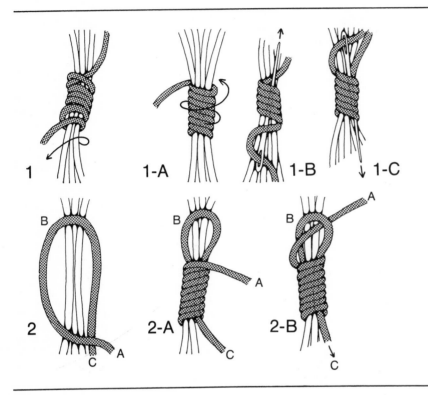

Wrapping can be used to join cords, finish ends off, or add color or unusual textural areas to your macramé work.

1. For soft, pliant cords, this method works best: group 2 or more cords into a bundle; then use one of the cords to wrap or cover this bundle, starting from the top or the bottom and working down (1) or up (1-A). When the wrapping is long enough, thread the cord end through the eye of a blunt tapestry needle and use it to pull the cord end through the wrapped coil (1-B and 1-C). Cut off cord end.

2. When heavy or slippery cords are being used, group them into a bundle; then cut a separate cord about 36 inches long. Loop the cord next to the bundle and bring end A across the bundle and end C (2). Begin wrapping with A, covering the bundle *and* loop B, working upward until only about an inch of loop B is left free (2-A). Thread end A through loop B and pull down on end C until A and B are pulled inside (2-B). Cut off cord end.

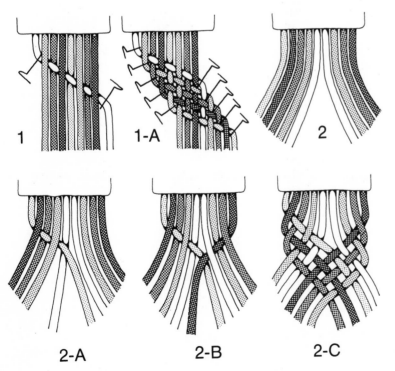

Though employed with macramé in the form of belts, straps, handles, or pattern filler, plaiting is actually a fancy form of braiding. Two versions of this method, flat and French, are shown at left.

1. For flat plaiting, cut an even number of cords, each 1½ times longer than the desired finished length. Line them up along one edge of your working surface and secure them with a clamp.

Weave the far left cord through the remaining cords (1), using T-pins as shown.

Working from left to right, continue to weave each far left cord through the remaining cords, incorporating at the right edge all previously woven cords (1-A).

2. For French plaiting, repeat step 1 but use an odd number of cords divided into 2 groups, the left-hand group having the extra cord (2).

Follow figures 2-A, 2-B, and 2-C, working individual cords alternately left to right, right to left. Continue in this manner, incorporating all previously woven cords into the design at the center (2-C).

Working Techniques

When you're "building" a project, you need more than just the basic know-how of tying macramé knots and patterns—these are only the raw materials. To join them into a working unit, you must also apply special techniques. This chapter offers you a selection of methods for starting, finishing, enlarging, diminishing, shaping, and fastening your macramé projects. Some of the methods are particularly suited to specific types of macramé; others can be employed in almost any project.

Starting from a point

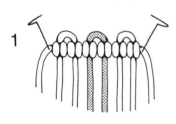

1

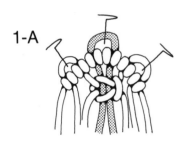

1-A

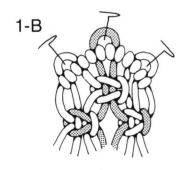

1-B

Choosing Working Surfaces

Is your macramé project long or short? Is it wide or narrow, flat or three-dimensional? Will you carry it with you or work on it exclusively at home? Consider all of these factors when you're choosing a working surface.

Small projects (jewelry and belts, for example) are most easily constructed on clipboards or on small pieces of fiberboard or foam. A lap board is a good choice for bracelets, chokers, and narrow belts.

Larger projects, such as purses, pillow covers, or small hangings, require a larger working area. Since fiberboard is available in any number of sizes, it ranks high as a larger working surface. Stretcher bar frames in various sizes can also be used, though they don't give the support of fiberboard.

Three-dimensional pieces require individual solutions. Hats are most successfully constructed on a wig or hat stand. Clothing, though, can be approached in two ways: one-piece construction (using a dressmaker's form for support) or pattern-piece construction. The latter breaks a design down into individual patterns, such as sleeve or bodice pieces; these are pinned or drawn onto the working surface, and the knotting is worked to fit the shape of the pattern.

Plant hangers and three-dimensional sculptures can be suspended from hooks or bars attached to a ceiling beam or to the overhead portion of a door jamb. Or they can be worked in stages on a large, flat piece of fiberboard or foam. If the project is a specific shape, it can be worked over a jig, or form. Jigs can be adapted from existing jars, boxes, or pillows; special jigs can be cut from plywood or fiberboard.

If you plan to make a valance, window covering, or doorway curtain, it's best to knot the project "on location" to assure proper fit and design suitability. If you can't attach your work directly to the window or door frame, devise a method for mounting your cords on a removable support that can be hung or set into the existing door or window frame.

Beginning a Project

Once you've decided to knot a specific item, the next decision you'll face will be choosing a suitable way to begin. Will you attach your cords to something or will they be self-supporting? If you decide to use a support, what will it be, and how will the cords be attached?

Macramé mounts vary with the type of project. Metal or wooden rings and hoops, bars and dowels, driftwood and tree branches, wire armatures and wooden frames, even hole-punched leather (note the cape on the facing page) or fabric can be used as starting points.

Cords can easily be mounted in the conventional way (see page 11) or attached with double half hitches at any point on the mount. Some mounts, such as driftwood and purse handles, will require drilling or punching in order to hold cords. Other mounts can take the form of purchased belt buckles, beads, or jump-ring closures. These are frequently used in the construction of jewelry and belts.

Some projects won't require a separate mount; rather, they will transform the mounting cord into a working cord, eventually incorporating it into the body of the piece. Since no discernible starting point will exist if this method is used, a piece may be started either at the middle or at one end. Belts, jewelry, purses, some garments, and some decorative macramé can be worked in this manner, as can a number of three-dimensional constructions.

Purses, belts, and watch straps will often begin at a point which later forms an end or a flap. One method for starting from a point is shown in figure 1 at left; the following starting methods are illustrated on the facing page: self-mounting cord (fig. 1), self-loop cord (fig. 2), continuous neck cord (fig. 3), loop-and-bead mount (fig. 4), and the jump-ring mount (fig. 5). Self-mounting cords and self-loop cord mounts can be used for almost any type of macramé; the three latter methods are used almost exclusively for jewelry making.

Starting from the center is a technique employed most frequently for knotting

Leather cape *with punch-mounted macramé fringe. Design: Lois Ericson.*

Purse started *from a pointed flap. Design: Gerta Wingerd.* **Close-up** *of belt point.*

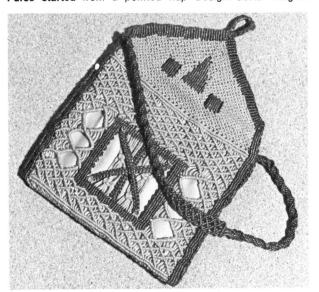

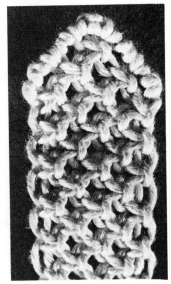

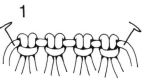

Self-mounting cord

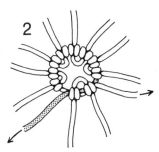

Self-loop cord

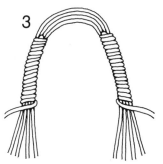

Continuous neck cord

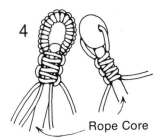

Rope Core

Loop-and-bead mount

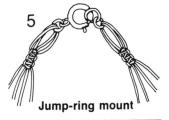

Jump-ring mount

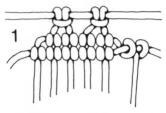

Adding new holding cords

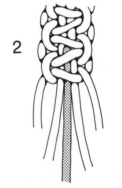

**Adding new cord
to a square knot chain**

**Adding new cords
between square knots**

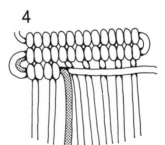

Adding new working cord

belts or jewelry. The unused portions of the cords can be draped over the top of the working surface or held in a paper bag, as shown below, right, on this page. Starting from the midpoint of a piece of jewelry often means beginning at the point where the pendant and the neck strands meet. A good example of this approach is shown at lower left on this page.

Adding or Subtracting Cords

Changing the size of a project, filling in or removing an open area, introducing or eliminating color, adding extra cord where the original working cord has run short, or deleting cords where they are no longer needed—these are situations that require specific solutions. Following—and illustrated at left—are several possibilities.

To enlarge the dimensions of a project, you can mount new cord lengths in available spaces, increase width by adding in new working cords in the form of holding cords (fig. 1), add new cord to the core of a square knot chain (fig. 2) or between 2 alternating square knots (fig. 3), or add new working cord by knotting the short end of the cord into the holding cord (fig. 4).

Extra space can be made for new cords in a double half hitch pattern area row by knotting triple or quadruple half hitches in the preceding row. In a square knot pattern area, cords can be added between individual alternating square knots.

When working or holding cords run short, new cords can be discreetly introduced in several ways; all are shown on the facing page. In a row of double half hitches, you can lengthen the holding cord by adding in new cord as shown in figure 1. Use this method also when a double half hitch working cord is running short (see fig. 4, this page). If the holding cord of any square knot runs short, add a new length of cord as in figure 2, this page. If a square knot working cord is short, exchange it for one of its longer holding cords (fig. 2, page 27) and then add a new holding cord.

Vertical double half hitches tend to use up cord very quickly. To lengthen a rapidly diminishing working cord, cut the existing cord to 3 inches after a completed row; then add in a new working cord to begin the next row, leaving a 3-inch end free at the start. These two ends can be glued to the back of the work when it is completed.

If a too-short cord is made of firm material, it can be spliced to a new cord with glue or thread. To splice with glue, cut both cords at an angle with a sharp knife, dip each end into glue, and bind the ends together with thread until dry.

To sew cords together, cut the ends at an angle and hold them together; then, with matching thread, stitch through one end at a point directly below the splice and wrap the thread up over both cord ends, keeping it in the spaces between the plies of the coil. Stitch through the

Graceful oriental necklace *of waxed nylon and jade was begun where the pendant meets the neck strands. Design: Grace Chinn.*

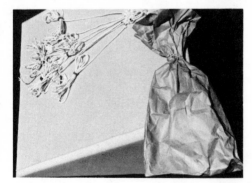

Loose cord ends *can be held in a plastic or paper bag to keep them from tangling while you knot a piece begun from the center.*

end above the splice and knot off the thread.

Cords will sometimes need to be eliminated, either gradually or suddenly. Here's how. The simplest way to drop a cord is to knot over it, leaving it hanging unused at the back of the piece where it can later be cut off. Knotting off is a means of gradually dropping cords by overhand knotting each unwanted cord and clipping off the excess end (fig. 3).

Another method for gradual elimination is the use of two or more cords as one working or holding cord until the extra cord(s) can be safely clipped off.

To abruptly eliminate a group of cords, try the cumulative edge method: group the excess cords into a bundle and use them all as one holding cord for a row of double half hitches, clipping off one excess end every three or four knots (fig. 4) until all cords but one are eliminated.

Three-dimensional Shaping

Working in more than two dimensions requires planning and some experience.

Unless plans are made to gradually introduce new cords, either your project will become very open and structurally weak or its size will be limited to the general dimensions of the mount you use.

To provide extra support and more cord-mounting surface as the piece grows, you can add new mountings, such as the hoops in the tiered hanging shown at the lower left on this page. Covering existing three-dimensional objects—such as bottles, flowerpots, and lamp shades—is easier than creating a sculpture from scratch.

Basketry techniques will produce any number of three-dimensional shapes, such as the hanging shown in the photograph at lower right on this page; refer to the basket project on page 54 for more detailed information on this subject.

Overknotting is a method of forcing holding cords into a tight, random pattern by experimenting with the tension, placement, and number of double and vertical half hitches knotted within a given area. This is a freeform approach, and the best way to understand it is to experiment with it; an example is shown on page 28.

Plant hangers are probably the most

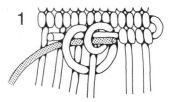

Lengthening the holding cord

Exchanging a working cord for a holding cord

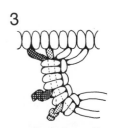

Knotting off unwanted cord ends

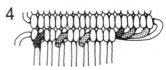

Cumulative edge method for eliminating cords

Three-dimensional macramé sculpture *in tiers grows with the addition of wooden hoops in graduated sizes. Design: Jacee Johnson.*

Coil work *incorporates double half hitches, wrapping, beads, and fringe to produce this natural basket form. Design: Susan Lehman.*

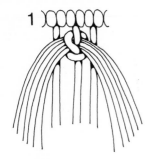

Thickening fringe

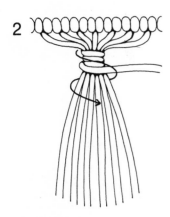

Wrapping fringe

familiar form of three-dimensional macramé. They can be started in two dimensions, then expanded to a third dimension. The addition of hoops or bars will accomplish this; so will division of the working cords into chains that are later regrouped into one bundle to form a loose "cradle" for the flowerpot. Both solutions are shown on the facing page. Other approaches are covered in the projects given on pages 43 and 59.

One of the most popular macramé projects is the covered bottle, an easy accomplishment if you keep the following points in mind: 1) Start at the neck of the bottle with a circular self-mount; 2) Keep knotting tight, evenly spaced, and consistent; 3) Add cords as needed to conform to the swell of the lower bottle; 4) Finish off the bottom in a diminishing concentric spiral of double half hitch rows, clipping off and tucking under cord ends as the spiral decreases (see facing page).

Purses can be considered three-dimensional. There are basically three ways to shape a purse: 1) Two separate pieces are knotted, then later sewn together or attached at the sides to a continuous side/shoulder strap (see facing page); 2) One long piece is knotted, then folded in half and joined at the sides; 3) The bag is

worked over a jig for an initial three-dimensional shape (see below).

Finishing Techniques

The natural finish for a macramé piece is fringe, but if this doesn't suit your design, consider these alternate treatments.

Existing fringe can be altered in several ways: 1) Thicken the fringe by adding extra lengths of cord as in figure 1, at left; 2) Divide fringe into bunches and wrap them into bundles (see fig. 2); 3) Divide fringe into tassels either by wrapping slightly below the point at which a bundle of cords has been attached (fig. 2, at left) or by using a gathering knot to bind each bundle (fig. 1, page 29).

Where you don't want fringe, cut cord ends to not less than 1 inch, depending on the size and pliability of the cord, and either glue all ends to the wrong side of the project with white glue or weave the fringe ends back into the body of the piece, keeping them to the wrong side (fig. 2, page 29).

To join edges where there is fringe, simply knot together the fringe from both sides. Where there is no fringe (the sides

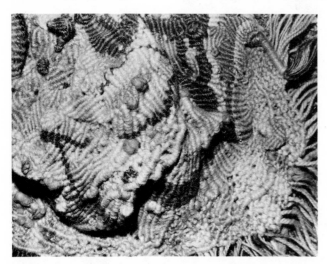

Sculptural quality of "Meteora," a small hanging, is emphasized by overknotting (see page 27). Colors are added, worked through the piece, and gradually removed; the technique is similar to that used in the basket project on page 54. Design: Marion Ferri.

A purse jig is made from an empty oatmeal box that has been filled with dry sand and taped shut with masking tape. The bag will have no side seams when worked with this method since knotting continues uninterrupted around the jig.

of a piece or edges that are glued or woven), edges can be either knotted together with an extra cord (fig. 3, this page) or interlaced with an extra cord (fig. 4, this page).

Some cords—especially nylon, rayon, and cotton cable—will need to have their ends sealed in some manner to prevent them from unraveling. Tie an overhand knot at the end of each cord or (for cotton or rayon) dip cord ends into white glue.

Nylon cord ends can be melted into a ball over a match flame, but be very careful—they can burn your fingers.

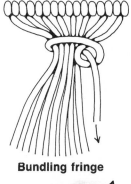

1

Bundling fringe

Back of DHH Knots

2

Woven edge finish

Bottle bottom *is tightly covered with a decreasing spiral of double half hitches from which cords are gradually eliminated.*

Knotted shoulder strap band *can be attached along both sides of a knotted handbag to add width and support. Design: Gerta Wingerd.*

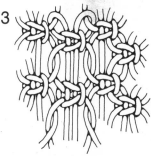

3

Joining edges of square knotted projects

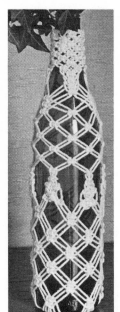   

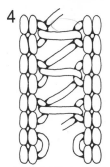

4

Covered bottles *can be started at the neck for complete coverage (***left***), or at the shoulder to avoid adding extra cords (***right***). Designs: left, Alison Jones; right, E. R. Vorenkamp.*

Plant hangers *are sculptural macramé. Support pots by joined cords (***left***) or by hoops knotted into the hanging (***right***). Designs: left, Winkie Fordney; right, Esther Parada.*

Joining edges of double half hitch knotted projects

Design and Color for Macramé

If you yearn to design a truly unique macramé project of your own or to alter one of the projects included in this book, the following information on design and color will help guide you through the decision-making process.

Planning Your Project

Asking yourself a few questions is a logical prelude to actually beginning a project. What shall I make? What size will it be? What color or colors would be suitable? What materials will give it the correct texture and body?

Try to keep the size of the project and the complexity of the design and the knotting pattern in balance with your abilities and the amount of time you'll want to spend working on the piece.

Because of its flexible nature, macramé can use color in very simple or very complex ways, depending on the manner in which a knotting progression is developed. Unless you have a great deal of experience with color, the best rule to follow is this: keep it simple.

If the knotting pattern of the piece is its most important element, then limit the number of colors. If color movement and blending are paramount to the success of the project, choose shades that either complement each other or blend for a harmonious overall effect.

The type of project you want to make, its size, the colors you'll use, and the knotting progression you'll follow—all of these decisions will influence your choice of materials. If, for example, you decide to make a macramé drapery for a window, choose materials that are thick enough to prevent the knotting process from taking months on end. The materials should also be colorfast so they won't fade in sunlight (primary or strong colors have a greater tendency to fade than do natural shades).

When selecting materials for use in articles that will either receive a great deal of wear or require occasional cleaning, check for shrinkage, colorfastness, shedding properties, and (in the case of apparel) comfort. A jute vest may be bright and bouncy in appearance but impossible to wear because of the roughness of the fiber.

To prevent bagging or a droopy look, avoid soft, stretchy cord or yarn in a garment unless it is closely knotted or has some extra support.

Planning may seem less important to you than the actual knotting process. But, as you will see, many mistakes and problems can be prevented if all factors are thought through ahead of time.

The Concept of Design in Macramé

Though any number of interesting knots can be used to construct a macramé piece, the manner in which these knots are combined can make a startling difference. For satisfactory results in macramé a simple appreciation of design basics is necessary. A well-planned piece will combine all elements of design into a harmonious whole that could become unbalanced if anything were added or taken away (the purse at right is a good example).

Design can be reduced to three basic elements: line, shape, and space. Though design is consciously used in handcrafted or machinecrafted articles, its pure form exists in nature.

Take time to really observe the things around you that go unnoticed in day-to-day life: the linear qualities of tree trunks and limbs, shape in the form of a squirrel or bird, space in the delicate web of a spider (note the bottom photographs on page 31). Size, density, texture, and color add dimension to these basic factors.

Size, of course, should be appropriate to the function and placement of the article; density will determine its weight, drape, and flow. Texture and color are used to guide the hand and the eye.

A smooth texture and monochromatic color scheme enhance the knots used in a project (see the lower left photograph on page 32 for an example of this approach); a rough, ropy, or nubby surface, though, will have the effect of emphasizing the overall form of the piece (as in the upper right photograph on page 31). Color can be used sparingly (to highlight only certain pattern areas) or boldly (to set a mood or to create a visual theme).

To learn more about such qualities as texture, density, and color, select several macramé works that appeal to you from the gallery on page 74. Break them down into their basic elements. Start with the knotting patterns used and figure out how they have been combined. Then go on to isolate and explore the uses to which line, space, and shape are put.

Note the natural divisions characteristic to macramé; horizontal, vertical, and diagonal lines or pattern areas are the most common. Curves, circles, and undulating lines require a sure hand and some previous knotting experience (see the lower right photograph on page 32).

When you sit down to think out a project, keep in mind the knowledge you've gained from these explorations. There are two ways to work: from a plan or cartoon or in a freeform manner. A cartoon can be as sketchy or as detailed as you wish. Usually it's executed on graph paper ruled with a certain number of squares to the inch and includes a sketch marked with information on size, colors to be used, and any knotting or shaping details pertinent to the construction of the project.

A freeform approach, on the other hand, requires greater versatility and foresight on the part of the artist. Greater spontaneity in the finished work is your reward for taking chances with your design idea and the materials you plan to use (note the example at lower center on page 33).

Freeform macramé is a medium demanding discipline and patience; if something doesn't work, be prepared to reknot the offending area until it satisfies you. This discipline also calls for shunning the stock solutions to standard problems. Being creative in your approach to problem solving will elevate your work to the plane of individuality (see the center photograph on page 32).

Using Color in Macramé

Color is a very personal aspect of design. Often people will have a natural sense of color without knowing any of the so-called color "rules." Though it's not necessary to memorize rules, it *is* important to have

Shoulder bag *displays basic design elements in proper balance* **(left).** *Overall form of amber bead necklace* **(right)** *is emphasized by a nubby surface texture. Designs: left, Gerta Wingerd; right, Paul Johnson.*

Rough ridges *of an aged palm tree* **(right)** *could have inspired the tightly knotted rows present in the hanging at left. Design: Marion Ferri.*

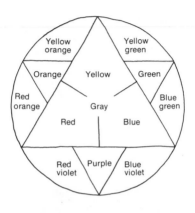

a basic knowledge of what color is, what it can do, and how you can apply it to the craft of macramé.

Understanding the composition of colors gives you confidence in your medium; it allows you to employ colors so that they work well in your macramé projects.

Color is best understood in terms of a color wheel (shown at left). The wheel positions colors in an order that shows how each color relates to its adjacent and its complementary colors. The primary colors of red, blue, and yellow (shown at the center of the wheel) can be combined to make the secondary colors of orange, green, and purple. These colors, in turn, can be mixed with their adjacent hues to make tertiary colors, such as red violet, yellow green, or blue violet.

This principle of mixing certain hues to achieve new colors can be applied directly to macramé. Experiment by twisting several lengths of red and yellow cord together; you'll find that the resulting cord appears to be orange.

The color wheel has what is termed "warm" and "cool" sides. Oranges and reds are considered warm colors; blues and greens fall into the category designated as cool colors. Because warm colors are associated with sunlight and brightness, they appear to be closer and larger than they actually are. Cool colors, on the other hand, tend to recede. These are hues associated with water and shadows.

The texture of the knotting cords will also play a part in altering the appearance of colors. Different surface qualities and diameters of cord will create different high

Simplicity in design and color *can be very effective, as displayed in this double half hitched cascade necklace. Brightly colored wool trimmed with fringe adds drama. Design: Lois Ericson.*

Beaded chains of knots *are gathered into a necklace so natural it might have grown rather than having been constructed. Design: Joyce Barnes.*

Doorway drapery *presents the complex problem of working cords into the center of a circle and out again. Design: Virginia Summit.*

and low areas on the face of the piece, adding subtle shadings to an area that would otherwise appear as solid color.

Effectively using color in your macramé can be handled in three ways. The first is to add in new colors at any point along the way by some of the techniques explained on page 26. Other colors can be removed or simply held back in a certain area—just leave them hanging at the back of the piece until they are again needed.

A second method is to manipulate existing color (the color that was originally knotted into the piece) across the face of the project in a number of ways. Sinnets and chains can move colors; each cord in a two or a four-cord unit can be a different color and can be interchanged as a working or a holding cord to either display or conceal its hue (see below, left).

The Cavandoli knot is a classic approach to using more than one color in a specifically knotted pattern area. The color of the holding cord can be varied to introduce color variety (see below, right).

A third way of using color is to move it out of its original alignment by using chains, sinnets, or diagonal rows of double half hitches. Keep color groups together but work them across or through one another for visual interest.

Think about the colors that will surround the finished project when it is displayed. For contrast, choose colors opposite on the color wheel from those appearing in the setting. For a blended effect, use related colors instead.

Remember—colors are never just ugly or beautiful; it's how you use them that counts.

"Allaciare" *displays solidly interwoven color areas, one method of moving color successfully through a macramé piece. Design: Marion Ferri.*

"Lighter than air" look *is achieved here by designing with the fluid draping quality of the cord in mind rather than the knots themselves. Design: Estelle Carlson.*

Texture and color movement *are heightened by combining Cavandoli knotting with a flat linear background in this hanging. Design: Jane Dodge.*

Macramé Projects: A Selection

p. 64

p. 54

p. 73

p. 60

p. 52

p. 68

p. 62

Macramé Projects for Everyone

You'll see by previewing some of the projects on the following pages that macramé has many faces. Here are colors and forms to delight the eye, function and versatility to satisfy the mind. Now that you know the basics, try your hand at macramé; but first give some attention to the information given on this page. It will help in your preparations for knotting.

Planning Ahead

Determining the cord lengths you will need for practice and for projects involves a little simple arithmetic. Cord lengths can't be calculated to the inch, for they must take into account your individual knotting style, the material you plan to use, and the pattern you choose. A good rule is to calculate and then add an extra yard or so for error. Suggestions for replacing over-shortened cord appear on pages 26 and 27.

By considering the following questions, you can approximate the length of cord you'll need.

How long is the project? Each cord should be at least four to five times the finished length of the project. However, since each cord is usually doubled when it is mounted on the heading piece (such as a buckle or frame), it should be cut eight to ten times the length of the finished project.

Is the pattern you've chosen lacy or close? If the pattern is very loose, you may need only six to seven times the finished length.

Is your cord thick or thin? Figure a longer length for thicker cords and a

Once you are acquainted with the basics of macrame, the real fun begins. On the pages that follow are some beautifully designed macrame projects for you to try . . . some decorative, some functional; some easy, some advanced.

You'll find clear instructions and easy-to-follow drawings to make your knotting more enjoyable. Bon appetit!

shorter length for very fine cords.

Will there be many vertical double half hitch knots in the piece? This knot uses up cord very rapidly, so plan accordingly.

Wrapping a Bobbin

Long cord ends have a tendency to tangle and get in the way, and a "butterfly bobbin" is the best method of wrapping up excess cord, avoiding tangles. Start at the free end of the cord and pull it in a figure 8 path around your thumb and index finger. Continue until you have wrapped to about six to eight inches below the mounting knot. Slip the cord off your hand by grasping it in the center of the figure 8. Put a rubber band or twist-tie around the center of the bundle to hold it securely. The bobbin will now feed off cord as you need it during knotting.

Project Directions

To clarify the macramé process, we've devised a simplified knotting and directional code. Instead of spelling out the name of each knot and the direction in which it is angled, we've used abbreviations. A list of the knots and their symbols appears below.

Note: Equipment has not been specified for individual projects. Refer to page 24 for suggested working surfaces for different types of projects. The use of pins and accessories is an individual matter; choose the approach that works for you.

Knotting Key:

ADDHH—Alternate Diagonal Double Half Hitch
AHH—Alternate Half Hitch
ASK—Alternate Square Knot
DHH—Double Half Hitch
HC—Holding Cord
HK—Half Knot
JK—Josephine Knot
LH—Lark's Head

MC—Mounting Cord
MK—Mounting Knot
OK—Overhand Knot
RDHH—Reverse Double Half Hitch
RMK—Reverse Mounting Knot
SK—Square Knot
VDHH—Vertical Double Half Hitch
WC—Working Cord

C—Center
L—Left
R—Right
UC—Upper Center
UL—Upper Left
UR—Upper Right
LC—Lower Center
LL—Lower Left
LR—Lower Right

Openwork Pillow Cover

(Color photo on page 39)

A beautiful accent for any sofa or chair, this macramé-covered pillow in earthy colors is an easy project for beginners.

Materials: Twenty-three 5-yard lengths and one 30-inch length of brown rya rug yarn; six 5-yard lengths of orange rya rug yarn; five 5-yard lengths of black rya rug yarn; ¾ yard of closely woven white wool fabric; white thread; needle.

How to make:

1. Fold the 30-inch length of brown yarn in half to make the MC, and pin 1 of the halves to the working surface with the fold at the R edge and the remainder of the cord hanging free.

2. Mount all cords at their midpoints, repeating the following sequence 5 times from L to R: 2 brown, 1 orange, 2 brown, 1 black; end with 2 brown, 1 orange, 1 brown.

3. Working from the L, knot 1 row of DHH. Follow with 1 row of DHH from R to L. Pin both HC aside.

4. Knot 3 rows of alternating triple SK, concealing the orange and black cords by using them throughout as HC **(fig. 1)**.

5. Knot 5 rows of ASK, allowing the colors to show in every other row, where they are used as WC **(fig. 2)**.

6. Repeat step 4.

7. Repeat step 5.

8. Repeat step 4.

9. Secure the lower edge by knotting 2 rows of DHH, using the far L or R WC for both HC; then OK each WC just below the last row of DHH and cut off extra cord.

10. To make a simple pillow, cut two 13 by 11-inch rectangles of closely woven white wool fabric. Sandwich the macramé cover between the two rectangles, placed with their right sides together. Stretch and pin the macramé piece at all edges until it is evenly held in place. Using a ½-inch seam allowance, sew around 3 sides of the pillow, beginning and ending slightly into the 4th side **(fig. 3)**. Turn the pillow right side out, being sure that the knotted piece is right side up. Stuff the pillow with dacron and slipstitch along the opening to close it **(fig. 4)**.

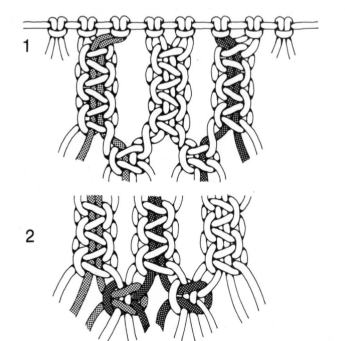

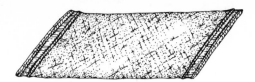

Pretty Placemats

(Color photo on page 39)

Materials: One 30-inch length of royal blue jute; forty-seven 5-yard lengths of royal blue jute; one 10-yard length of royal blue jute; white glue.

How to make:

1. Fold the 30-inch length of jute to make a 15-inch-long double HC; then pin it firmly to the working surface. Mark off into thirteen 1-inch intervals with T-pins, leaving 1 inch free at each end of the double HC **(fig. 1).**

2. Working from L to R, mount each 5-yard length of jute at its midpoint to the HC.

3. When all 5-yard cords are mounted, fold the 10-yard length of jute into 2 lengths, one of 7 yards and one of 3 yards. Mount this cord at its fold to the HC, following the last MK at the right. The long cord should be placed to fall at the outside R edge.

4. Space the MK as evenly as possible along the HC (for smaller cord more lengths may be needed; add in multiples of 4); then, using the long cord on the R edge as HC, knot a horizontal row of DHH from R to L.

5. Tie 4 rows of VDHH with the long cord as WC and the remaining cords as HC.

6. Knot 1 row of DHH with the long cord as HC.

7. Tie 35 rows of alternating 1½ SK **(fig. 2).** This section of the project should measure from about 13½ inches to 14 inches in length.

8. Using the long cord on the L edge, knot a row of DHH from L to R.

9. Repeat step 5.

10. Repeat step 6, but knot *single* HH instead of DHH, except for the 1st and the last knots on either edge; these should be individual DHH.

11. Trim off all ends about 1 inch from final row of knots; then glue all ends to the wrong side of the placemat. Allow glue to dry overnight before using.

Richly knotted in royal blue, this smart yet sturdy jute placemat makes a good beginner's project. Only three knots are used: the double half hitch, the vertical double half hitch, and the alternate square knot.

Left Edge

1

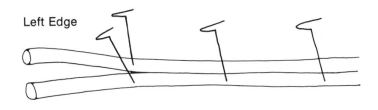

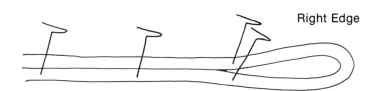

Right Edge

2

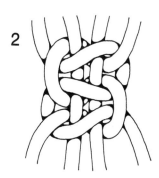

Miniature Rainbow Hanging

(Color photo on page 39)

Perle cotton in myriad colors criss-crosses this petite but powerful hanging, making it a perfect means for learning how to move colors in macramé. The design itself is an easy to medium-level challenge using only four knots: the double half hitch, the vertical double half hitch, the half knot chain, and the square knot.

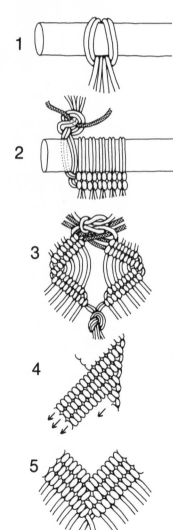

Materials: 90-inch lengths of perle cotton in the following quantities and colors: 6 turquoise, 4 grape, 8 mauve, 4 orange, 8 blue, 4 red, 10 gold, and 4 lime green; twenty-two 18-inch lengths of blue perle cotton; two 15-inch lengths of gold perle cotton; a 4½-inch-long wooden bar, dowel, or other mount.

How to make:

1. Find the midpoints of all cords and mount them *in pairs* with RMK onto the bar **(fig. 1)** in the following order (L to R): 1 grape, 2 mauve, 1 orange, 2 blue, 1 red, 2 gold, 1 lime, 2 turquoise, 1 lime, 2 gold, 1 red, 2 blue, 1 orange, 2 mauve, 1 grape, 1 gold.

2. Center 1 strand of turquoise below the RMK and across the entire width of the piece, leaving an equal length of cord on either side. Using this cord as HC, knot a horizontal row of DHH, using not individual cords but *pairs* of cords as WC.

3. Repeat step 2 with a 2nd strand of turquoise; then at either side, below the bar, cross the ends of both turquoise HC. Next, go above the bar, recross the ends, and tie an OK with both cords to secure. At their midpoints, add in the two 15-inch lengths of gold, 1 at either side **(fig. 2)**.

4. Using pairs of cords as single WC, tie a 2-inch HK sinnet on each edge, using the gold cords as HC.

5. Join the chains with a SK; then, using the individual gold cords as HC and individual turquoise cords as WC, knot a diamond motif as in **figure 3.** Cut off ends 1 inch below diamond.

From this point on, *all* knots are tied using *pairs* of cords as WC and as HC.

6. Using the grape cords at L and the gold cords at R as WC, tie 1-inch HK sinnets over 2 mauve HC at L and 2 grape HC at R.

7. At C, angle last turquoise cord at R of central group from UC to LR. Using cords lime through mauve, knot 8 diagonal decreasing DHH rows, ending with mauve

knots and leaving HC ends free at R.

8. Repeat step 7 for L side, starting with last turquoise cord as first HC and ending with mauve knots.

9. From UR to LRC, knot 11 diagonal rows of VDHH, using all cords from the gold HK sinnet as the first 4 HC; follow with 1 turquoise, 2 lime, 4 gold, and 1 red as HC.

10. Repeat step 9 for L side, working from UL to LLC and using all cords from the mauve HK sinnet as the first 4 HC; follow with 3 turquoise, 2 lime, and 4 gold as HC.

11. At C, group cords red through orange on R and knot a ½-inch HK sinnet, using blue cords as WC and red and orange cords as HC. Repeat for L side, grouping gold through blue cords with blue cords as WC and red and gold cords as HC.

12. Join the blue HK sinnets at C and knot ½ inch of HK sinnet, using 2 blue cords as WC and remaining cords of 1st sinnets as HC.

13. Use HC from last 3 VDHH rows on R as first HC for a series of 8 diagonal DHH rows from UR to LC **(fig. 4)**; follow the mauve knots with cord from the center sinnet in this order: 1 blue, 1 gold, 3 red, 2 blue. Repeat for L side, following orange knots with cords from central sinnet in this order: 2 blue, 1 orange, 2 blue, 1 orange, 1 blue.

14. Divide the HC from the first 5 rows of DHH on either side into 2 equal groups; then tie a SK with the 2 upper groups as HC and the 2 lower groups as WC.

15. Use these cords to complete the last 3 rows of DHH on either side of C, coming to a point at the very center **(fig. 5)**.

16. Group the turquoise and lime cords at the point; then add in two 18-inch blue cords by looping them at their midpoints through the last DHH knot. Tie a ½-inch HK sinnet with the deep blue cords as WC and secure the end of the WC with an OK. Clip WC ends 4½ inches from end of sinnet.

17. Divide cords to R of sinnet into 5 equal groups and repeat step 16 for each group.

18. Repeat step 17 for L side.

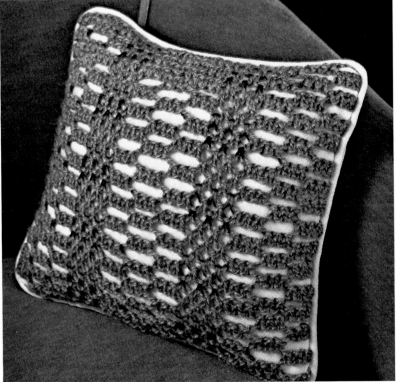

A. Openwork Pillow Cover, page 36
A latticelike design is produced in this softly muted pillow cover when variations are made on the alternate square knot pattern.
Design: Kathryn Arthurs.

C

C. Miniature Rainbow Hanging, page 38
Colors and curves abound in this pretty little perle cotton wall hanging. Tack it up wherever you want to add a bright spot of color.
Design: Helen Freeman.

B. Pretty Placemats, page 37
Only two knots are needed to make a smart indigo blue placemat in rough jute cord.
Design: Kathryn Arthurs.

B

Eden Pattern Tablerunner

(Color photo on page 42)

Kin to a sampler, this table runner is a versatile project. Instead of leaving it a continuous length, you can cut it into individual place mats. Or create an ornate shawl by doubling the number of cords used.

Materials: Fifty 8-yard lengths of orange 3-ply knitting worsted.

How to make:

1. This project is begun at its center point. Pin the midpoint of each WC to the top of your working surface, hanging one half of each cord behind the board and the other half at the front of the board. Number the cords from L to R; then use the far L WC as HC for 1 row of DHH knotted from L to R.

2. Pattern 1: Using cord 26 as HC, knot a diagonal row of DHH from UC to LL. Follow with a diagonal row of DHH from UC to LR, using cord 25 as HC.

3. Repeat step 2, using cords 24 and 27 instead of cords 25 and 26 as HC.

4. Tie a SK bundle with the C 22 WC; use 3 WC at either side for the WC and the remaining 16 cords as HC **(fig. 1)**.

5. Use WC 38 and 15 as HC for diagonal rows of DHH from UL and UR, crossing, and meeting at LC.

6. Repeat step 5, using WC 39 and 14 as HC for the cross.

7. Tie 2 SK bundles as in step 4, 1 with the L group of WC and 1 with the R group of WC.

8. Complete the diamond-shaped areas in step 7 by first continuing the diagonal rows of DHH begun in steps 5 and 6 from UC to LLC and LRC; then use the HC from the diagonal rows of DHH knotted in steps 2 and 3 as HC to knot diagonal rows of DHH from UL and UR to LLC and LRC, meeting the diagonal rows coming down from UC.

9. Use the far L WC as HC for a row of DHH from L to R.

10. Pattern 2: Count in 8 WC from the L; then use the next 4 WC to knot 2 JK as in **figure 2**. Count over 6 more WC; then use the next 4 WC to knot 2 JK. Repeat for the R side, working inward from the R edge.

11. Repeat step 9.

12. Pattern 3: Divide the WC into 5 equal groups of 10 cords each. Knot each group as in **figure 3** for the 1st row of the pattern. Repeat this sequence 2 more

times to complete the pattern.

13. Repeat steps 9, 10, and 9.

14. Pattern 4: Divide the WC into 5 equal groups of 10 cords each. Use the C 2 WC of each group as HC for diagonal rows of DHH from UC to LL and LR. Repeat 4 times as in **figure 4** to complete the 1st row of this pattern, crossing the last pair of HC before beginning the next pattern row. Repeat 1st row 2 more times to complete the entire pattern.

15. Repeat steps 9, 10, and 9.

16. Pattern 5: Divide the WC into 5 equal groups of 10 cords each. Use the far L WC in each group as HC to knot a slightly upward-curving diagonal row of DHH from UL to LR; follow this row with a 2nd row of DHH knotted in the same manner but with a downward curve **(fig. 5)** to complete the 1st row of the pattern.

17. Use the 6th WC of each group as a HC to knot a slightly upward-curving diagonal row of DHH from UR to LL. Follow this row with a 2nd row of DHH knotted in the same manner but with a downward curve **(fig. 6)** to complete the 2nd row of the pattern.

18. Repeat steps 16 and 17 one more time to complete this pattern.

19. Repeat steps 9, 10, and 9.

20. Pattern 6: Divide the WC into 5 equal groups of 10 cords each. For the 1st row, knot a double-X pattern in each group, using the outside cords of each group as HC as in **figure 7**. Repeat 2 more times to complete this pattern.

21. Knot a row of DHH from L to R, using the far L WC as HC; then knot a row of DHH from R to L, using the same HC. Follow with a final row of DHH knotted from L to R over the same HC.

22. Trim fringe to desired length.

23. Roll up the completed knotting and place it in a plastic bag. Turn the work around and again work through steps 1 through 22 for the 2nd half of the runner. Refer frequently to the completed half to check dimensions, length of rows, and design placement.

To make individual place mats, cut through the center of each repeat of Pattern 2 and trim all fringe to an even length.

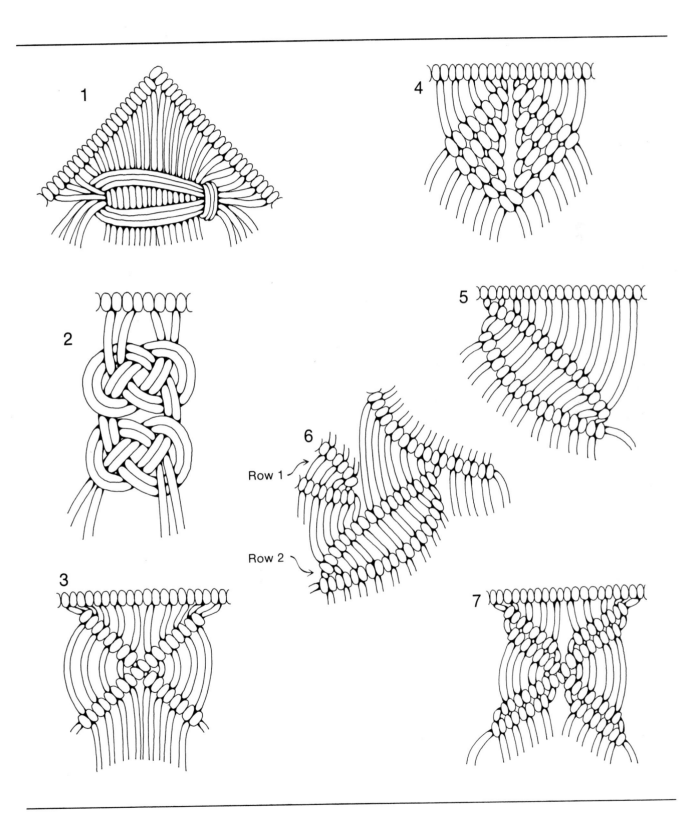

1

2

3

4

5

6

Row 1

Row 2

7

A. Outdoor Plant Hanger, page 43

White cotton welting and brown wooden beads combine in a sturdy but attractive plant hanger. A bamboo ring holds up its end beautifully. Design: Kristi Carlson.

B. Eden Pattern Tablerunner, page 40

Designed to keep table conversation running along complementary lines, this centerpiece is knotted in soft woolen yarn. Overall patterns of leaves and lozenges create a floral motif. Design: Ginger Summit.

A

Outdoor Plant Hanger

(Color photo on page 42)

Materials: Ten 11-yard lengths of ⅛-inch-diameter cotton welting; six 7-inch-long, ⅜-inch-diameter, walnut-stained wooden dowels; one 4½-inch-diameter bamboo or wooden ring; one 2½-inch-diameter brass ring; forty-one 14 mm light brown wooden beads and thirteen 24 mm dark brown wooden beads, each with a large hole.

How to make:

1. Mount the midpoints of all 10 cords to the bamboo ring with MK to make 20 WC.

2. Using the far L cord as HC, tie 1 row of DHH from L to R, curved to follow the ring. Using the same HC, knot 1 curved row of DHH from R to L.

3. Divide the WC into 5 equal groups. Knot 3 SK in groups 1 and 5, and 1 SK in group 3. Onto the 2 HC in each of these 3 groups, thread 1 light brown (hereafter referred to as "LB") bead, 1 dark brown (hereafter referred to as "DB") bead, and 1 LB. Knot 1 SK below each bead group.

4. In groups 2 and 4, knot sinnets of 15 HK each.

5. Knot a row of DHH tightly over one 7-inch dowel.

6. String 1 LB over each of the following cord pairs (L to R): 2, 3; 6, 7; 10, 11; 14, 15; 18, 19.

7. Repeat step 5.

8. Pin the 2 far L and the 2 far R WC aside and then divide the remaining WC into 4 equal groups. Knot 4 decreasing rows of double SK, ending with 1 double SK at C (**fig. 1**). Use the 2 far L and the 2 far R WC to knot 2 diagonal rows of DHH from UL and from UR to LC (**fig. 2**).

9. Divide the WC into 5 equal groups and knot each group into HK chains. Groups 1 and 5 have 17 HK; groups 2 and 4 have 11 HK; group 3 has 7 HK.

10. Repeat steps 5 through 7.

11. Divide the WC into 5 equal groups. Knot chains of 4 SK each with groups 1 and 5; then thread 1 LB, 1 DB, 1 LB on the 2 HC and follow with 4½ SK.

12. With the remaining WC groups, knot 7 rows of alternating double SK.

13. Repeat steps 5 through 7.

14. Divide the WC into 5 equal groups. Knot 2 SK in each group.

15. Repeat step 8.

16. Divide the WC into 5 equal groups. In groups 1 and 5, knot chains of 6 SK each; then thread 1 LB, 1 DB, and 1 LB onto the HC of each group. Follow with 33 SK in each chain.

17. Knot 3 SK in groups 2 and 4, and 1 SK in group 3. Pin aside 2 WC on the far L and 2 WC on the far R; then redivide the WC into 2 equal groups and knot 2 double SK in each group. Again, drop 2 WC at each side and knot 1 double SK at C with the remaining 4 WC.

18. Knot 2 diagonal rows of DHH from UL and from UR to LC.

19. Divide the WC into 3 equal groups and knot 11 HK in groups 1 and 3.

20. Tie 1 SK in group 2; then add 1 LB, 1 DB, and 1 LB over the HC. Follow with 1 SK.

21. Knot 1 diagonal row of DHH from UL and from UR to LC.

22. Divide WC into 3 equal groups and knot 58 HK in group 1 and group 3. Knot 24 SK in group 2. All chains should end at the same point.

23. Divide each chain into 2 pairs of WC. Measure 4 inches from the chain ends and knot a circle of double SK using pairs of WC from adjacent chains (**fig. 3**).

24. About 4 inches below this point, attach the WC with DHH to the brass ring.

25. Divide the cords into 5 equal groups and knot 5 rows of alternating double SK rings, forming a tube. To do this, knot double SK in each of the 5 groups; then divide each group into 2 pairs. Take 1 pair from 1 group and 1 pair from an adjacent group and knot them into double SK. This will start a 2nd ring of knots alternating with the 1st ring. Complete the 2nd ring; then knot rings 3, 4, and 5 in a similar manner.

26. Cut all cords approximately 14 inches below the last row of double SK. Divide the remaining beads into 5 groups, each with 1 DB and 2 LB. OK the beads onto 5 ends; OK the remaining ends, leaving 2 inches free.

Soft cotton welting cord and large wooden beads team up for a plant hanger with the look of outdoors. To protect the cotton from dampness and rot, avoid unglazed pots with drainage holes and locate this hanger in a dry, protected area.

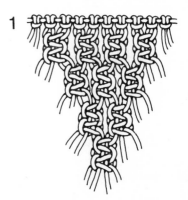

1

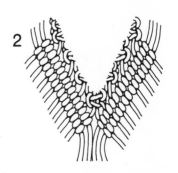

2

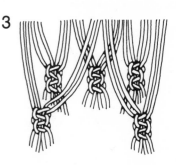

3

Borromini Hanging

(Color photo on page 47)

If you're an advanced knotter, consider an exercise in sculptural form. This intricately curving wall hanging will be a fitting reward for your investment of time and patience.

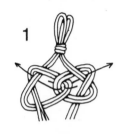

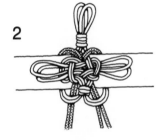

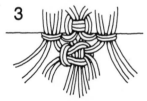

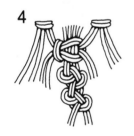

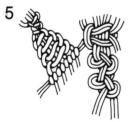

Materials: Eighty 12-yard lengths of #4 Venetian blind cord; two 1⅜-inch-diameter closet dowels, each 2 feet long; 4 wooden drawer pulls whose bases measure 1⅜ inches; 4 ping-pong balls; epoxy glue; white acrylic paint; small paint brush.

How to make:

1. Paint dowels and knobs white and allow to dry overnight.

2. At their midpoints, mount all but 6 cord lengths *in pairs* with MK to make 148 WC. Use the remaining 6 cords to form 3 decorative picot headings.

3. Form 1 picot by folding 2 cords at their midpoints and tying both into 1 OK. As in figure 1, interlock the 2 WC pairs thus formed. To make the large side loops, pull on the C part of the knot (as in **figure 1**) until the entire knot is tight. Secure the picot by knotting a final OK with all 4 WC knotted as 1 cord.

4. Repeat step 3 two more times.

5. Attach each picot to the dowel as shown in **figure 2**. Position 1 picot at a point 1 inch in from *each* dowel end; attach the remaining picot at the very C of the dowel with 78 WC to either side. Use 1 WC pair at either side of this picot to tie a SK over the 4 WC coming from the picot **(fig. 3)**. 5. Knot two 16-inch-long HK sinnets, 1 at far L and 1 at far R, using 12 WC as HC and 4 cords *in pairs* as WC. Set these 2 sinnets aside until step 11.

6. From the C picot, knot a 10½-inch AHH chain, using the 4 WC *in pairs* **(fig. 4)**.

7. Except for the AHH chain in step 6 and the 2 WC immediately at L and at R of this chain, divide the remaining WC into 30 groups of 4 WC each (15 groups on either side of the AHH chain). Starting at the far L, knot 8 inches of HK sinnet; then pull the sinnet over to the C and, using the pair of WC coming out of the SK at C as HC, start to tie individual DHH over the *pair* of HC **(fig. 5)**. Continue to knot HK sinnets and to bring them over to the pair of HC gradually to knot a diagonal row of DHH from UC to LL.

Knot sinnets 2 through 15 in the following lengths: 7 inches, 6 inches, 5 inches, 6 inches, 7 inches, 8 inches, 9 inches, 10 inches, 11 inches, 12 inches, 13 inches, 14 inches, 15 inches, 16 inches, and attach each completed sinnet immediately to the HC.

When the L side is completed, repeat this procedure on the R side, starting with the WC on the far R and numbering inward to C.

8. Knot another pair of diagonal rows of DHH, 1 row from UC to LL, the other from UC to LR, exactly like the previous rows. Use the 1st 2 WC at C on each side as 1 HC **(fig. 6)**.

9. Knot another pair as in step 8, but use only 1 cord from UC as HC in each case. Curve this row slightly downward; then at the end, line it up with previous rows.

10. Using the 1st 20 WC from UC to LL as WC and the 21st WC as HC, knot a diagonal row of DHH from UL to LC, *starting at far L with WC 1* and ending at LC with WC 20. Repeat on R side.

11. Join the main body of the hanging to the large HK sinnet at far L by first knotting a chain of 12 AHH with the HC pairs from the 1st and the 2nd diagonal DHH rows as WC; then divide the 16 WC from the large sinnet into 8 pairs and knot pairs 2, 3, 4, 6, 7, and 8 into chains of 7 AHH each. Knot 2 AHH in chains 1 and 5; then pass the AHH chain from the main body *between* the 2 WC of chains 1 and 5 and secure it in place by OK both chains below the opening thus formed **(fig. 7)**.

Push 1 ping-pong ball up inside of the AHH chains from the large sinnet and tighten the AHH chain from the main body around the ball. Secure this chain by using each of its 4 WC to knot a DHH over the HC of the 3rd diagonal row of DHH in the main body. Regroup all cords from the original large HK sinnet to knot another sinnet of 24 HK. Repeat for the R side.

12. Divide all WC at UC on the L side of the hanging into 5 equal groups of 4 WC. Also divide all WC coming in from the L side into 9 equal groups of 4 WC; the 10th group falls at the LL and has only 3 WC, since the last 2 cords will be used later as HC. Interweave each group as 1 **(fig. 8)**, working from top to bottom. Repeat for R side.

13. Using 2 of the 4 WC from the C AHH chain (see step 6) as 1 HC, knot a diagonal row of DHH from UC to LLC, using all woven cords as WC. Repeat for R side.

14. Using the 1st 14 WC on each side (28 cords in all) as HC, tie a large SK bundle at C with cords 15 through 20 as WC.

15. Knot a slightly curving diagonal row of DHH from UL to LC, using WC 21 as HC. Repeat for R side and join this HC with the HC from the L diagonal row at C when both rows are completed.

16. Using the last 2 cords remaining at far L in step 12 as 1 HC, knot a diagonal row of DHH from UL to LLC, linking with the diagonal row of DHH from UC to LLC in step 13 **(fig. 9)**. Repeat for R side.

17. Divide the 20 WC used for the DHH row in step 16 into 5 equal groups of 4 WC each and knot each group into a sinnet of 24 HK. Repeat for R side.

18. Continue to use the double HC from step 16 as HC for a row of DHH from ULC to LL. Take the WC from the sinnets tied in step 17, working first with the far L sinnet and knotting from ULC to LL.

19. Repeat step 11 for both sides, but follow each with a sinnet of 35 HK.

20. At CL (center left) of the hanging, make 1 more large SK bundle. Use 24 cords as HC (12 from UL and 12 from UC) and 6 cords from each side as WC. Repeat for R side.

21. Continue the crossed diagonal rows of DHH in step 15, working from UC to LLC and LRC; use *all* cords from the SK bundles as WC for each row.

22. Repeat step 20 at C instead of CL.

23. Knot a diagonal row of DHH from UL to LC, starting from the point illustrated in figure 9. Repeat for R side. When both rows are completed, join them at C **(fig. 10)** and use the 4 HC from these 2 rows to knot a chain of 22 AHH at C.

24. Repeat step 12, changing "UC" to read "UL"; also change "in from the side" to read "in from C" and "LL" to read "LC."

25. Using the cords from the woven areas as WC and the 2 centermost cords as HC, knot diagonal rows of DHH, 1 from UC to LLC and 1 from UC to LRC.

26. From UL to LC, knot 1 slightly inward curving diagonal row of DHH over a single HC, incorporating the HC from step

25 as a WC. Knot in reverse order the last 21 WC to be DHH over this HC—that is, start with the top cord and work downward from there. The last WC to be knotted in is the cord closest to the curving diagonal row of DHH. Repeat for R side.

27. Knot 2 more diagonal rows of DHH from UL to LC, using a double HC for the 1st row and a single HC for the 2nd row. Repeat for R side. Use the HC from the last L and R diagonal rows of DHH to knot a SK over the 4 WC from the C AHH chain.

28. Divide the WC into 15 equal groups of 4 WC each and knot HK sinnets in each group. Use the sinnet lengths listed in step 7, working backward from 17 inches to 7 inches. Start at the far L edges and knot the sinnets from UL to LC.

29. To attach all ends to the bottom dowel, start at C and work outward to L edge. Loop *pairs* of cords from back to front around the dowel; then pass them around themselves and knot them into a SK on the wrong side of the hanging **(fig. 11)**. Start with the C AHH chain; then tie on the 2 WC from the C SK.

The next cords to be tied on at C should come from the 1st HK sinnet at far L. Tie on sinnets 2 through 15 in numerical order but tie on from C to *far L* edge. This creates a thick, curved area of sinnets. Repeat for R side.

30. Divide the 8 longest HC from the large HK sinnet at far L into 2 equal groups and knot 1 sinnet of 45 HK with each group. Divide the remaining 8 cords into 2 equal groups and knot 1 sinnet of 3 HK in each group. Attach the cords from these last 2 sinnets to the dowel as in step 29. Loop the remaining 2 cords from front to C back of the dowel, attaching them to previously tied SK. Repeat for R side.

31. Cut cord ends to 1 inch. Secure all knots behind the dowel with epoxy.

32. Attach wooden knobs to all 4 dowel ends with epoxy and allow to dry overnight.

33. To make 1 hanger loop, fold a 2-yard length of cord in half and OK it 2 inches from the fold. Knot a chain of AHH as long as you desire. Repeat for 2nd hanger loop. Tie hangers to upper dowel with SK and secure the knots with epoxy.

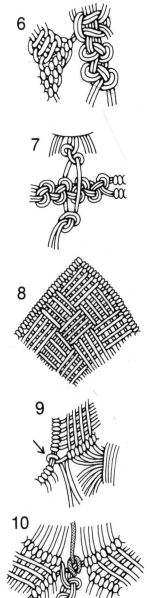

6

7

8

9

10

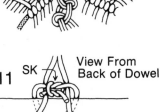

11 SK View From Back of Dowel

Pagoda Bell Chimes

(Color photo on page 47)

The unique appearance of these wind chimes is due to their spiraling three-dimensional bell cords. The simple technique used here is explained in detail on page 16.

Materials: Six 10-yard lengths of gold or blue jute cord; one oval-shaped iron link or equivalent; one large beaten brass bell or cow bell; white glue.

How to make:

1. Group all 6 WC together at their midpoints. One inch away from the midpoint, at each side, knot two 7-inch-long sinnets of HK, using the two outside cords in each group as WC and the remainder as HC **(fig. 1)**. Be sure to knot both sinnets to twist in the same direction.

2. When the sinnets are completed, slip the link onto the sinnets and hold it at the 2-inch unknotted section between sinnets while you twist them together to form a tubelike shape **(fig. 2)**.

3. To begin the larger spiral section, knot 11 decreasing rows of DHH from R to L, using the far R WC as the first HC and working downward from there **(fig. 3)**.

4. Upon completion of this 1st triangular shape, turn and repin your work so that the WC hang downward. Again start from the right as in step 3 and knot a triangle of 11 decreasing rows of DHH.

5. Repeat step 4 seven more times, turning your work as you progress, for a total of 9 spiraling triangles, each with 11 rows.

6. From this point on, the number of rows in the triangles will decrease: triangle 10 will have only 10 rows; triangles 11 through 16, 9 rows each; triangles 17 and 18, 8 rows each; and triangles 19 and 20, 7 decreasing rows each. Follow triangle 20 with a single row of DHH from R to L to secure all WC. To delete extra cords, knot the first rows of triangles 10, 11, 17, and 19 over 2 HC from the far R edge. Two-thirds into the row, cut off the extra cord and complete the row of DHH **(fig. 4)**.

7. Using the 2 outside cords as WC and the remaining cords as HC, knot 3 SK, each separated by a 1-inch interval. Loop the 8 cords through the bell ring and double them back on themselves 4 inches down from the last SK. Working up from the bell ring, knot enough SK over all WC to reach the last SK. Clip excess cord and glue the knot.

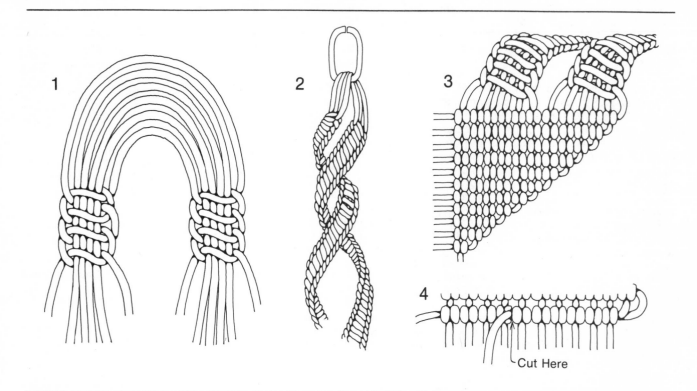

1

2

3

4

Cut Here

A. Borromini Hanging, page 44

Inspired by the unusual structural designs of a 17th century Italian Baroque architect, this unique knotted and plaited hanging of cotton clothesline cord flows into soft, three-dimensional surfaces based on geometric relationships. Design: Gertrude Reagan.

B. Pagoda Bell Chimes, page 46

Reminiscent of tier-roofed Japanese temples, these spiraling bell chimes will hold small hanging plants if extra cord is added. Design: Sandra Cummings.

Mexican Olé Rebozo

(Color photo on page 50)

Wrap yourself in color when you wear this Mexico-inspired rebozo. Its loose, open macramé pattern makes it an ideal shawl for cool summer evenings. If you'd like something with more density, knot only horizontal rows of double half hitches set more closely together. This means that you'll need a holding cord at least three times longer than the length indicated at right.

Materials: 7-yard lengths of 3-ply rope-like wool yarn in the following amounts and colors: 6 lengths of blue green, 10 of light blue, 10 of royal purple, 10 of lemon yellow, 20 of red orange; one 21-yard length of red orange, 3-ply, ropelike wool yarn.

How to make:

1. Using a 36-inch square of fiberboard as your working surface, pin the midpoint of each cord to the top edge of the board in this order (L to R): 4 light blue, 8 red orange, 2 blue green, 2 lemon yellow, 2 royal purple, 2 light blue, 2 lemon yellow, 4 red orange, 2 lemon yellow, 2 blue green, 2 royal purple, 2 light blue, 2 royal purple, 6 red orange, 2 lemon yellow, 4 royal purple, 2 light blue, 2 blue green, 2 lemon yellow, 2 red orange.

Half of each length should fall behind the board, and half should fall to the front of the board. Bundle the cords that are behind the board into a paper bag to keep them out of your way while you work.

2. Find the midpoint of the 21-yard-long red cord and pin it at C of the top of the fiberboard square. This cord will be used strictly as a HC, the only one used throughout the project. All other cords will be used only as WC.

3. Knot a horizontal row of DHH from R to L over the red HC. Move the R half of this long cord to the back of the board and enclose it in the bag with the other extra cord lengths. It will be used for the 2nd half of the shawl. From this point on, use only the L cord end for this half of the shawl.

4. At a point 5 inches below the 1st row of DHH, knot a 2nd horizontal row of DHH from L to R.

5. Knot a row of 3½ deep Vs from R to L; each side of 1 V should have 8 WC (16 WC for each V), and the bottom of the V should fall at a point 5 inches below the last horizontal DHH row **(fig. 1)**.

6. From L to R, knot a row of 3½ shallow Vs, following the procedure outlined in step 5. This row of Vs should meet the previous row of Vs to make a row of open diamonds, as in **figure 2**.

7. Knot a row of 3½ shallow Vs from R to L to meet the previous row of Vs in a way that produces broad, open diamonds **(fig. 3)**. Each side of 1 V should have 8 WC (16 WC for each V).

8. Repeat step 5 but work from L to R. The bottom of each deep V should fall at a point 7 inches below the top of each shallow V in the previous row **(fig. 4)**.

9. Knot a horizontal row of DHH from R to L, directly below the bottoms of the deep Vs in the last row.

10. Five inches below the horizontal row of DHH in step 9, knot 3 horizontal rows of DHH.

11. Follow this horizontal row of DHH with 3½ shallow Vs knotted from R to L. The bottom of each V should fall 3 inches below the horizontal row **(fig. 5)**.

12. Divide the WC into 14 groups of 4 WC each; include the red HC in the far L 4-cord group to make a bundle of 5 cords.

13. OK each bundle as though it were 1 cord at a point 4 to 5 inches below the last row of shallow Vs. Redivide the WC into new groups of 4 cords each by taking 2 cords from each adjacent OK and making a new, alternate bundle **(fig. 6)**.

14. Knot a total of 5 rows of alternate OK to end the shawl.

15. Cut all cord ends to 10 inches; then carefully unravel each 3-ply cord into its separate plies to fringe the shawl.

16. For the 2nd half of the shawl, repeat steps 4 through 14.

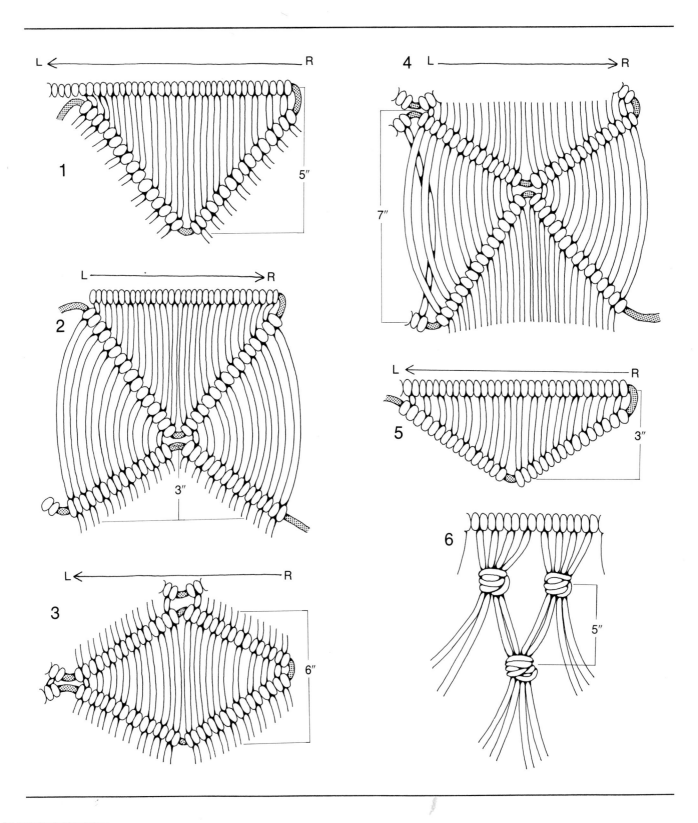

A. Artful Apothecary Jar, page 51
Give instant interest to your kitchen by covering an apothecary jar with openwork macramé. Design: Ginger Summit.

A

B. Mexican Olé Rebozo, page 48
Earthy, primitive colors flow across this dramatic fringed rebozo. Based on a traditional Mexican macramé technique, this variation uses ropelike, woolen yarns. Design: Alyson Smith Gonsalves.

B

Artful Apothecary Jar

(Color photo on page 50)

Materials: Apothecary jar 9½ inches tall by 4½ inches square (with cap); thirty-two 6-foot lengths and sixteen ½-yard lengths of ¼-inch braided nylon cord; white glue.

How to make:

1. RMK 25 cords at their midpoints at a point equidistant from both ends of one 6-yard length of cord (used here as both a MC and a WC). To form a large circle, RMK the remaining 7 cords at their midpoints over *both* ends of the HC **(fig. 1)**. Drape the MC around the neck of the jar and pull both ends of the MC to cinch the cords up around the neck.

2. Knot 3 rounds of ASK around the entire jar to cover the neck.

3. Divide the 64 WC into 4 equal groups, each arranged to correspond to one flat side of the jar. Work a side at a time.

4. Number the 16 WC from L to R. Using WC 8 and 9 as HC, knot 2 SK with WC 7 and 10; set them aside. Continue to knot SK in this manner, using the following cord pairs as WC; 6 and 11, 5 and 12, 4 and 13, 3 and 14, 2 and 15, 1 and 16. Set each WC pair aside after its SK is tied.

5. For the 2nd half of the design, set aside WC 1 and 16. Start tying single SK, using the following cord pairs in this order: 2 and 15, 3 and 14, 4 and 13, 5 and 12, 6 and 11, 7 and 10. Allow the loose cords to form a soft, oval shape between the upper and the lower design areas (see photo on page 50).

6. To complete the design, knot 3 rows of ASK, starting with the C 12 WC in the 1st row and increasing to include all 16 WC in the 2nd row. Follow with a 3rd row of 3 ASK.

7. Repeat steps 4 through 6 three more times, once for each side of the jar.

8. When all 4 sides are completed, turn the jar upside down and join all WC into 1 continuous round of SK.

9. To cover the jar bottom, knot successive rows of ASK, pushing the knots against the bottom as you work.

10. As rounds become smaller, cut WC ends to 1 inch but *only* after they have been used as HC for an ASK. Tuck these cord ends under the previously knotted portion. Continue in this manner until the entire bottom is covered.

11. To cover the jar cap, fold 2 of the ½-yard cords and pin them next to each other on a piece of fiberboard. Tie a SK as in **figure 2**. Repeat 3 more times to form 4 individual SK.

12. Pin these 4 SK in a circle, with knots at C and WC radiating outward. Join the 4 SK by using 1 WC from each of 2 adjacent SK as HC and using a *new* WC at its midpoint to tie a SK **(fig. 3)**. Join all SK in this manner to form a round of 8 SK chains. Knot 4 SK in each of the 4 original SK chains and 3 SK in each of the secondary SK chains. If needed, add extra SK to each chain to cover the cap to its lip. Remove cords from fiberboard and place over jar cap.

13. To secure the knotting to the jar cap, use 1 WC as HC for a round of DHH snugly fitting the base of the cap. Pull on the HC to tighten the fit. Follow with a 2nd row of DHH knotted over the same HC.

14. Tuck the end of the HC firmly under the knotting; then clip all cords as close to the last DHH round as possible. To secure the cut cord ends, apply white glue below the last DHH row all around the cap.

Here's a decorative idea that's quick and relatively easy: a large apothecary jar is covered with lacelike openwork macramé in braided nylon cord. The covered jar is especially attractive when filled with brightly colored candies or dried fruit.

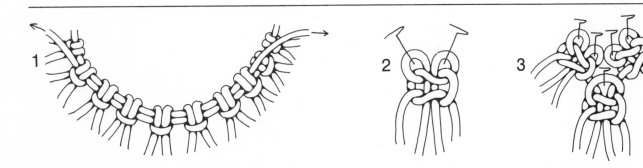

Starburst Necklace

(Color photo on page 55)

Design elements separated by square knot chains give this necklace an air of sophisticated simplicity. Begun from the clasp, the neck strands are joined at the bottom into a single diamond-shaped pendant with half hitch spirals for fringe. This is an intermediate-to-advanced project.

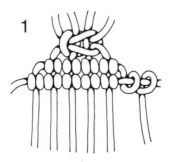

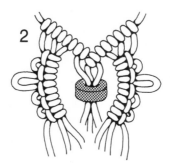

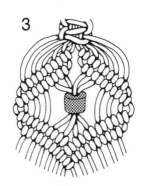

Materials: Eighteen 3-yard lengths and one 48-inch length of beige #18 waxed nylon cord; one 48-inch length of chocolate brown #18 waxed nylon cord; 18 small copal blue glass beads; 16 medium copal and light blue striped barrel beads; 6 small brown beads; 3 large brass beads; 1 clasp; 2 jump rings; white glue.

How to make:

1. Pin the midpoints of two 3-yard lengths of beige cord to the working surface; then, starting ½ inch down from the pin, knot 35 SK. Secure the 1st SK with white glue.

2. Add in WC 3 and 4 as shown in **figure 1.** Thread 1 small blue bead onto the C 2 WC; then knot 2 diagonal rows of DHH from UL and UR to LC below the bead, joining the rows at C.

3. Slide a small brown bead onto the C 2 WC. With the remaining WC, knot 1 chain of 5 LH on either side of the bead, leaving a large loop following knot 2 **(fig. 2)**.

4. Use 1 far L and 1 far R WC to knot 8 SK, using remaining WC as HC.

5. Attach WC 5 and 6 as in step 2.

6. Thread a medium blue bead over the C 4 WC; then knot 1 chain of 8 LH on either side of the bead, leaving large loops following knot 2 and knot 5 on each side.

7. Repeat step 4.

8. Using the C 2 WC as HC, knot 1 diagonal row of DHH from UC to LL and to LR. Repeat. Thread a small blue bead onto the C 4 WC; then knot 2 diagonal rows of DHH from UL and from UR to LC **(fig. 3)**.

9. Thread a medium blue bead over C 4 WC and knot 1 chain of 11 LH on either side of the bead, leaving large loops following knots 2, 5, and 8 **(fig. 4)**.

10. Repeat step 4.

11. Slide a small blue bead over the C 4 WC; then knot 1 chain of 5 LH on either side of the bead, leaving a large loop following knot 2 on each side. Thread 1 small blue bead onto all cords of each LH chain.

12. Using the C 2 WC as HC, knot 1 diagonal row of DHH from UC to LL and to LR; repeat. Follow with a 5-strand Berry Pattern (see page 20), leaving free the L and R HC from the last diagonal DHH rows. When the Berry Pattern is completed, use the free L and R HC to curve single rows of DHH around the berry, leaving the HC uncrossed at the end. With the outermost WC on each side as HC, knot a second curving row of DHH from UL and from UR to LC, crossing them at the end **(fig. 5)**.

13. Knot 1 chain of 8 LH on either side with the 2 far L and the 2 far R WC, leaving large loops after knots 2 and 5; then knot 1 chain of 3 LH with the next 2 WC on either side. Leave the last 2 WC free.

14. Repeat step 12, continuing to use the 2 crossed C cords as HC and starting to knot with the 2 free WC in step 12. Divide the WC into 3 equal groups and thread 1 small blue bead onto each group. Knot 1 chain of 8 LH with the L group and with the R group, leaving large loops after knots 2 and 5 on each side.

15. Repeat step 4.

16. Slide 1 large brass bead over the C 4 WC; then knot 1 chain of 11 LH at L and at R, leaving large loops after knots 2, 5, and 8.

17. Repeat step 4.

18. Repeat step 8, but use 1 barrel bead.

19. Repeat step 13.

20. Repeat step 8, but use 1 barrel bead.

21. Knot 1 chain of 8 LH with the 4 WC at L, leaving large loops following knots 2 and 5. Knot 3 SK with the C 4 WC; then knot 5 LH with the R 4 WC.

22. Repeat steps 1 through 21 for the 2nd neck strand, reversing order of chains.

23. Thread both beige and brown 48-inch lengths through 1 small brown bead and position the bead at the midpoints of the cords. Pin the bead and cords to the working surface with the beige color above the chocolate color; then pin the ends of both finished strands adjacent to the bead and cords in a slight (15°) diagonal position **(fig. 6)**.

24. Using the beige cord as HC on both sides, knot 1 slightly diagonal row of DHH from UC to LL and to LR, using the cords from both strands as WC.

25. Knot 1 diagonal row of VDHH directly under the previous row of DHH, using the chocolate cord as WC and working outward from UC to LL and to LR.

26. Using the C 2 WC as HC, knot 1 slightly diagonal row of DHH from UC to LL and to LR.

27. Thread 1 small brown bead onto both the beige and the chocolate HC at both outside edges.

28. Thread 1 large brass bead onto the C 4 WC. Knot 1 chain of 10 LH with the adjacent 2 WC at either side of the brass bead.

29. Thread 1 small blue bead over the next 4 WC at either side. Knot 2 LH with the next 2 WC at each side. Leave the last outer WC free.

30. Repeat step 26, but work from UL and UR to LC, using the HC from the last diagonal row of DHH as HC.

31. Repeat step 25, working inward from UL and UR to LC.

32. Repeat step 24, working from UL and UR to LC. Complete the diamond shape as in **figure 7**, passing the chocolate and the beige HC from the L and from the R through a brown bead at the center.

33. Divide the WC into 8 groups, 3 WC in the 2 outside groups at either side and 4 in the remaining 2 groups at either side. The chocolate and beige HC should finish in the 2 groups immediately adjacent to the C brown bead.

34. Using the longest beige cord as WC and the remaining cords as HC, knot 1 chain of HH spirals **(fig. 8)** measuring 1¾ inches long with each of the 2 groups adjacent to the C bead. Working outward from this point, knot at each side 1 HH spiral measuring 1½ inches in length.

35. Knot the next 2 groups of 3 WC into single HH spirals, each 1¼ inches long. The last 2 outside groups of 3 WC are knotted into 1-inch-long HH spirals.

36. Thread 1 medium blue barrel bead onto all cords of each chain and knot all cords in each group as 1 into an OK below each bead. Cut off excess cord and dip knots in white glue to hold.

37. Attach jump rings and clasp to loops at ends of necklace strands.

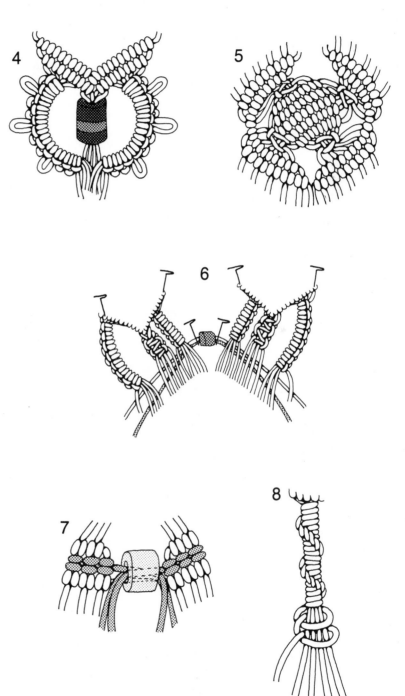

Hopi-Style Rope Basket

(Color photo on page 55)

Macramé doesn't have to be limited to two dimensions—sculptural pieces like this coiled basket are surprisingly easy to construct. Double half hitches are knotted over an outwardly spiraling rope core to hold the basket together, while secondary colors are added as the basket expands.

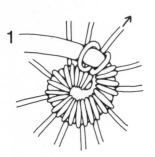

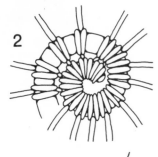

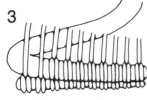

Basket Lip

Materials: One 50-foot length of ¼-inch-diameter sisal rope; 304 yards of white 18-thread cotton cable cord; 40 yards of maroon 18-thread cotton cable cord; 30 yards of orange 18-thread cotton cable cord; 20 yards of yellow 18-thread cotton cable cord; crochet hook; white glue.

How to make:

1. Taper off 1 end of the rope by cutting it at a slant.

2. Cut the white cotton cord into 4-yard lengths and, with RMK, attach 12 lengths at their midpoints to the tapered end of the rope core.

3. Force the knot-covered tapered end into a very tight circle, approximately 1 inch across, and secure the circle by knotting a DHH over the core with the first WC that was mounted on the core **(fig. 1)**.

4. To continue the flat outward spiral of the core, use the mounted WC to join the next round of rope to the previous round with continuous DHH **(fig. 2)**. Work the knots as tightly as possible, keeping the rounds moving outward on a flat plane.

5. As areas open up on the core between the WC, attach new WC as in step 2 and use them just as the original WC are used. Continue to add cords as needed until the shape of the basket begins to taper inward.

6. After 6 complete rounds have been knotted, gradually adjust the core to lie slightly above the previous round **(fig. 3)**. Continue this method for 2 more rounds, gradually expanding the basket as you go.

7. At the 3rd round, introduce the pattern by cutting an 8-yard length of maroon cord and looping it at its midpoint over the core of the basket. Continue to work rounds until the opposite side of the basket is reached; then position a 2nd 4-yard maroon cord over the rope directly opposite the first maroon cord.

8. Continue to coil and knot the core to a point 2½ inches before the original

maroon cord; then attach a 3rd maroon cord as in step 7. When the original maroon cord is reached, knot a single DHH with one maroon WC, leaving the 2nd maroon WC unused. Follow this with a 4th maroon WC added at a point 2½ inches past the maroon DHH.

9. Repeat step 8 for the opposite design.

10. Continue to work upward on the basket, adding in orange and yellow cords to colored designs where needed (see photo on page 55).

11. Begin to decrease the diameter of the basket and to taper the designs back in the 11th row up from the bottom of the basket. To delete cords, work them to the inside of the basket, leaving about 2 inches hanging free and cutting off any remaining cord.

12. From row 17 onward, work the rounds into a cylindrical shape with straight sides. Small color patterns should be completed by row 18, main patterns by row 19.

13. When the last color cord has been deleted, knot 1 more round of DHH to a point falling between the 2 design groups. Cut WC ends and glue to the inside of the basket neck. Leave the core uncut.

14. To make the handles, cut four 2-foot lengths of white cord and insert them from the outside of the basket between rounds 12 and 13, 2 cords at each side of the basket. SK each pair of cords inside the basket and glue them down.

15. Cut two 4-inch lengths of rope and use each of these as a core over which 14 SK are tied, using the glued-in cords as WC **(fig. 4)**.

16. Pass the rope ends and cords between the last 2 coils of the neck and knot into place with the WC. Fringe the ends of the rope at the inside of the basket and cut off the WC.

17. To finish the mouth of the basket, wrap the core with cord for an inch or so; then cut the rope and glue it to the round below, holding the cotton cord to the inside of the basket. When glue is dry, cut off the remaining length of rope.

A. Starburst Necklace, page 52

Staccato starbursts of copal blue and brass beads punctuate this necklace of seemingly intricate, interlocked, Celtic-style motifs made with berry knots and square knot chains. Design: Barbara DeOca.

B. Hopi-style Rope Basket, page 54

Southwestern colors and Indian motifs decorate this jug-shaped basket. Made almost entirely with cotton cord double half hitched over a rope core, it's surprisingly firm. Design: Nilda Duffek.

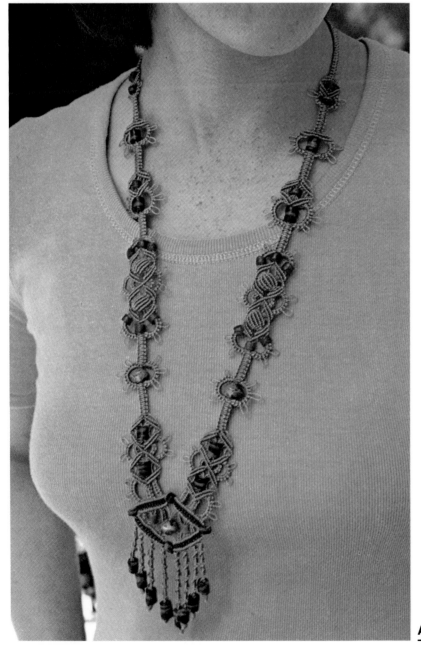

A

Nubby Textured Rug

(Color photo on page 58)

Think big! Make yourself a beautifully durable macramé rug of heavy jute cord. An intermediate-level project, the rug measures 26 by 44 inches when completed and employs only two knots—the alternate diagonal double half hitch and the double half hitch.

Materials: Fifty-two 32-foot lengths of beige 3-ply heavy jute cord; sixteen 32-foot lengths of brown 7-ply heavy jute cord; sixteen 32-foot lengths of black 7-ply heavy jute cord.

How to make:

1. This project is started in the middle and worked outward to the ends. Pin the midpoint of each cord to the top edge of a 36 by 36-inch square of fiberboard, one half of each cord falling behind the board and one half falling in front of the board, in the following order (L to R): 2 beige. Repeat this sequence 8 times—1 brown, 1 beige. 16 beige. Repeat this sequence 8 times—1 brown, 1 black. 16 beige. Repeat this sequence 8 times—1 beige, 1 black. 2 beige.

2. Knot each of the 2 groups of all beige cords into a decreasing triangle of ADDHH, starting with 8 knots and ending with 1 knot **(fig. 1)**.

3. At L, use beige cords as HC and brown cords as WC to knot 8 increasing diagonal rows of DHH followed by 8 full rows of DHH from UL to LR **(fig. 2)**.

4. Repeat step 3 for the C group of brown and black cords, knotting from UC to LR. Start with black HC and move to beige HC, using brown cords as WC.

5. For 8 diagonal rows of black DHH knotted from UC to LL, use the beige WC from the L ADDHH area as HC.

6. In the far R black cord group, knot 8 increasing diagonal rows of DHH followed by 8 full rows of DHH, using beige as HC and black as WC.

7. Knot 17 *increasing* rows of ADDHH (note in **fig. 3** that each row of knots is repeated once, as: 1st row, 1 knot; 2nd row, 1 knot; 3rd row, 2 knots; 4th row, 2 knots; etc. up to 9 knots on row 17; follow with decreasing rows) at far L and at far R; use beige HC from diagonal brown and black rows at L and at R *plus* 2 beige cords at *each* outside edge as WC. Follow with 16 *decreasing* rows of ADDHH at far L and far R; drop 1 cord from row ends nearest colored WC in each successive row. A triangular area pointing toward C of rug will appear at each edge.

8. At C, knot 15 rows of ADDHH in a diamond shape, using beige HC from C black and brown areas as WC **(fig. 4)**.

9. In L group of brown cords, knot 16 diagonal rows of DHH from UL to LC.

10. In the C group of brown cords, knot 16 more diagonal rows of DHH, followed by 8 diminishing rows of DHH **(fig. 5)** from UL to LR.

11. In the L group of black cords, knot 8 diagonal rows of DHH, followed by 8 diminishing rows of DHH **(fig. 6)** from UC to LL.

12. In C group of black cords, knot 16 diagonal rows of DHH from UC to LL.

13. Knot each group of beige cords at CL and CR, as in step 8.

14. In the L black cord group, knot 8 increasing rows, then 8 full rows of DHH from UL to LLC, using beige cords as HC.

15. Knot 8 diagonal rows of DHH from UC to LL in the C group of black cords, using beige cords as HC.

16. Join both black areas by knotting, in sequence, diminishing chevron-shaped rows, 8 rows on L side, 7 rows on R side, using black for WC and HC **(fig. 7)**.

17. In C group of brown cords, knot 8 diagonal rows of DHH from UC to LR.

18. In the R group of brown cords, knot 8 increasing rows of DHH, followed by 8 full rows of DHH from UR to LC.

19. Join both C and R areas of brown cords by knotting 8 diminishing chevron-shaped rows, using brown for WC and for HC (refer to step 16 and fig. 7).

20. Knot 17 increasing rows of ADDHH (see step 7) in both L and R groups of all beige cords. Follow with 8 decreasing rows of ADDHH and 2 diagonal DHH areas **(fig. 8)**. Use beige cords for all WC.

21. Repeat step 8 at bottom C, referring to figure 4. Knot remaining cords at L and at R of this diamond into 8 diagonal DHH rows at each side (as in fig. 8).

22. Use the far L beige WC as a HC for a horizontal row of DHH from the L to the R edge of the rug.

23. Divide all cords into pairs and OK each pair as 1 cord below the DHH row in step 22. Incorporate the HC in step 22 into the far R OK bundle. Clip all cords to 2 inches.

24. To make the 2nd half of the rug, repeat steps 2 through 24 but change to read "brown" instead of "black" and "black" instead of "brown." The black area will start at L and the brown area will start at R. The only other change will be in step 4—knot the rows of brown from UC to LR.

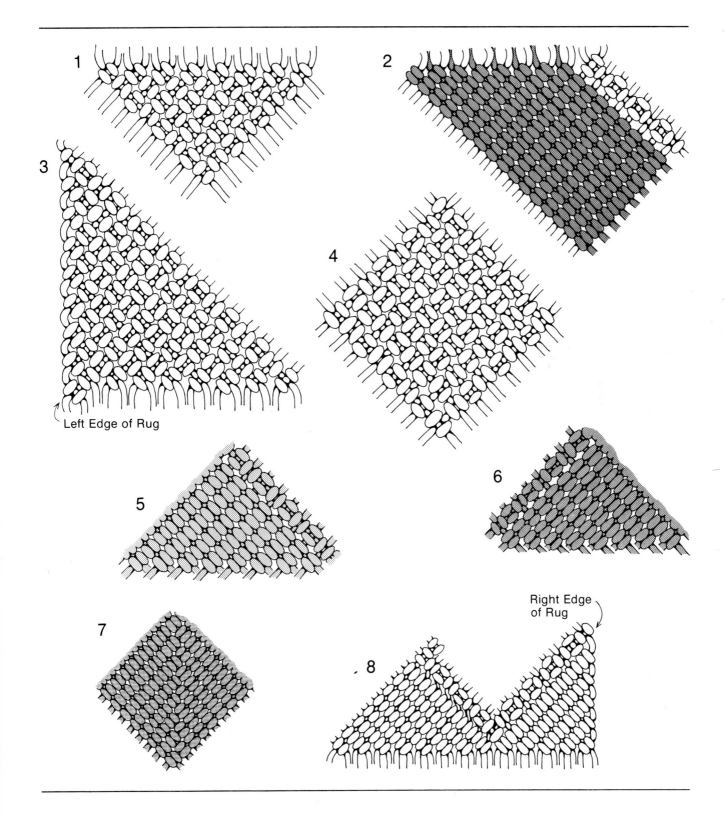

1

2

3

4

Left Edge of Rug

5

6

7

8

Right Edge of Rug

A. Sculptural Plant Hanger, page 59

Spectacular, with the effect of a carved temple column, this plant hanger of Chinese red jute is an effective foil for your indoor greenery. Design: Joy Coschigano of Hidden House.

B. Nubby Textured Rug, page 56

Bold arrowhead designs are interlocked across the face of this knotted jute rug. Alternate diagonal double half hitches form a seemingly irregular background surface pattern in contrast to the regular ribbing of the two-color, double half hitched arrowheads. Design: Ginger Summit.

A

Sculptural Plant Hanger

(Color photo on page 58)

Materials: Six 11-yard lengths, one 4-yard length, two ½-yard lengths, three ¾-yard lengths, and one 3½-yard length of red 5-ply jute cord; six 16-yard lengths and fourteen 1½-yard lengths of orange 5-ply jute cord; two 4-inch-diameter wooden (or metal) rings; six 6½-inch lengths of coat hanger wire; white glue.

How to make:

1. RMK six 16-yard orange cords and six 11-yard red cords to 1 ring in this order: 3 red, 6 orange, 3 red.

2. Wrap the remainder of the ring from L to R with the 4-yard red cord as explained in step 1-A, page 23. When completed, tuck the end through the closest MK on the back; glue and cut excess cord.

3. Using a ½-yard length of red as HC, knot a row of DHH from L to R, following the curve of the ring. Clip both HC ends to 3 inches and glue to wrong side.

4. Repeat step 3.

5. Divide WC into 6 equal groups and knot 4½ SK in groups 1 and 6; 2½ SK in groups 2 and 5; and 1 SK in groups 3 and 4.

6. Using one ¾-yard length of red as HC, knot 2 rows of DHH, 1 from L to R and 1 from R to L.

7. Knot 8 AHH with cords 1 and 2, then with cords 23 and 24; knot 3 AHH with cords 3 and 4, then with cords 21 and 22; knot 2 AHH with cords 5 and 6, then with cords 19 and 20. (Number WC from L to R.)

8. Divide orange WC into 3 equal groups; tie 3 decreasing rows of ASK, **(fig. 1)**.

9. Using the red WC as HC, knot 6 diagonal rows of DHH from UL and from UR to LC, dividing the orange WC into 2 equal groups and using them as DHH WC **(fig. 2)**. Divide the red WC into 6 pairs and knot 3 AHH with each pair. Add extra knots if needed to even out lengths.

10. Knot 14 AHH with orange cords 1 and 2, 23 and 24; knot 9 AHH with orange cords 3 and 4, 21 and 22.

11. Cross the 2 C red cords and knot 1 diagonal row of DHH from UC to LL and to LR, using the remaining red cords as WC.

12. Make a Berry Pattern, using 5 red WC at L as HC and 5 red WC at R as WC (see page 20). Follow with 1 diagonal row of DHH from UL and from UR to LC.

13. Using the orange cords to the R and to the L of the Berry Pattern, tie 8 rows of DHH on each side as shown in **figure 3**. Divide the red WC into 6 pairs and knot 3 AHH in each pair.

14. Repeat steps 10, 9 (1st sentence only, but work from UC to LL and LR), 8 (knot 3 *increasing* rows of ASK), 7.

15. Repeat step 6 through 14.

16. Divide the red WC on L and R into 6 pairs and knot as follows: cords 1 and 2, 23 and 24—8 AHH; cords 3 and 4, 21 and 22—5 AHH; cords 5 and 6, 19 and 20—6 AHH. Knot 3 diagonal rows of DHH from ULC to LL at L and from URC to LR at R.

17. Repeat step 8.

18. Knot 3 diagonal rows of DHH from UL and from UR to LC, using only orange cords.

19. Divide all WC into 8 equal groups. Knot each red group into a 9-inch-long HK sinnet. Then join each pair of red sinnets with 2 SK **(fig. 4)**. Redivide the red WC back into 4 equal groups and add 9½ inches of HK to each sinnet.

20. Knot each group of orange WC into a 20-inch-long HK sinnet.

21. DHH all 4 orange sinnets to the back of the remaining ring and all 4 red sinnets to the front of the ring. OK all WC below the ring.

22. RMK the 14 doubled 1½-yard lengths of orange cord as follows: 4 RMK between red sinnets 1 and 2 and between red sinnets 3 and 4; 3 RMK to the L and to the R of the orange sinnets.

23. Repeat step 8 at the front of the ring, using C red cords and 1 pair of orange cords at either side as WC.

24. Repeat step 9, knotting only 3 diagonal rows of DHH; use orange cords as HC.

25. Repeat steps 23 and 24 at the back of the ring, using only orange WC and HC.

26. Using the 3½-yard length of red, wrap all ends together directly below the bottom DHH rows. Wrap for 2 inches, following the method given in step 2 on page 23. Cut all ends 14 inches from wrapping.

27. Weave lengths of wire in behind each horizontal row of DHH in the plant hanger.

28. Glue down all loose cord ends.

This red jute plant hanger deserves star billing in your home as well as on our cover. A stately column of knots ripples downward from a covered ring into a cuplike pot holder garnished with long fringe.

1

2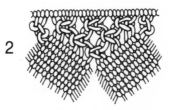

3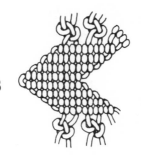

4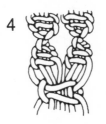

Cavandoli Clutch Purse

(Color photo on page 63)

Cavandoli knotting originated in Italy, where it was first taught to schoolchildren. This technique employs only two knots to create a two-color design. Our folk art clutch purse is decorated with two simple designs, both of which can be worked from the pattern graphs on the facing page. Each empty square on the graph equals one double half hitch knot; each filled square indicates one vertical double half hitch knot.

Materials: Thirty-nine 2½-yard lengths, nine 1-yard lengths, and two 20-inch lengths of black 3-ply wool rug yarn; one 30-yard length, one 4-yard length, and two ½-yard lengths of red 3-ply wool rug yarn; ¼ yard of heavy black lining material; 7-inch black zipper; blunt tapestry needle; regular sewing needle; black sewing thread.

How to make:

1. The body of this purse is begun at its center, which will later form the bottom of the finished purse. Pin the midpoint of the 30-yard length of red cord (hereafter referred to as "pattern cord," or "PC") to the working surface and mount twenty 2½-yard black WC at their midpoints to the L of the pin with DHH **(fig. 1)**; then mount the remaining 2½-yard lengths to the R of the pin with DHH. Pin the R PC end aside, for you will be working with the L PC.

2. Starting from the L, work row 2 in this order: 3 DHH * 3 VDHH, 3 DHH *. Repeat starred sequence 6 more times to complete the row.

3. Knot a row of DHH from R to L.

4. For the next 19 rows, follow the graph for the main design pattern, *working from the bottom up*. The design will appear in an upside-down position.

5. Knot a row of DHH from R to L.

6. Knot a row of VDHH from L to R, working over 2 HC at a time. The last knot in the row has only 1 HC, for a total of 20 VDHH.

7. Knot a row of DHH from R to L.

8. For the final row, knot a series of individual LH over the PC **(fig. 2)** and cut all cord ends (including the PC) to 1½ inches, folding them to the wrong side of the purse.

9. For the 2nd half of the purse, turn the piece upside-down and again work out from the center of the purse. Repeat steps 2 through 8, reading L instead of R and R instead of L.

10. Begin one side panel in the fol-

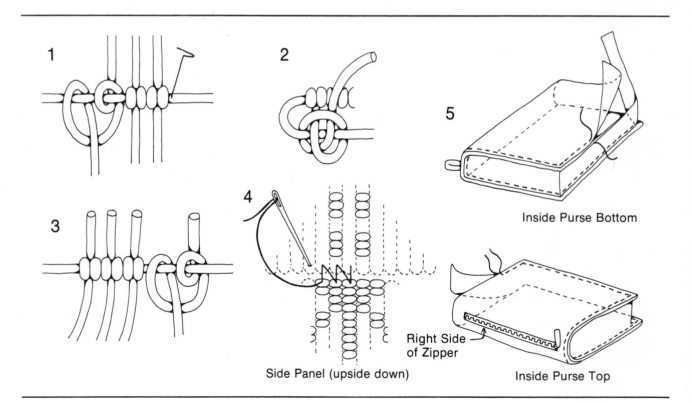

Side Panel (upside down)

Right Side of Zipper

Inside Purse Bottom

Inside Purse Top

lowing manner: At the R end of the 4-yard PC, tie an OK and pin it to the working surface.

11. Mount the nine 1-yard WC to the PC from R to L, using RMK and leaving 1½-inch ends above the PC **(fig. 3).**

12. Work downward from the top of the secondary design (20 rows). When the panel is completed, trim all ends (including the PC) to 1½ inches.

13. Repeat step 12 for other side panel.

14. To construct the purse, thread a 20-inch length of black yarn onto the tapestry needle; then start at the corner of one end of the purse body and attach it to the centermost row (the stem of the flower) of 1 side panel as shown in **figure 4**. As you work, shape the bottom, sides, and top of the purse body around the side panel so that both ends meet evenly at the purse top.

15. Repeat for the other side panel.

16. To line the purse, cut the following from the lining fabric: two 2½ by 4½-inch rectangles; two 5 by 7-inch rectangles; and one 2½ by 7-inch rectangle.

17. Attach the 7-inch zipper to the 2 large lining pieces along the longest sides, following package directions.

18. Using a ½-inch seam allowance, sew the two 4½-inch-long rectangles to either end of the 2½ by 6-inch rectangle to make one continuous strip. To form the boxlike lining, attach this strip to the wrong side of the zippered lining pieces as in **figure 5**, starting on one short end and ending at the other. This means that the zipper tongue will be on the same side as the seam allowances.

19. To make purse loop, knot a 6-inch chain of AHH. Double the chain and knot the 4 strands together firmly; then pass 2 ends under and 2 ends over the PC of one of the side panels to meet on the inside of the purse. Knot with 2 SK to attach the loop firmly to the purse.

20. *Do not* turn the lining but drop it into the purse, fitting it into place as snugly as possible with raw edges facing the wrong side of the macramé.

21. Hand-stitch the lining to the open lip of the purse with black thread.

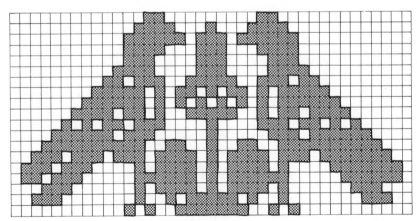

Main Pattern

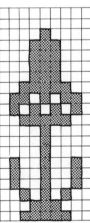

Side Pattern

Lacy Choker Necklace

(Color photo on page 63)

Demurely delicate, this lacy choker band is an ideal project for a beginner. The band is based on a simple repeat pattern using only one knot, the double half hitch.

Materials: Two 5/16-inch-diameter glass beads; eight 2½-yard strands of black #18 waxed nylon cord; white glue.

How to make:

1. Find the midpoint of each cord; then, holding all cords together, knot them as 1 into an OK 1 inch from their midpoints **(fig. 1)**. Pin OK to working surface.

2. Pass 1 bead onto the 2 centermost WC, leaving 3 WC on each side of the bead.

3. Using the outside cords on either edge as WC, tie a series of 6 RMK over each of the remaining pairs of cords as shown in **figure 2**, spacing knots 2, 3, 4, and 5 each ¼ inch apart. Push head up tight against OK; then push all RMK's up against each other to surround bead with tight knots and loops.

4. Leaving the outermost cord on each edge free, divide the remaining 6 cords into 3 pairs and tie a SK over the C pair, using each of the remaining 2 pairs as though they were 1 cord **(fig. 3)**.

5. Divide the cords into 2 groups of 4 cords each; then work diagonally out from UC to LL and LR, tying 3 diminishing rows of DHH on each side **(fig. 4)**.

6. Repeat step 5 from UC to LL and LR, crossing the 2 centermost cords and using them as the 1st HC.

7. Repeat steps 4 through 6 eight times.

8. Again repeat steps 4 through 6; then use the far L and far R cord on each edge to tie 2 pairs of diagonal rows of DHH from UL and UR to LC. Knot off each WC end tightly against the last DHH row. Clip off WC ends and dip knots in white glue.

9. For 2nd half of necklace, remove the OK at choker midpoint; then repeat steps 4 through 6 ten times.

10. Repeat step 5; then OK, clip off, and glue each of the 3 outside WC on each edge, leaving the 2 WC at C uncut.

11. Slip the clasp bead onto both remaining cords; then bring each cord end up, over, and around itself above the bead. At this point, tie a firm SK **(fig. 5)**, clip the 2 cord ends, and coat the SK with white glue to secure it.

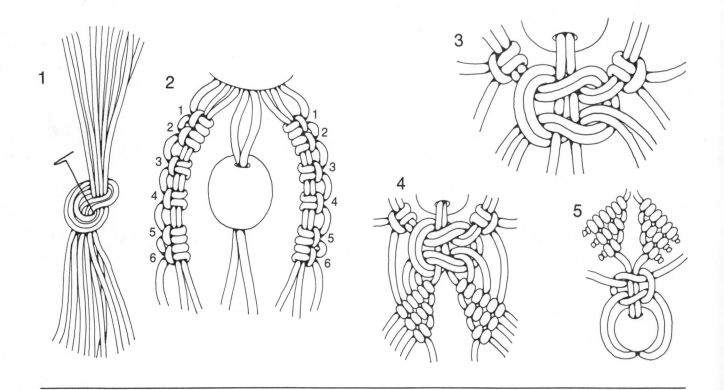

B. Lacy Choker Necklace, page 62

A delicate Victorian period piece, this tiny lacelike choker harkens back to the days of throat ribbons and cameos. Fine waxed nylon cord determines its diminutive scale. Design: Luisita Amiguet.

B

A. Cavandoli Clutch Purse, page 60

An Italian macramé technique reproduces charming folk art patterns on the sides of this red and deep gray woolen clutch purse. Only two knots are used to create a two-color effect. Design: Hannalies Penner.

Sampler Shoulder Bag

(Color photo on page 66)

This unusual purse will give you a chance to use some interesting repeat patterns, macramé and otherwise. Latticework, modified diamonds with gathering knots, alternating bobble knots, and even simple weaving come together in the texturally rich overall appearance of this advanced project.

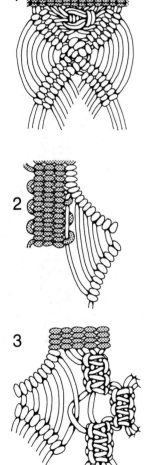

Materials: One 10-inch length, twenty-four 6-yard lengths, two 5-yard lengths, and eight 2-yard lengths of 3-ply purple rug yarn; two 15-yard lengths, two 2-yard lengths, two 5-yard lengths, two 1½-yard lengths, and one ½-yard length of 3-ply gray rug yarn; 2½ yards each of gray, orange, and yellow 3-ply rug yarn; ½ yard of ocher yellow cotton lining fabric; yellow thread; needle.

How to make:

1. OK each end of the 10-inch length of purple cord (to be used as HC) and pin both knots to the working surface.

2. Mount cord lengths in this order (from L to R): one 15-yard length of gray folded to make one 14-yard WC and one 1-yard WC (the 14-yard WC should be on the L edge), one 2-yard gray length at its midpoint, twenty-four 6-yard purple lengths at their midpoints, one 2-yard gray length at its midpoint, and one 15-yard length folded to make one 1-yard WC and one 14-yard WC (the 14-yard WC should be on the R edge).

3. Using the R 14-yard cord as WC, knot 2 rows of VDHH, 1 from R to L and 1 from L to R.

4. Divide the purple WC into the following 3 groups (L to R): 12, 24, 12.

5. To begin the column of modified diamonds using the L group of 12 WC, hold the C 4 WC in a bundle and tie 1 SK over them, using each pair of cords directly to the R and to the L as 1 WC. Using the 2 remaining outside WC on both sides as HC, knot 2 curving diagonal rows of DHH in from UL and UR, joining all 4 rows at LC.

6. Following this join, continue to use the outside WC pairs as HC by crossing them and knotting 2 more curving rows of DHH outward from UC to LL and LR **(fig. 1)**.

7. Repeat steps 5 and 6 on the R side.

8. Repeat steps 5 and 6 three times on the L side and 8 times on the R side.

9. At this point, use the long gray cords at either side of the piece as WC to knot 52 rows of VDHH down each edge of the purse, interlocking every other inner loop with the far L and far R WC of the 2 modified diamond columns **(fig. 2)**. Finish with the WC at the outside edges; then set all gray cords aside.

10. For the alternating bobble pattern (see page 20) at the middle, divide the 24 C purple WC into 6 groups of 4 WC each and knot 6 bobbles, 1 in each group.

11. Redivide the 24 WC into 5 groups of 4 WC each, linking the 2 unused outer WC at each side with the outside loops of the adjacent modified diamond patterns **(fig. 3)**, and knot a second row of 5 bobbles.

12. Repeat step 10.

From this point on, for stability, interlock every other loop of any pattern with the nearest loop or cord of its adjacent pattern throughout the purse.

13. Use the outside purple WC from the last far R bobble as a HC for 2 rows of DHH, from R to L and from L to R below the bobble pattern area only. Interlock the HC at the L after the first DHH row.

14. Mount one 2-yard length of purple to the outside purple WC from the far L bobble, as in **figure 4**. Use this cord as WC to knot twenty 2-knot rows of VDHH, using the 2 outermost cords on the L as HC and making 2 vertical columns. Leave slight loops at the inside of the 2 columns and interlock every other outside loop of the WC through the nearest cord of the adjacent modified diamond pattern. When the rows are completed, eliminate the added WC.

15. Repeat step 14 on the R side, mounting the 2-yard length of purple on the far R bobble WC.

16. Following the color photograph on page 66 for color placement, weave lengths of orange, gray, and yellow into the purple WC at the center of the purse **(fig. 5)**. Leave 3 inches free at the beginning and at the end of each color length and cut off any excess colored cord, setting it aside for later use.

17. Use the far L purple HC from the VDHH columns as HC for 2 rows of DHH below the woven area, 1 from L to R and 1 from R to L.

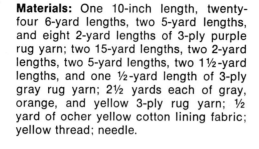

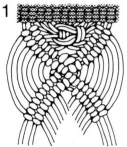

18. Repeat steps 10 through 12 for lower bobble area.

19. Using the outside cord in the far R bobble knot as HC, knot 2 rows of DHH, 1 from R to L and 1 from L to R. These rows should run below the bobble and the left modified diamond sections to and from the gray area along the L edge.

20. Repeat step 9, knotting these columns as you work. The easiest way is to knot them in 3 steps, working them simultaneously with the central design areas.

21. As in **figure 4**, mount one 2-yard length of purple to the 15th purple cord in from the L. Use this cord as WC and cords 1 and 2 as HC to knot 3 inches of VDHH in 2 columns. Leave loops along the R side of the column and link the L loops of the column to the adjacent gray column.

22. Mount one 2-yard length of purple to the far L purple WC; use this cord as WC and cords 1 and 2 as HC to knot 3 inches of VDHH in 2 columns. Leave loops along each side of the column.

23. Following the color photograph on page 66, weave strands of orange, yellow, and gray through the area between both vertical columns of VDHH, interlocking them with the loops of the columns at either side.

24. Divide the purple cords falling between the modified diamond column and the VDHH column to the R of the woven area into 5 equal groups of 4 WC each. As in **figure 6**, use the far R WC of each group as HC and knot 5 diagonal segments of 3 DHH each from UR to LL.

25. Use the 2nd WC in each group as HC and knot 4 diagonal segments of 3 DHH each from UL to LR, knotting a partial row at the far R **(fig. 7)**.

26. Repeat steps 24 and 25 four more times to complete this section.

27. Repeat step 24.

28. Use the far L purple WC as HC to tie a row of DHH from the gray area at L to the column of modified diamonds at R.

29. Repeat step 28, working from R to L and ending at the gray area.

30. Repeat steps 21 through 29, but reverse the woven and the latticework areas. The VDHH columns in step 20 should fall on the R edge, the woven area

should cover 16 purple cords, and the VDHH columns in step 21 should fall immediately to the L of the woven area. For the 2nd latticework area, work as follows: divide the 16 purple WC on the L into 4 equal groups and repeat steps 24 and 25 six times to complete the section.

31. Repeat steps 21 through 29, but knot 2-inch-long VDHH columns and repeat steps 23 and 24 four times.

32. Using the far L WC as HC, knot 1 row of DHH from L to R, incorporating all WC.

33. Knot 2 rows of VDHH, using the far L gray cord as WC and working 1st from L to R, then from R to L.

34. Using the outside L and the outside R cords as WC, knot 1 final row of VDHH in each gray column.

35. Using the far L purple WC as HC, knot 1 final row of DHH from L to R; end the DHH row when the last purple WC is used.

36. Clip all cord ends to 2 inches and iron them toward the wrong side of the purse.

37. To line the purse, cut the lining 2 inches larger all around than the purse body. Iron under a 1-inch seam allowance on all sides of the lining; then slipstitch the lining to the wrong side of the macramé, keeping the lining slightly back from the loops along each edge.

38. To join the sides of the purse, fold it in half, wrong sides together, and use 1½-yard lengths of gray cord to lace the loops together as in **figure 8**. Knot off the ends at the inside of the purse on each joined edge.

39. Form the handle of the purse as follows: mount two 5-yard lengths of purple and of gray at their midpoints to 1 corner of the purse, making 4 purple WC and 4 gray WC. Knot 2 separate 16-inch-long HK sinnets, 1 in each color; when the sinnets are completed, twist them around each other to form a 2-color handle. OK each WC and thread ends out through the opposite corner of the purse. Use a ½-yard length of gray cord to group the cord ends into a tassel, wrapping for 1½ inches directly below the top edge of the purse. Trim the tassel to measure 6 inches.

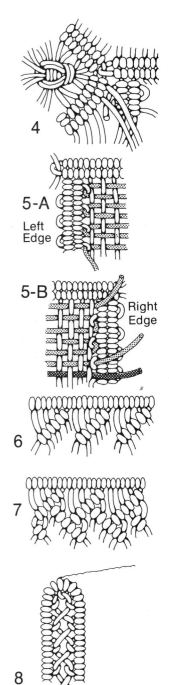

4

5-A
Left Edge

5-B
Right Edge

6

7

8

A. Reverse of the purse: *Simple weaving is mixed with interwoven macramé bars on the back of this intricate bag, pictured here to make its construction an easier task.*

B. Sampler Shoulder Bag, page 64

Bobbles, braids, and interwoven segments combine in an intriguing series of surface treatments on this small but striking shoulder bag. Resembling a macramé sampler when knotted together, the patterns are nevertheless arranged in a predetermined manner. Design: Gerta Wingerd.

B

Leather Thong Belt

Materials: Four 7-yard lengths of square-cut, 3/16-inch-wide leather thong; two 2-inch-diameter brass belt rings.

How to make:

1. Fold each 7-yard length of thong in half; then attach each doubled length at the fold to both rings at once **(fig. 1)**. This will give you 8 WC. Bobbin each WC and secure with a rubber band; then anchor the rings to your working surface.

2. Divide the WC into 2 groups of 4 cords each and tie 2 SK as shown in **figure 2**.

3. Using the center 4 lengths and, leaving the outer pairs free, tie 1 SK **(fig. 3)**.

4. Repeat steps 2 and 3 until the belt is long enough to go around the waist and through the loop with about 3 inches extra. Cut cord ends as desired for fringe.

This belt has some good things going for it: expandable design, simple construction, and the use of a durable material—leather thong. Made completely with alternating square knots, this is a good project for the beginner. If you can't locate leather thong, cut your own from a single large piece of 1/8-inch-thick leather. Draw a circle on it and, starting at the outside edge work spirally to the center, cutting a continuous, 3/16-inch-wide thong with a sharp knife or heavy-duty scissors.

No knotty problems *here; just a simple alternate square knot pattern to give you a rugged belt of leather thong. Design: The Leatherworks.*

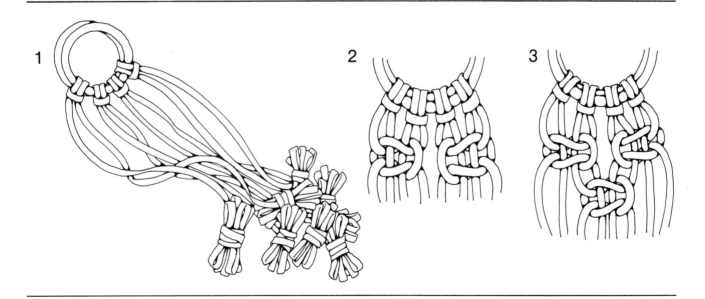

Sea and Sand Necklace

(Color photo on page 70)

*Shades of the beach—
they're all here in this
pleasingly precise necklace.
A true tour de force for the
advanced knotter, this piece
depends on planning and
careful workmanship for a
professional look.*

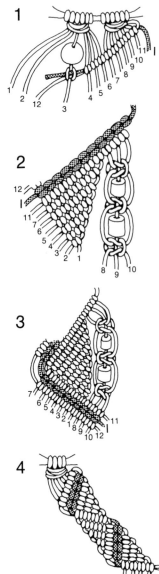

Materials: Twenty 3-yard lengths, sixteen 1½-yard lengths, and three 1-yard lengths of taupe #18 waxed nylon cord; two 2-yard lengths and three 1-yard lengths of warm ivory #18 waxed nylon cord; one cross-section and one slab-cut side of a mitra or other shell; 23 orange Wili Wili seed beads (referred to as orange); 48 cylindrical shell beads (referred to as black); 28 round mother-of-pearl beads (referred to as white); white glue.

How to make:

1. For one *neck cord,* fold two 3-yard lengths of taupe cord in half and mount individually to L edge of shell cross-section.

2. Begin the cord in this manner: 1 SK; 2 black beads, 1 on each outside cord; 1 SK; 1 orange bead over both center cords together; 1 SK; 2 black beads, 1 on each outside cord.

3. Tie 8 inches of AHH chain, using pairs of cords as single cord units (see Half Hitch Chains, step 2, page 15).

4. Tie an OK with all 4 cords; then thread a black bead onto each cord end and secure each bead with an OK. Dip each knot in white glue to secure it.

5. Repeat steps 1 through 4 for 2nd neck cord, working at R edge.

6. To begin pendant portion of necklace, divide sixteen 3-yard lengths of taupe cord into 4 groups of 3 cords each and 2 groups of 2 cords each. Using each group as though it were a single unit, fold in half and mount at fold to R and L sides of shell cross-section, working from *outside* in. L side: 3-cord group, 3-cord group, 2-cord group. R side: 3-cord group, 3-cord group, 2-cord group, leaving 1¼ inches of shell free at the LC edge.

From this point on, only the left-hand side of the pendant will be explained; for the right side, work simultaneously, reversing all directions to read R instead of L and L instead of R.

7. Number L cords from outside in (1 to 16); cords for the C shell pendant are explained in step 43. Hold cord 12 diagonally to LL, then lay in 1 end of a 2-yard length of ivory cord. Using both cords as 1 HC,

tie a diagonal row of DHH from R to L **(fig. 1)**, adding an orange bead to cord 3 before knotting it on. Trim off short end of ivory cord.

8. With the ivory cord, tie a diagonal row of VDHH from UR to LL, leaving the last cord free; follow it with a diagonal row of DHH, using UR taupe cord as HC. Leave the 2 outside cords free.

9. Using cord 9 as HC, tie a SK with cords 8 and 10; add a black bead; tie a SK; add another black bead; tie a last SK.

10. Tie 6 diagonal decreasing rows of DHH from UR to LL, leaving cords 12, ivory, and 11 free **(fig. 2)**.

11. Working diagonally from UL to LR, use cord 11 as HC and tie a row of DHH followed by a row of VDHH ending in a DHH. Finish with a diagonal row of DHH, using cord 12 as HC **(fig. 3)**.

12. Work cords 13 to 16 as shown in **figure 4**, using a 1-yard length of ivory cord at its midpoint as the initial HC for row 1. Join right and left sides of this part of the design by tying a SK with the ivory cords **(fig. 5)**.

13. Using both L ivory cords coming from the SK as one HC, tie 4 horizontal decreasing rows of DHH from R to L; then tie 4 vertical decreasing rows of DHH from top to bottom, moving to L **(fig. 6)**.

14. Repeat step 13; then cut away 1 of the 2 ivory HC. Join the 2nd completed section to the 1st completed section. To do this, use the far L taupe cord of the 2nd section to tie 1 DHH over the ivory HC from the 1st section and 1 DHH at the end of the last diagonal row of knots in the 1st section.

15. Thread 1 orange bead onto the far L taupe cord.

16. Using the far R ivory cord as a HC, work a row of DHH horizontally from R to L. After tying 3 knots in the row, include the second ivory HC, using it as one with the taupe HC. After tying 5 more knots cut away the 2nd ivory HC.

17. Tie a horizontal row of VDHH from L to R with the ivory cord.

18. Repeat 1st sentence of step 16.

19. Thread 1 white bead onto each of the following cords: far L ivory cord, taupe cords 5, 11, and 16.

20. Repeat 1st sentence of step 16.

21. Repeat step 17.

22. Repeat step 18.

23. At *each side* of the section being worked, use 4 cords to knot a chain of beads and SK as follows: 1 SK; 1 black bead on 2 C cords; 1 SK; 1 orange bead on 1 C cord; 1 SK; 1 black bead on 2 C cords; 1 SK. Conceal the ivory cord on the R side by running it down through the centers of the knots and beads in the R chain.

24. With the remaining 8 cords, tie 10 rows of ASK.

25. Repeat 1st sentence of step 16.

26. Repeat steps 17 through 19.

27. Repeat 1st sentence of step 16; then with HC held diagonally down from L to R, add eight 1½-yard lengths of folded taupe cord at their midpoints. Use the picot mount described on page 22, step 1. At the center of the necklace, cross holding cords as in **figure 7**.

28. Using all cords, repeat step 17, but work upward diagonally and then horizontally from LRC to UL edge.

29. Repeat step 16, working from R to L and using cord 16 as HC.

30. Repeat 3 times the section shown in **figure 8**, using taupe cord 1 as the continuous zigzag HC and incorporating the ivory HC from the diagonal row of VDHH only when moving from UR to LL. At end of the 3rd repeat, cut away the ivory cord.

31. Tie 7 rows of ASK with the remaining 12 cords.

32. Working on the central portion, use the 1st added cord on the L edge to tie a diagonal row of DHH from UL to LRC. Follow with 2 more rows, using 2nd and 3rd cords respectively as HC. Join *only the last row* to its mate at C of the necklace **(fig. 9)**.

33. Using cord 4 as HC, tie a diagonal row of VDHH from UL to LRC; join it to its mate at C **(fig. 9)**.

34. Knot a final diagonal row of DHH from UL to LRC, using cord 5 as HC. Join it to its mate at center of the necklace **(fig. 9)**.

35. Divide cords on L side of C into 4 groups of 4 cords each. Tie 1 SK with each group of 4 cords; add 1 black bead to C 2 cords of each group and secure each with a SK. Tie an OK with the 2 C cords

and thread on an orange bead, securing it with an OK.

36. Beginning from the L edge of the ASK area worked in step 24, continue to knot rows of ASK, gradually incorporating all remaining cords on the R except the 2 WC through the orange bead. After the last group of 4 cords is tied in, work 5 more rows of ASK. Incorporate the 2 C cords and join both sides of the necklace in the 5th row **(fig. 10)**.

37. To join all sections at the bottom, add in a 2-yard length of ivory cord, starting it 6 inches to the L of the lower edge of the necklace. Hold the longer end horizontally and tie a row of DHH from L to R with all WC.

38. Follow with a horizontal row of VDHH from R to L.

39. Repeat last sentence of step 37.

40. Repeat step 39, working from R to L.

41. Divide L half of cords into the following groups, working from L to C: 5, 6, 5, 5, 6, 5. On each group use the 2 outside cords as WC and the rest as HC for a sinnet of HK. Include ivory cord in the core of the far L sinnet to conceal.

42. Tie each sinnet as follows: 25 HK, add 1 black bead; 5 HK, add 1 white bead; 8 HK, add 1 orange bead; secure with OK; trim excess cord; dip knot in glue.

43. To add inner shell pendant: attach 3 folded 1-yard lengths of taupe cord as 1 group to the very center of the shell cross-section with a MK.

44. Using 2 center cords as HC, tie 2 matching diagonal rows of DHH from UC to LL and LR.

45. Center a 1-yard length of ivory cord under the rows in step 44; then use it to tie 2 matching diagonal rows of VDHH from UC to LL and LR.

46. Repeat step 44.

47. Using outside taupe cords as HC, knot 2 diagonal rows of DHH from UL and UR to LC, using all cords.

48. Pass all but the 2 HC through the *front* of the shell pendant and adjust placement of shell to necklace. Pull ends upward *behind* shell cross section and knot 4 SK with remaining 2 HC over all cords holding the shell. Cut off and glue the WC to secure. Cut off all HC as close as possible to the top SK.

5

6

7

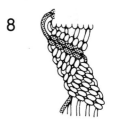

8

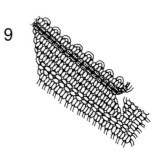

9

10　Center Cords

Sea and Sand Necklace, page 68

Framed in waxed nylon knotting, sliced mitra shells echo in the burnt orange and black bead accents dotted throughout this elegant piece of beach-colored body jewelry.
Design: Edwina Hawbecker.

A. Snappy Strap Bracelet, page 73
Variety is the spice of life. And variety's what you get when this monotone waxed nylon strap bracelet is enlivened with the addition of cords in one, two, or three extra colors.
Design: Barbara Jee.

B. Oriental Belt, page 72
Overlapping diamond and sphere elements form a filigreelike belt length of golden nylon twine. Based on a repeat pattern, this belt is well within the scope of the beginner.
Design: Barbara Jee.

B

Oriental Belt

(Color photo on page 71)

Add style to your slacks with this openwork belt of nylon twine. A simple repeat pattern easy enough for a beginner to tackle forms the main design of the belt. For waist measurements over 28 inches (the belt size presented here), add 8 inches per cord for each additional inch needed.

Materials: Eight 10-yard lengths of gold nylon twine; one belt buckle with a 1¼-inch-wide buckle bar; needle with large eye; white glue.

How to make:

1. Hold the buckle with its back side *toward* you, making sure that its tongue in its correct position hangs downward. Mount the midpoint of each cord onto the buckle bar with MK. This gives 16 WC.

2. Use the 2 centermost cords as HC for diagonal rows of DHH worked from UC to LL and LR. Repeat twice for 3 consecutive rows **(fig. 1)**.

3. Using the 2 outside cords on either edge, tie 2 chains of 6 AHH **(fig. 2)**.

4. Use the remaining 12 cords to make a diamond-shaped area of 5 rows of ASK, starting ¼ inch below the last design area

(see **figure 3**, below, right).

5. Using all 16 cords, leave another ¼-inch space and tie 3 consecutive diagonal rows of DHH from UL and UR edges to LC **(fig. 4)**.

6. With the 2 outermost groups of 3 cords each from either side, tie chains of 12 LH and 8 LH **(fig. 5)**.

7. Tie a chain of 4 SK at C, with 2 cords as WC and the 2 C cords as HC.

8. Repeat steps 2 through 7 nine times, ending with the pattern given in step 2.

9. Starting with the center 4 cords and gradually increasing outward until all cords are in use, tie 38 rows of ASK. Tie 3 more rows of ASK decreasing to 3, then 2, and ending with 1 central SK **(fig. 6)**.

10. Repeat step 5, but tie only 2 rows.

11. Press cords to the back of the belt and sew them down with matching thread. Trim off excess cord and glue into place.

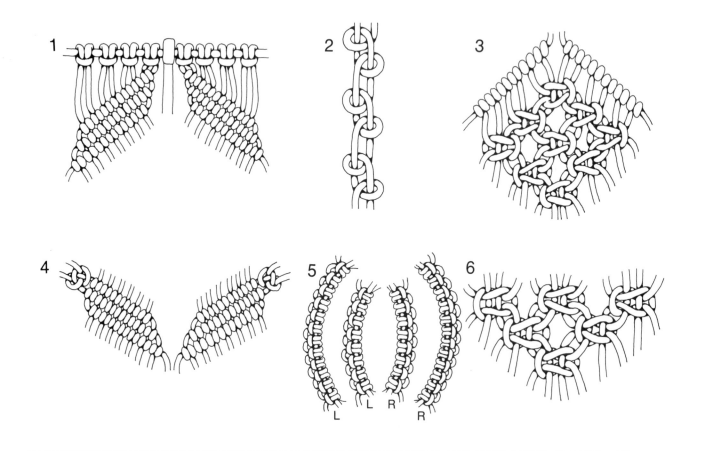

Snappy Strap Bracelet

(Color photo on page 71)

Materials: 20 yards of buff-colored #18 waxed nylon cord cut into eight 2½-yard strands (for the other straps shown, use 2½-yard strands of each color desired in the following orders: 3 black, 2 ivory, 3 black; 1 green, 1 orange, 2 yellow, 1 orange, 1 green; or 1 green, 1 light green, 1 blue, 2 white, 1 blue, 1 light green, 1 green); ⅝-inch brass buckle; 2 small ¼-inch-diameter beads; needle with large eye; white glue.

How to make:

1. Hold the buckle with its back side *toward* you, making sure that its tongue in its correct position hangs downward. Mount each cord at its midpoint onto the buckle bar, 4 cords to a side (giving 16 WC).

2. Tie 16 rows of ASK, starting row 1 with 4 SK and ending row 16 with 3 SK. This will leave both outside cord pairs in row 16 hanging free and untied.

3. For rows 17 and 18, knot as indicated in **figure 1**, coming to a point at C.

4. Using the outside cords as HC, tie diagonal rows of DHH, crossing them at C **(fig. 2)**.

5. Repeat step 4.

6. Using the outside cords as WC, tie diagonal rows of VDHH, crossing at C **(fig. 3)**.

7. Repeat step 4 twice.

8. Thread a bead onto the 2 C cords.

9. Tie 2 matching SK chains of 5 knots each with the 3 cords at either side of the bead **(fig. 4)**.

10. With the 4 outside cords at each edge, tie 2 matching SK chains of 8 knots each.

11. Using the 2 C cords as HC, tie diagonal rows of DHH from UC to LL and LR edges **(fig. 5)**.

12. Repeat step 11, crossing HC.

13. Tie 19 ASK rows from this point on, beginning with the 4 C cords and gradually increasing to the use of all 16 cords.

14. For the 2nd half of the strap, repeat the preceding steps in the following order: 3 (change to read " . . . rows 20 and 21 . . ."), 4, 8, 9, 10, 11, 12, 6 (use the 2 C cords as WC), 11, 12, 13 (knot 27 rows), 3 (change to read " . . . rows 28 and 29 . . ."), 4, and 5.

15. Turn the strap on its face and press the WC flat against the back. Holding down the cords, sew them to the back side with a thread pulled from an unraveled length of nylon cord. Cut off loose ends and secure them with white glue.

Designed for the talents of an intermediate macramé buff, this wrist strap depends on firm, regular knotting for its good looks. If you're feeling adventurous, try expanding it into a choker or a belt.

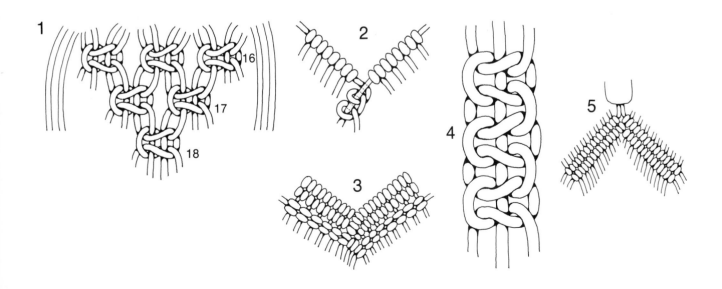

Macramé Masterworks

In a very short time span, macramé has progressed from revived craft to sophisticated art form. To inspire and intrigue you, we present here a selection of current works by some of the finest artists in this field.

A. "Berries and Beads" necklace employs golden picots, Berry knots, and chains intermixed with jade-blue beads. Design: Elaine Seely.

B. Josephine knot necklace of waxed linen displays old Chinese coins. Plaited-in red cord runs through several knots. Design: Nilda Duffek.

A   B

C

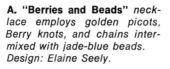

C. Exploding colors arc outward from the center of this spontaneously worked pendant. Design: Helen Bitar.

D. Earthy, found-object-laden necklace is macraméd with waxed linen and leather. Design: Joyce L. Barnes.

E. Sweep of hackle feathers frames 76 carats of smoke topaz quartz double half hitched together with waxed linen. Design: Paul Johnson.

D   E

A. Lion-faced mask *was looped, knotted, and woven of rope and cord into an exciting, three-dimensional shape. The techniques used to make the mask are based on those practiced by the primitive native artists of New Guinea. Design: Rubin Steinberg.*

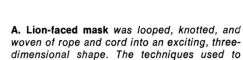

B. Tree hanging *is a floating Cavandoli work in brown jute knotted with double half hitches from a pattern taped to the mounting dowel. Design: Susan Peters.*

C. "Persian Collar" *could be an ancient artifact; instead, it's a modern piece worked in Cavandoli knotting with fine copen blue and gold cords. Old carnelian points, beads, and brass filigree lend a feeling of antiquity. Design: Sylvia Cook.*

A   **B**

A. A fiber "sketch" or study in manipulating fibers without armatures or contrivances, this bas-relief wall piece is sculptured in a trompe l'oeil manner with braided nylon fiber.
Design: Joan Michaels Paque.

B. "Nesting Place" resembles an ancient clothing fragment. Sisal, suede, carpet shag, and feathers are combined in this unusual exploration of negative and positive space.
Design: Nancy Robb Dunst.

C. "Intellectual-in-the-Clouds," a potpourri of macramé, weaving, assemblage, and porcelain ceramic work, was constructed over a welded steel form. Mink tails appear in the tassels.
Design: Edwina Drobny.

D. "Perchance to Dream" is the culmination of a number of techniques. Macramé and wrapping were used to construct the halo of hair and the dramatic wings of this angel.
Design: Nancy and Dewey Lipe.

C   **D**

A

B

A. Arched doorway curtain of white cotton cording was knotted entirely of square knots and double half hitches in matching panels. Design: Peggy Stone.

B. Baby's "bed" is completely handcrafted, down to the butternut wood frame. Soft cotton welting is knotted across the frame, anchored, and then wrapped in areas with colored jute. Design: Susan Peters.

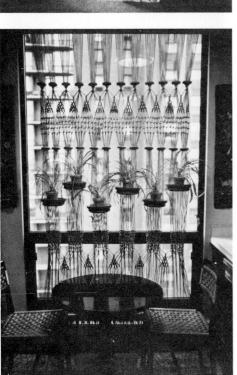

C. Refined design elevates to the realm of art this practical window planter of upholsterer's cord. Several wooden hoops knotted into the design support the plant saucers. Design: Esther Parada.

D. Clock face adds an element of surprise to this tarred marlin plant hanger. Knotting was worked around wooden plaque-mounted clock. Design: Donalie Orton.

C 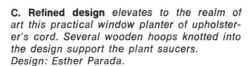 **D**

A. "Pocahontas Dress" *could have been worn by the lady herself. It's a totem of Indian ancestry with feathers, shells, deer horn, leather, and tiny bells joined by natural fibers. Design: Jack Dunstan.*

B. Muted colors *interlock in a soft vest of wool rug yarn. Peacock down and Peking glass beads adorn the 147 handwrapped yarn tassels. Design: Pat Henshaw.*

A

B

C

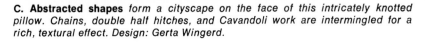

C. Abstracted shapes *form a cityscape on the face of this intricately knotted pillow. Chains, double half hitches, and Cavandoli work are intermingled for a rich, textural effect. Design: Gerta Wingerd.*

D

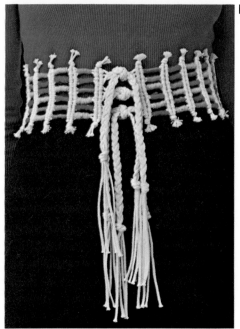

D. Multicolored belt *is a white and bright concoction of shoelace cotton braid, double half hitched in separate rows and then wrapped with odds and ends of colored synthetic yarns. Design: Penny Laing.*

A

B

A. Three months in the making, this 11-foot-tall fiber sculpture holds over 300 pounds of wrapped and knotted jute. *Design: Libby Platus.*

B. Linear background of vertical rows of double half hitches and wrapped openwork areas makes a graphic foil for the colorful, three-dimensional shapes knotted and interwoven across its surface with colored yarns. *Design: Marion Ferri.*

D

C

D. "Macramé Relief Number Two" makes use of entire lengths of half knot sinnets carefully arranged in blended color groups. Softly curved and folded back over itself, this piece has subtle surface changes and undulations, giving a three-dimensional effect. *Design: Michi Ouchi.*

C. Color control *is supremely exhibited in this impressive wall hanging. Note the tapestry-like vine and leaf motifs, serving as bridges between more solidly knotted areas. Design: Helen Freeman.*

Index

Photographers

Richard Anderson: 33 right. **Edward Bigelow:** 33 left. **Charles Bray:** 27 left. **Estelle Carlson:** 33 center. **Grace Chinn:** 26 left. **Edwina Drobney:** 76 bottom left. **Nancy Robb Dunst:** 76 top right. **Marion Ferri:** 28 left, 31 bottom left, 79 top right. **Winkie Fordney:** 29 bottom right center. **Alyson Smith Gonsalves:** 9 all, 25 all, 26 right, 29 top right, 31 top left, 32 left and center. **Mona Helcermanas-Benge:** 55 left, 70, 74 top left, 77 top left and bottom right, 78 all, back cover right. **Paul Johnson:** 31 top right, 74 bottom right. **William J. Kearns:** 74 bottom left. **Susan S. Lampton:** 28 right. **Dewey Lipe:** 76 bottom right. **Ells Marugg:** 7 all. **Jack McDowell:** 27 right, 31 bottom right. **John Satre Murphy:** 74 left center. **Museum of Fine Arts, Boston:** 4. **Akira Ouchi:** 79 bottom right. **Henry Paul Paque:** 76 top left. **Esther Parada:** 29 bottom right, 77 bottom left and top right. **Jack Peters:** 75 right. **Norman A. Plate:** 34, 39 all, 42 all, 47 all, 50 all, 55 right, 58 all, 63 all, 66 all, 67, 71 all, 74 top right, 75 bottom left, 79 bottom left, back cover left and bottom. **William C. Sedlacek:** 29 bottom left center. **William J. Shelley:** 29 top left, 31 bottom left, 32 right. **Rubin Steinberg:** 75 top left. **E. R. Vorenkamp:** 29 bottom left.